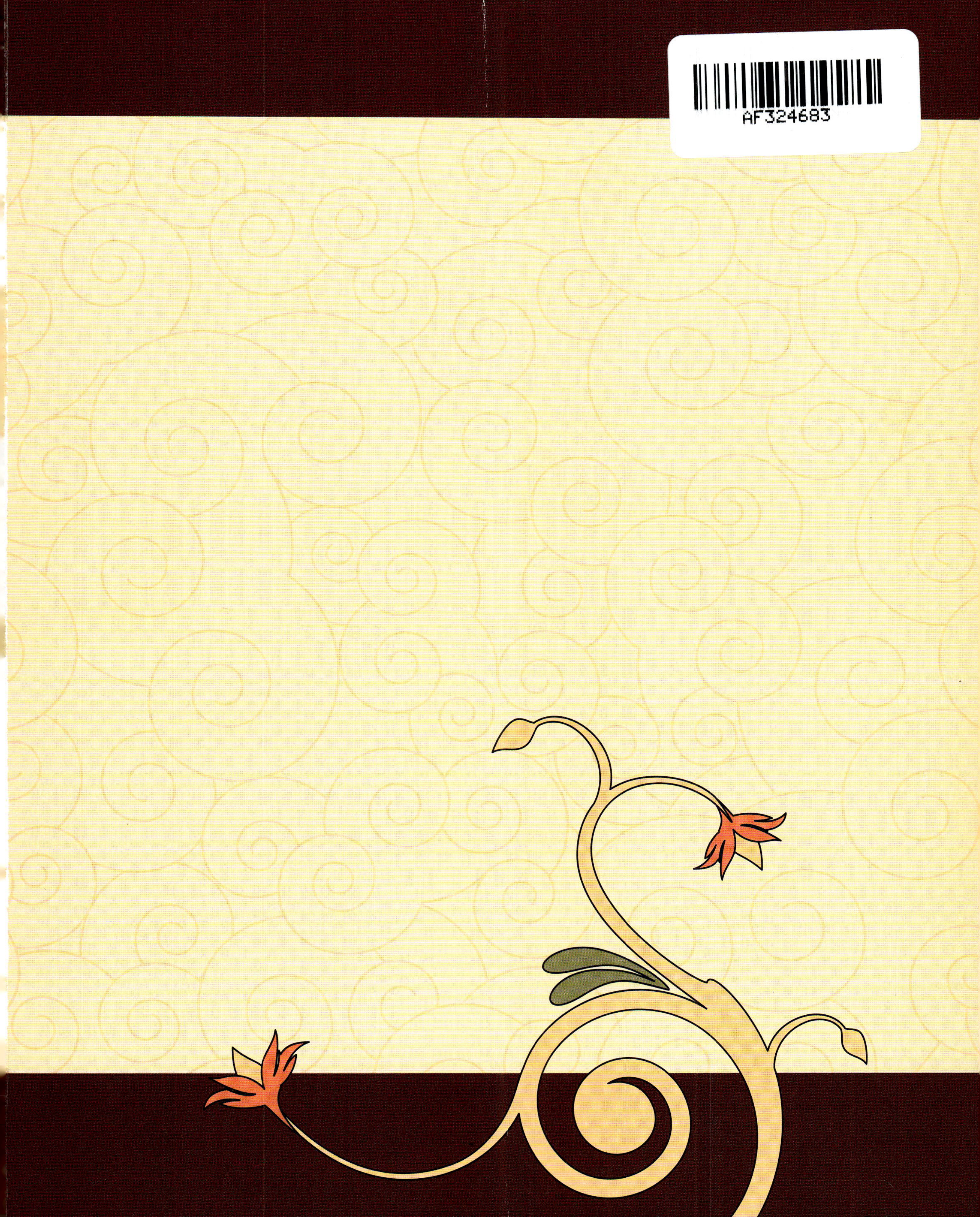
AF324683

REDEFINING the LINE

Art Nouveau & the Female Figure

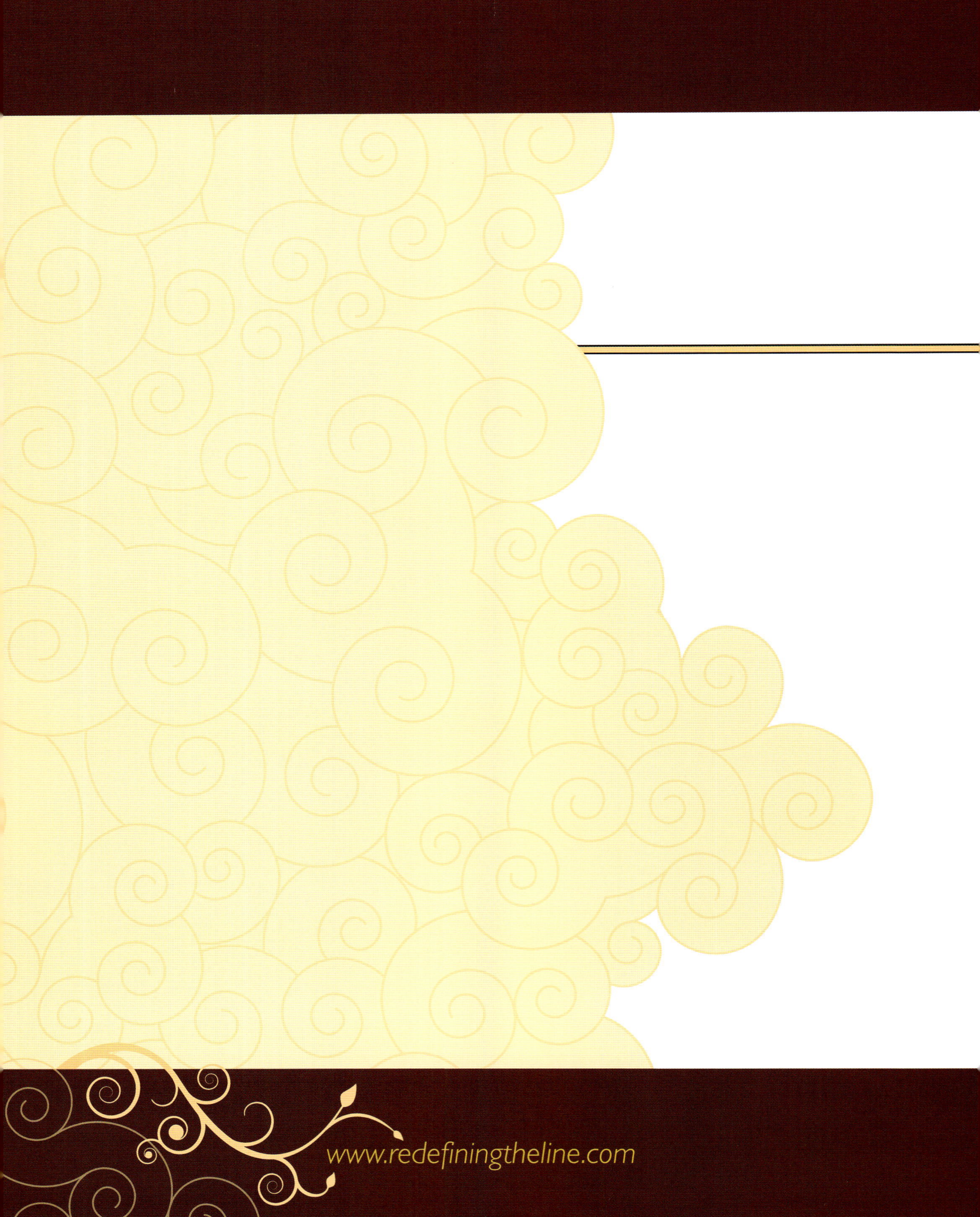
www.redefiningtheline.com

REDEFINING the LINE

Art Nouveau & the Female Figure

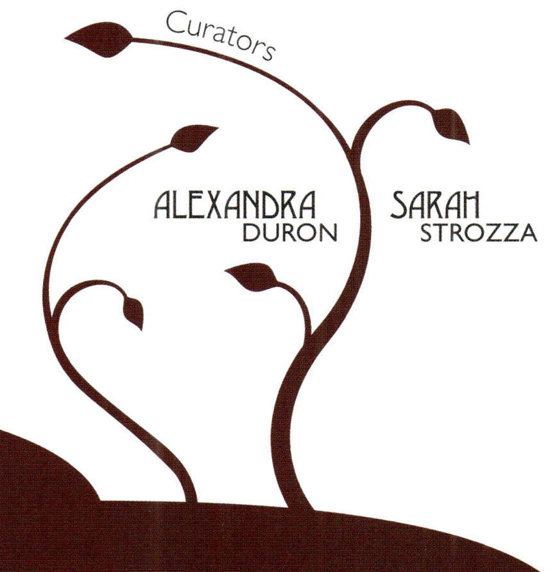

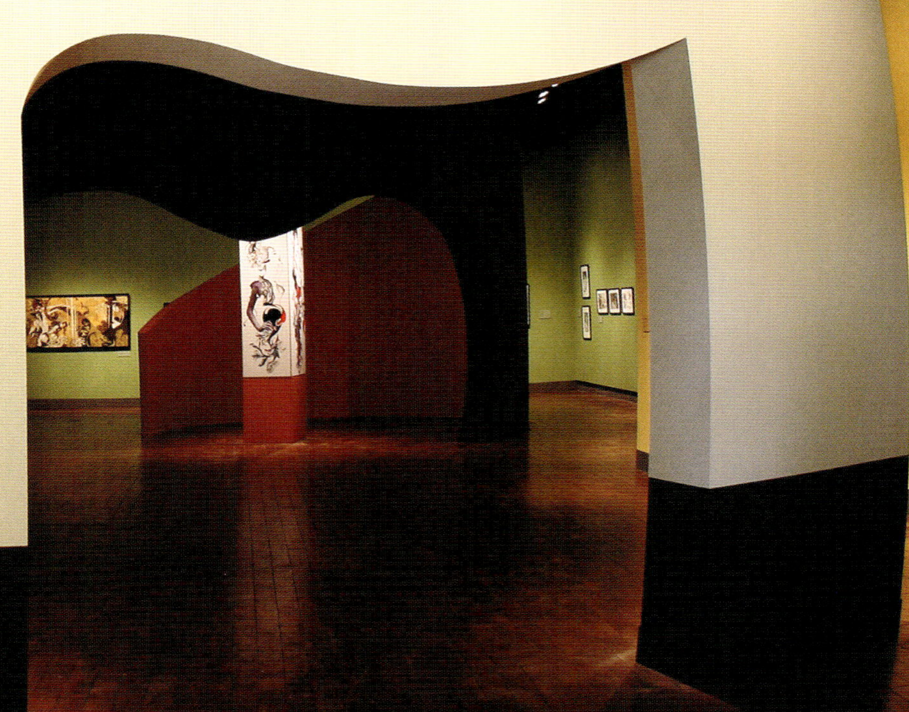
REDEFINING
the LINE
Art Nouveau & the Female Figure

CONTENTS

DIRECTOR'S FOREWORD
MIKE McGEE

When curators Alexandra Duron and Sarah Strozza approached me with their proposal for *Redefining the Line: Art Nouveau and the Female Figure*, I was a bit puzzled. I had seen artists using Art Nouveau references, but I had no idea that it was so pervasive. The more I learned about the project the more I realized that it was a youth-based development. So why are young people interested in Art Nouveau, and why now?

In Joanna Roche's essay for this publication she refers to "the power of line force." I think this is the most straightforward reason why young artists today are attracted to Art Nouveau. It is the power of the line and the desire to make their mark on our culture. The choice of a historical reference to a line that is by definition sensuous and decorative seems like an appropriate antidote to a culture that is becoming increasingly complex, cerebral, and removed from nature. And, as Duron, Strozza, and Roche have pointed out in their essays, one of the legacies of Art Nouveau is the depiction of the sensual female figure, thus giving contemporary artists the opportunity to create images that update female sexuality.

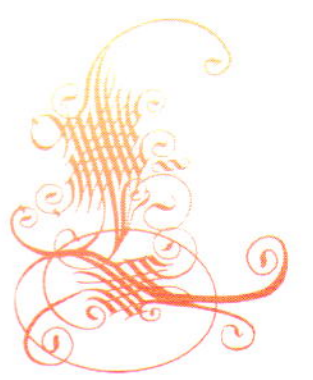

ike the original Art Nouveau, the current rediscovery is taking place at the turn of a century, albeit a hundred years later. Art Nouveau has roots in the Arts and Crafts movement and was initially intended to celebrate the value of the handmade over the mass-produced-by-machine products that resulted from the shift from an agrarian to an industrial economy. As we move into the twenty-first century, artists, like everyone else in our culture, are grappling with the shift from an industrial to a postindustrial, information-technology-propelled society. Concern about the value and power of the handmade seems like a distant dream at this point. Ironically, the computer today—with the advent of pen tablets and other digital interfaces—facilitates human gesture and handmade marks, and the Internet facilitates the international distribution of and discourse about art and design. Today's interest in Art Nouveau, like the response to Art Nouveau originally, is very much an international phenomenon.

There are so many people to thank for the success of this project, and, for some reason, the project seemed like a series of celebrations. Perhaps it was because the artists who participated were so delighted to be a part of the project and have been so responsive and willing to find creative solutions to the challenges of gathering artwork from around the globe, thus contributing to dozens of small victories. Ariel Aguilera and Andrea Benyi of Pandarosa were artists-in-residence during the exhibition, and they were, like the rest of the artists in the exhibition with whom we communicated remotely, wonderful to work with. Pomme Chan, Deanne Cheuk, Naja Conrad-Hansen, and Pandarosa created new, in some instances site-specific, artworks for the exhibition. Thank you to all the artists, Pomme Chan, Deanne Cheuk, Naja Conrad-Hansen, Aya Kato, Pandarosa, Marguerite Sauvage, Alberto Seveso, Sonya Suhariyan, Yoshi Tajima, and Eveline Tarunadjaja.

Art Nouveau as a style has always seemed celebratory to me. The design of the poster, the exhibition, and the publication for this project with the stunning colors, vinelike forms, and period fonts plays beautifully off that tradition. Kudos to Alexandra, Sarah, and graphic designers Paul Lam, Shana Lengyel, and Sawako Naganuma—and thank you to graphic design professor Theron Moore, who served as art director on this project, for his mentorship and guidance. Another thing that made this exhibition special was the dedicated web page artfully designed by Chris Varesi.

The design of the exhibition merits further recognition. Alexandra and Sarah's design for the space complemented the art and created an environment that echoed the traditions of Art Nouveau architecture. Building curvilinear walls and swooping curvature overhangs is a colossal challenge. Gallery technician Martin Lorigan and his assistants David Brokaw, Kimberly McKinnis, and Martha Lourdes Rocha deserve applause for so skillfully building to Alexandra and Sarah's ambitious plan. Other students in the exhibition design/museum studies program also helped with the buildout and installation of the exhibition, and Marilyn Moore worked dutifully behind the scenes to coordinate and make sure every aspect of the project went smoothly.

I want to thank Joanna Roche for her for her poetic take on Art Nouveau and the artists in this exhibition, and for her role as advisor for this project. This is the first time we have worked with artist and writer Annie Buckley; I thank her for her professionalism and scholarly essay that created historical context. As usual Sue Henger, as she has been doing for more than a decade, edited all the copy for this publication and made sure the text conformed to our standards and style.

Alexandra and Sarah worked extremely hard on this project, and one other aspect of their multifaceted efforts that deserves recognition is the fundraising they accomplished. Special thanks to all who contributed to the project; without this generous funding we could not have published a book of this size and quality.

....

Mike McGee, CSUF Main Art Gallery Director
Gallery Director and professor of art at California State University Fullerton, McGee has worked as an art writer, curator, and arts administrator since 1982. He is also founder of the CSU Fullerton Grand Central Art Center.

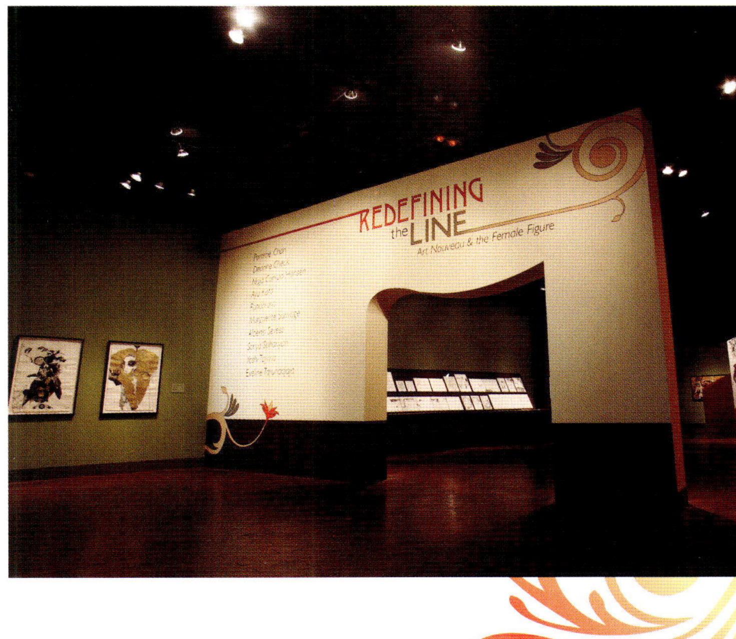

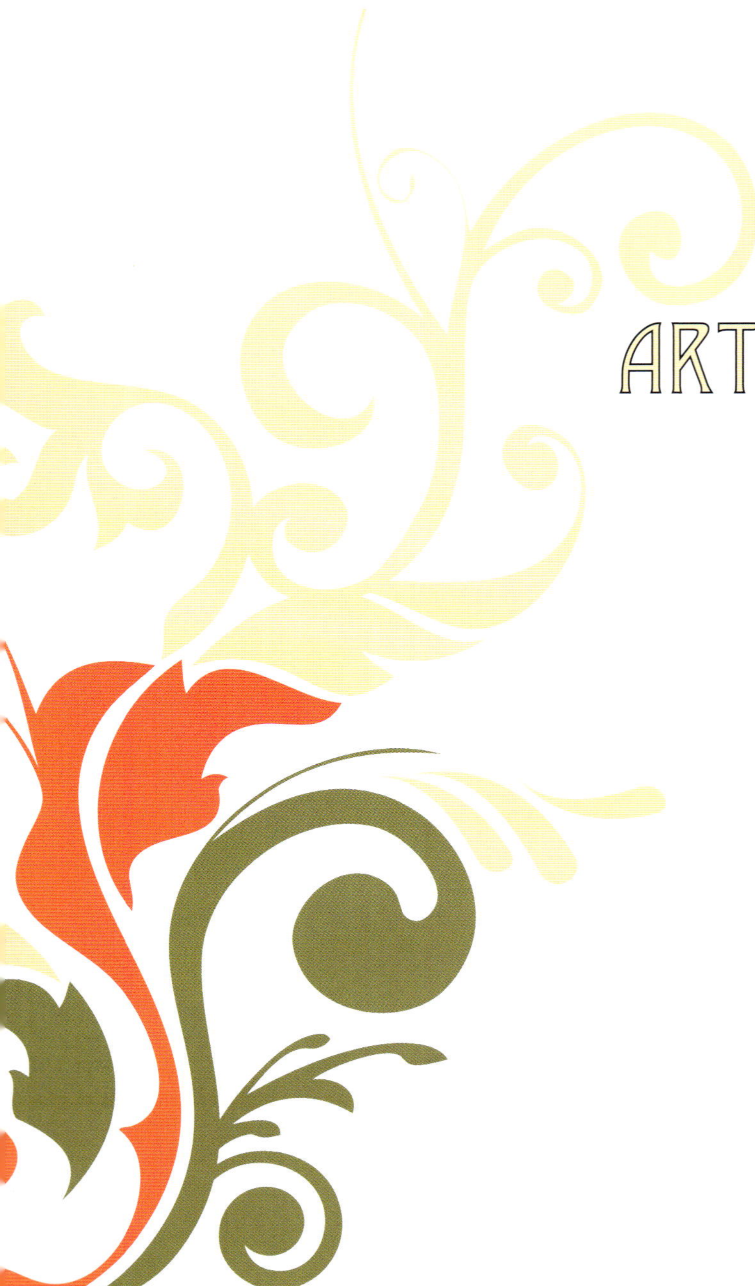

ART NOUVEAU REDUX
SARAH STROZZA

Featuring the graphic design, illustration, and installation work of eleven highly talented international artists, *Redefining the Line* investigates the influence of historical Art Nouveau on contemporary artists working in both the fine and commercial art worlds. In recent years, advances in digital technology have provided contemporary artists with new design practices, media, and printing methods. The artists presented in this exhibition—Pomme Chan, Deanne Cheuk, Naja Conrad-Hansen, Aya Kato, Pandarosa (Ariel Aguilera and Andrea Benyi), Marguerite Sauvage, Alberto Seveso, Sonya Suhariyan, Yoshi Tajima, and Eveline Tarunadjaja—embrace both traditional and digital design practices and convey the aesthetics and attitude of their Art Nouveau ancestors. Where to draw the line between fine and commercial art and between female beauty and vulgarity has certainly been argued by many. This exhibition not only intends to redefine such lines but perhaps blur them entirely.

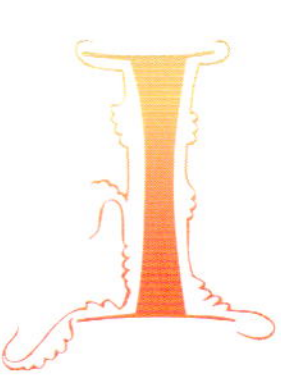

I n the late 1800s and early 1900s, Art Nouveau became a new art for a new age, uniting the fine and decorative arts and ultimately setting the stage for modern art as we know it. The industrial revolution offered artists not only new approaches to style, composition, and subject matter, but also new production methods such as color lithography. From Alphonse Mucha's graphic posters to Henri de Toulouse-Lautrec's theatrical advertisements, their work transformed the streets of Europe into galleries. Artists of the Art Nouveau era were famous for challenging academic standards of the day in their search for new forms that were capable of expressing this new, modern age.

Today, more than 100 years later, the artists showcased in this exhibition not only continue to lend their art to commercial avenues, like their Art Nouveau forefathers, but in ways never before imagined, as new digital media have joined the established realms of photography and lithography. In recent decades, the use of digital technology and computer programming has increasingly influenced our contemporary visual culture. Artists are able to exhibit their work in traditional forums such as museums and galleries, and to display their artwork more broadly—on billboards and T-shirts, iPods and skateboards, for example. Computer programs such as Photoshop and Illustrator give artists the capacity to digitally manipulate line as they please, resulting in images that can be conveniently mass-produced. Contemporary artists in this exhibition, like artists of the Art Nouveau era, take advantage of the ability to reproduce their artwork, reaching a broad range of viewers internationally.

In many ways, Art Nouveau set the stage for today's illustrators and graphic designers. It became the first true international art movement to embrace commercial art, as these earlier artists consistently used their images and designs to enhance the beauty of industrial products. Stylistically, Art Nouveau is famous for its emphasis on the graphic curvilinear line in the portrayal of the contemporary female figure. The use of linearity can also be seen in its incorporation of floral and organic plant-inspired motifs. Artists of this era, such as Jules Chéret, Alphonse Mucha, Aubrey Beardsley, Gustav Klimt, and Henri de Toulouse-Lautrec, were ultimately interested in taking the notion of ornament and pushing it beyond the decorative. They often explored new trends in their choice of subject matter; depicting women who conveyed an erotic yet innocent disposition. In many ways these artists liberated women from their Victorian restraints. Illustrated with bold lines and striking colors, reminiscent of Japanese woodblock prints, their works conveyed the modern, elegant woman who simultaneously radiated sensuality and self-confidence.

The artists in *Redefining the Line* similarly represent the female as symbolic of beauty, grace, elegance, and sensuality; however these artists depict the present-day, contemporary woman. These artists further seek to reclaim the traditional domination of the "male gaze" and to reinterpret the significance of female beauty. The attractive woman is no longer simply an object to be desired; rather she can own and take pride in her sexuality.

Ultimately, these artists successfully merge the fine and commercial art worlds. Inspired by both art historical ideas and contemporary media, they are redefining the line between fine art and commercial art while literally redrawing the lines of feminine beauty.

Sarah Strozza, Co-Curator
  Redefining the Line: Art Nouveau and the Female Figure

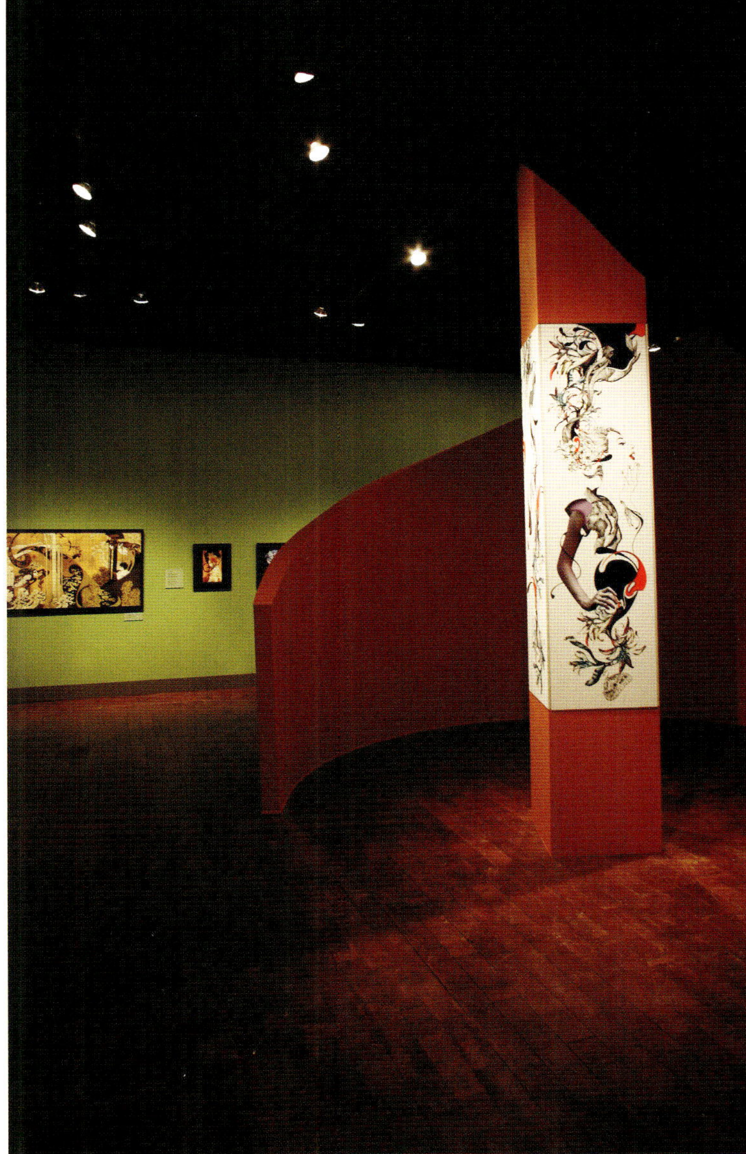

EMBRACING THE EMPOWERED FEMALE FIGURE IN ART NOUVEAU

ALEXANDRA DURON

Art Nouveau marked a pivotal moment in the representation of women. During the years from 1890 to 1910,[1] illustrators and graphic artists portrayed the feminine with a newfound sense of self-confidence and sensuality. Artists from this movement liberated depictions of the female figure from the conservative standards of the Victorian era and redefined the portrayal of women in art at the turn of the twentieth century. Today, approximately 100 years later, *Redefining the Line: Art Nouveau and the Female Figure* brings together a talented group of international contemporary artists, Pomme Chan, Deanne Cheuk, Naja Conrad-Hansen, Aya Kato, Pandarosa, Marguerite Sauvage, Alberto Seveso, Sonya Suhariyan, Yoshi Tajima, and Eveline Tarunadjaja, who celebrate and continue to reinvent the empowered female figure in their twenty-first-century artworks.

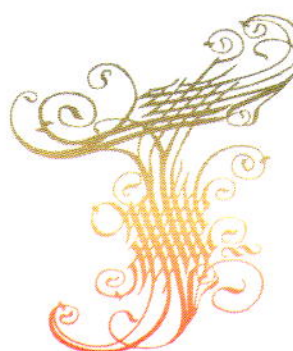

he most popular illustrators and designers associated with Art Nouveau, Aubrey Beardsley, Henri de Toulouse-Lautrec, Alphonse Mucha, and Jules Chéret, depicted women in ways that challenged traditional notions of femininity. British artist Aubrey Beardsley created dark, sensual illustrations that were considered "taboo" and even "pornographic" by Victorian society.[2] French artist Henri de Toulouse-Lautrec depicted the dancer Jane Avril, whom essayist Gabriel P. Weisberg described as the "new woman," and one who was "able to escape women's otherwise voiceless position to enter a world controlled by men."[3] Author Philip B. Meggs described Czech artist Alphonse Mucha, the favored poster designer of legendary actress Sarah Bernhardt, as depicting "exotic, sensuous, and yet maidenlike" women.[4] Meggs also observed that the females in French designer Jules Chéret's posters, affectionately referred to as the "Chérettes," were "neither prudes nor prostitutes," noting that "these self-assured, happy women enjoyed life to the fullest, wearing low-cut dresses, dancing, drinking wine, and even smoking in public."[5]

Just as the Art Nouveau artists' portrayals of women rejected the constraints of past representations, the contemporary illustrators, designers, and installation artists of *Redefining the Line* depict female figures who are in control of their sensuality rather than subject to it, emphasizing the confidence, power, and eroticism of a twenty-first century woman. This internationally diverse exhibition presents the point of view predominantly of women artists whose female characters meet the gaze of the viewer with a cool indifference at times and a coy, alluring smile at others. These artists allow their women to be as sweet or as seductive as they please. For example, upon first glance of artist Marguerite Sauvage's *Cups of Tea*, one notices a woman wearing a high-collared, puffed-sleeve garment reminiscent of a Victorian woman's dress calmly sipping one of many cups of tea surrounding her. Upon closer investigation of her hair, one notices that it is composed of a layered mass of female bodies playfully intertwined. The teardrop-shaped forms of steam that rise from the teacups also emanate from her hair, perhaps representing the sensuality of her thoughts. This layered, stimulating imagery suggests a high degree of sexual energy. Meanwhile, the female subject, sitting with a confident upright posture, appears to gaze self-assuredly, and rather seductively, into the distance.

The framework that shapes these sensual female images stems from the intensity of the line. The attention to bold, graphic linework, a driving force behind Art Nouveau, originated with Japanese Ukiyo-e woodblock prints from the seventeenth century through the late nineteenth century. "Ukiyo-e" translates as "pictures of the floating world,"[6] a description that is appropriate both for Art Nouveau imagery, as seen in the voluminous hair and skirts of Chéret's and Toulouse-Lautrec's women, and for the contemporary images in *Redefining the Line*, as seen in Aya Kato's fantastical landscapes, in the dreamlike imagery of Deanne Cheuk's *Mushroom Girls Virus* series, in the equally voluminous hair of Eveline Tarunadjaja's women, and in the flowing fabrics that Pomme Chan and Yoshi Tajima illustrate. Ukiyo-e subjects included a range of sensual female figures, from "renowned courtesans and prostitutes" to common, humble beauties.[7] This exhibition aligns with *Beauty and Art* author Elizabeth Prettejohn's opinion that "...the picture can be called erotic not simply because it represents nude female flesh, but in the way that it compels the viewer to experience a vivid relationship with the figure."[8]

The artists in *Redefining the Line* create imagery that sparks an instant bond with contemporary audiences. Today's women and men can identify with the bold, multilayered organic forms and delicate lines evident in Sonya Suhariyan's and Pandarosa's mixed-media works, the high-fashion clothing and design motifs apparent in Naja Conrad-Hansen's large-scale works on linen, and the provocative depictions of the female figure embodied in the art of Alberto Seveso. These qualities explain why the exhibited artists' illustration, installation, and design work is continually in demand by popular culture and fine art publications, merchandise and fashion designers, music video producers, and gallery exhibitions. Within these media avenues, the artists effortlessly merge the fine art and commercial art worlds. They create artworks for international companies and art galleries alike. These artists further bridge the divide with artistic approaches that combine traditional media and digital media. Many of the artists begin their work in the form of an ink or pencil drawing, watercolor painting, or both, and complete their work by enhancing the initial image through the use of contemporary digital art programs such as Adobe Photoshop and Illustrator. In our contemporary society, we crave dynamic imagery that pushes boundaries both visually and technically. Art Nouveau artist Chéret similarly employed technology and contributed advancements in color lithography, a growing medium at the end of the nineteenth century.[9] Through varied innovative methods, the artists of *Redefining the Line* create vibrant, layered images in which female bodies, flowing tresses, billowy fabrics, and organic forms intertwine.

This interplay of imagery and lines, whether drawn, painted, or digitally created or manipulated, results in a powerful combination of sensual, curving forms. The artworks presented are accessible to a wide range of viewers: some can appreciate the relationship between the past and present, while others can appreciate the immediacy of color, line, and representation. Both the contemporary artists and their Art Nouveau predecessors entice viewers with bold, attractive female silhouettes and with the curved, flowing linework that surrounds them. The contemporary images exude a freedom of spirit and linear exuberance similar to historical Art Nouveau yet redefine the style in a way that resonates with audiences today.

Alexandra Duron, Co-Curator
Redefining the Line: Art Nouveau and the Female Figure

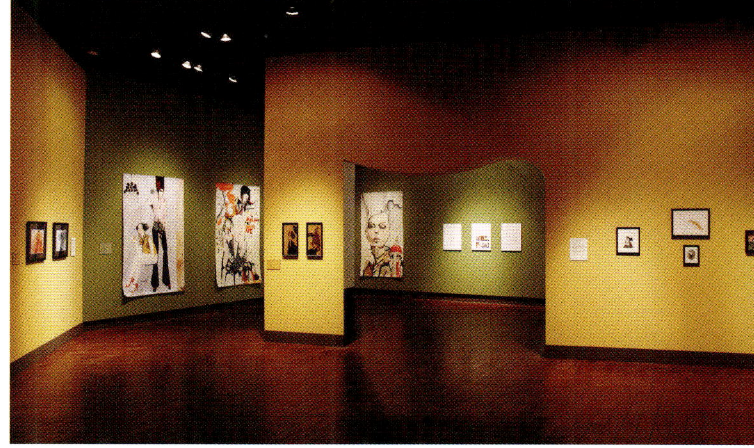

1. Philip B. Meggs, *Meggs' History of Graphic Design* (Hoboken: Wiley, 2006): 194.
2. Alastair Duncan, *Art Nouveau* (New York: Thames and Hudson, 1994): 20.
3. Gabriel P. Weisberg, "The Urban Mirror: Contrasts in the Vision of Existence," in *Paris and the Countryside: Modern Life in Late-19th-Century France* (Portland, Me.: Portland Museum of Art, 2006): 1.
4. Meggs, 205.
5. Ibid., 197.
6. Ibid., 190.
7. Ibid., 190-193
8. Elizabeth Prettejohn, *Beauty and Art* (New York: Oxford University Press, 2005): 132.
9. Meggs, 196-197.

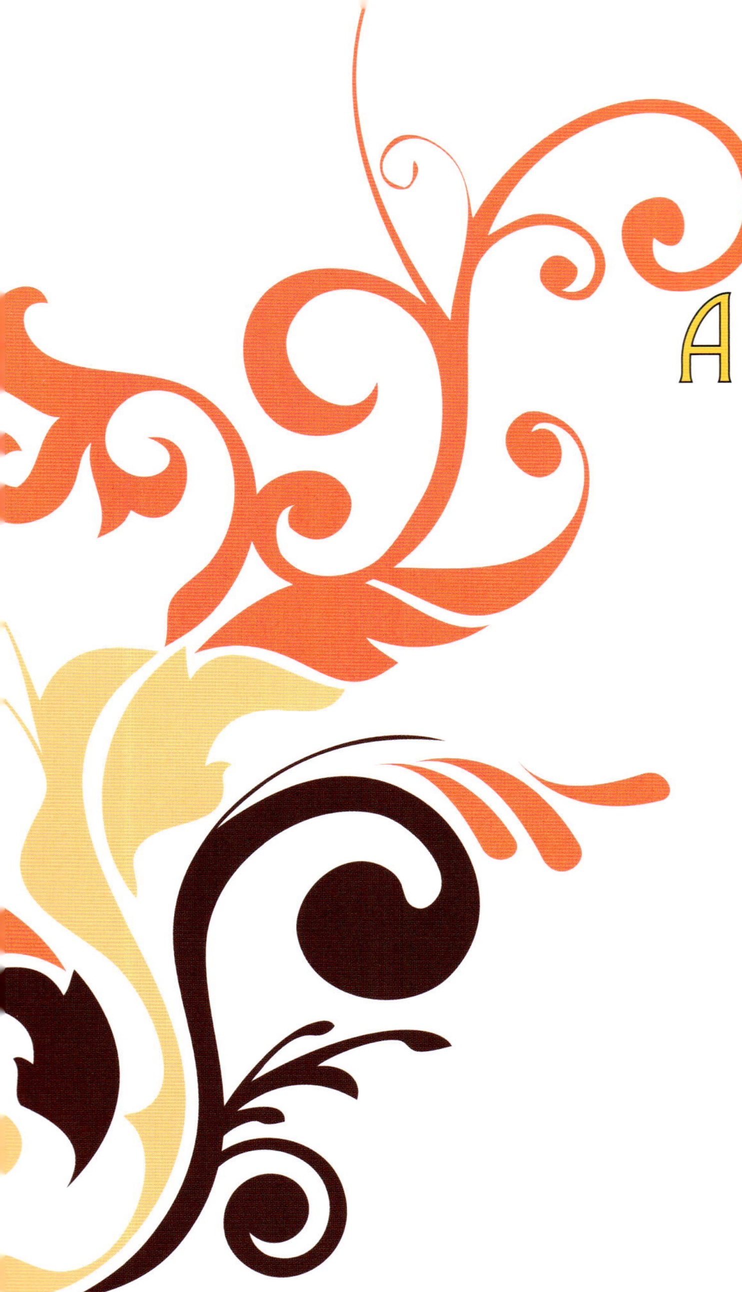

A 21ST-CENTURY

The late nineteenth century was a period of intense creativity and great invention in many fields. The electric light, the telephone, skyscrapers, movies, the Eiffel Tower, and Sigmund Freud's "The Interpretation of Dreams" all have roots this era. In the midst of this activity, the term "art nouveau" appeared in print for the first time in a Brussels newspaper. The year was 1884 and the new name caught on, capturing the essence of an international movement in art and design that spanned multiple creative disciplines for nearly two decades and culminated at the 1900 World's Fair in Paris.

The defining principles of Art Nouveau include embellishments and curvilinear lines along with flat color and bold, black lines. Japanese woodblock prints and Middle Eastern decoration were influential, as were botanical elements and the female form. But rather than don stuffy dresses or strike prim poses, women in these new pictures reflected the spirit of the times—they were joyful, expressive, and often erotic.

Art Nouveau was also notable for its wide embrace of disparate fields; painting and drawing, furniture making, jewelry design, architecture, graphic arts, performance, and glassware were all included. Art Nouveau practitioners envisioned a "total work of art" or *Gesamtkunstwerk*, but this idea faltered with the advent of Modernism and a renewed emphasis on fine art as distinct from—even elevated above—commercial arts and design.

In 2000, Paul Greenhalgh, head of research at the Victoria and Albert Museum, London, organized an Art Nouveau exhibition for the London Museum, an iteration of which was shown at the National Gallery in Washington, D.C. On a portion of the National Gallery's website dedicated to the exhibition, Greenhalgh explains, "We felt that the style itself had held the beginnings of modernity proper—that it was not just a weird aberration in the nineteenth century, or a false start to the twentieth century."

Today, the fine art versus commercial art divide has shifted again, with new technology urging a further blurring of the line. Artists paint with imaging-software and architects build with computer-aided design while training has become increasingly conceptual and theoretical, allowing those educated in the arts to apply their critical and aesthetic skills to

GESAMTKUNSTWERK

ANNIE BUCKLEY

various media and practitioners to move easily from one field to another.

Complicating this terrain is the increased accessibility of sophisticated technology for image manipulation, video editing, and design. These tools are available to anyone with a home computer, while the Internet provides a ready venue for showing creative work. This access to creative tools has arguably made the public more visually aware, but lacking historical and artistic understanding of what one is looking at—or making—changes the process. More people are certainly making more things, but are more people making art?

With *Redefining the Line: Art Nouveau and the Female Figure*, curators Alexandra Duron and Sarah Strozza address the possibility of a contemporary merging of multiple materials and fields, fueled by the use of digital media and the practitioners' ability to incorporate diverse disciplines. Duron and Strozza sought out an international group of talented individuals—from the United States, Japan, Australia, Italy, Denmark, France, Russia, and Great Britain. Each artist moves deftly between previously drawn categories in the fine and commercial arts and is inspired by the look and mindset of Art Nouveau.

reenhalgh explains, "All the famous makers of Art Nouveau objects were selling their ideas through magazines, journals, trade fairs, and exhibitions; they saw themselves as part of this larger world." Likewise, the artists in this exhibition are engaged in painting and drawing, publishing, installation, design, fashion, and illustration. The flowing lines and stylistic motifs of Art Nouveau are on view throughout, often in surprising new ways.

Like most of the artists included, Pomme Chan's multi-pronged practice mixes the digital and the handmade. The Thai-born, London-based artist draws lush imagery in pencil and finishes the work in the computer. Chan's drawings and illustrations have graced the pages of fashion and architecture magazines and the walls of the popular London store, TopShop. For this exhibition, Chan has transferred drawings, made with watercolor and pencil, to digital prints that are then applied onto a pillar in the gallery.

Australian born and New York-based Deanne Cheuk has a similarly hyphenated job description—designer, illustrator, art director, independent zine publisher, and artist—and also merges the lithe limbs of fashion models with graceful swirls and succulent flowers in her work. The line drawings included in Cheuk's first self-published book, *Mushroom Girls Virus*, are evocative of the elegant posters of Czech printmaker Alphonse Mucha, one of Art Nouveau's most prominent artists.

Sonya Suhariyan is a Russian artist, designer, and illustrator living in Rostov-on-Don, Russia. The long, thin women, clad in swirling garments, evident in many of her works also invoke Mucha, particularly Suhariyan's bright gouache, ink, and watercolor drawings of the seasons; the subject and vertical format reference Mucha's *Les Saisons*, but Suhariyan updates the universal theme and Mucha's earth-toned palette with jewel-like colors and ethnically ambiguous women.

With *Red Mask* and *Blue Mask* (both 2005), Suhariyan shifts away from a direct connection to Art Nouveau; the chaotic fusion of color and imagery here is evocative of the contemporary abundance of information and ideas. This visual overload is also apparent in the work of Japanese artists and designers Yoshi Tajima and Aya Kato.

Tajima studied in London and lives in Tokyo. He counts the Apple computer among his tools, alongside pencil, ink, watercolor, and gouache. In Tajima's work, flowers morph with clocks, swirls, and women wearing the perpetually stunned look of fawns. His use of Chinese ink, particularly in works like *Fairy 01* and *Fairy 03* (both 2008), is an intriguing take on Art Nouveau's signature black lines; here they wrap around imagery in a calligraphic swirl like a curling ribbon.

The profusion of flowers, lace, and limbs in Aya Kato's psychedelic prints is made from a combination of traditional and digital printing processes. The layered results, many featuring Kato's original take on fairytale characters like Rapunzel and Snow White, reference Disney and erotica at the same time. The truncated and bare-breasted women in *Cinderella (Metamorphosis)* cavort amidst a gold-and-black sea of artistic references—elegant waves à la Ukiyo-e woodblock prints, Klimt's signature gold, and stained-glass windows equally reminiscent of Art Nouveau and animated castles.

The photographic collages of Italian illustrator and graphic designer

Alberto Seveso stray yet further from the over-the-top decoration and lighthearted sensibility of Art Nouveau. Like Suhariyan and Kato, Seveso at times draws on traditional themes and personae. *The Three Graces (Grazia, Graziella e Grazie al Cazzo!)*, 2008, features three women, eyes and lips intact, cheeks and jaw composed of a maze of tendrils and petals.

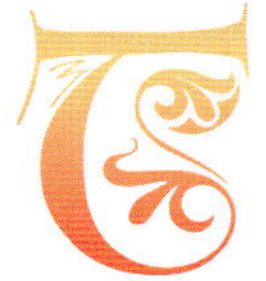

he minimal colors and surreal use of decoration in place of flesh veer toward the grotesque; Seveso challenges the conventions of beauty from within fashion and design.

In contrast, Naja Conrad-Hansen, an artist and designer from Denmark, exaggerates the tropes of contemporary beauty in her oil on linen paintings. In *Don't Call Me Girl*, 2009, two women with the elongated physiques and blank expressions of supermodels vamp on a subdued ground of washy grey. The strong shapes and powerful contrast of their long legs—one woman clad in black pants, the other with nude legs—approach abstraction.

In Conrad-Hansen's *Is It Real or Am I Confused?*, 2009, a woman's hair is made of a pattern of vertical lines. As it was in Art Nouveau, most notably in the work of Aubrey Beardsley, hair is used as a design and compositional element in many of the works in this exhibition. Marguerite Sauvage cleverly draws a giant up-do from a pile of cavorting women and their intermingled hair in *Cups of Tea*, 2007. The playful, idyllic female figures—often clad in the Converse-and-ballgown style of contemporary princesses—of this French artist, illustrator, and animator can be found in glossy fashion magazines and animated television shows. Like Kato and Tajima, Sauvage uses a mix of old and new technology, drawing in pencil and painting with the computer.

The central figure of *V is for Vices*, 2006, by Eveline Tarunadjaja, is surrounded by an oval composed of the subject's flowing locks; indeed, much of this Indonesia-born, Australia-based artist and illustrator's work involves an abundance of intricately drawn hair, like so many swirling snakes. In her ink-and-acrylic drawings, masses of excessively long, delicate hair are draped over petite shoulders, fancifully pulled by balloons or umbrellas, and blended poetically with the green waters of a lake or the long feathers of birds. The collaborative pair of artists from Australia, Pandarosa, also know as Andrea Benyi and Ariel Aguilera, often uses decorative hair in their installations and drawings—including the aptly titled *She tangled her hair in the clouds*, 2009.

Here Pandarosa creates a unique wall drawing with cut vinyl featuring an androgynous face with hair mutating into flowering vines. Set amid the glass and geometric architecture of the front window of the gallery, the sweetly fierce portrait and hair-meets-nature of Pandarosa's installation epitomize the updated take on Art Nouveau evident throughout this exhibition. Pandarosa—makers of website, animation, illustration, and installations—has a heady enthusiasm for media and a graphic take on decoration. Their aim, "to break the preconceived idea that design and art cannot co-exist," underlies Duron and Strozza's curatorial vision in *Redefining the Line*. ✦

Annie Buckley
Buckley is a writer, editor, and artist based in Los Angeles. She has contributed to Artforum *and* Art in America, *and has guest lectured at the San Francisco Art Institute and UCLA Graduate School of Education.*

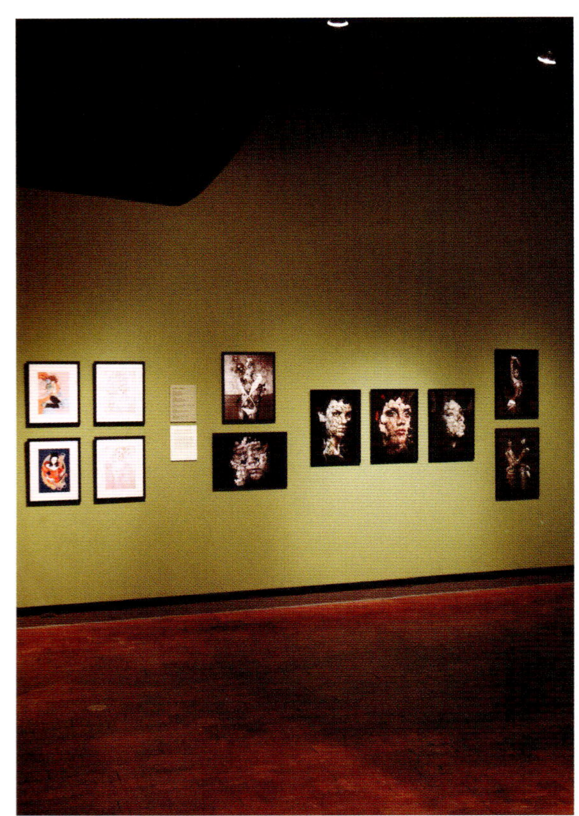

NEW PURSUITS: THE LURE OF THE CURVILINEAR

JOANNA ROCHE

Line is a force. [1]
Henri van de Velde

"Change and destroy the body which has given too much delight!" Daphne, pursued by Apollo, cried to her father, the river, for help. Responding to his daughter's despair, he transformed her into a laurel tree. The poet, Ovid, continues the tale:

> When her limbs grew numb and heavy, her soft breasts
> Were closed with delicate bark, her hair was leaves,
> Her arms were branches, and her speedy feet
> Rooted and held, and her head became a tree top,
> Everything gone except her grace, her shining.

[lines 548-552, book One, *Metamorphoses*] [2]

The eleven artists of *Redefining the Line: Art Nouveau and the Female Figure* change but do not destroy the body, which clearly gives so much delight. The dominant vision represented by this wonderfully varied, international group of artists is that of women as sentient and sexually charged beings, who, unlike Daphne, are in control of their transformation. Rather than losing breasts, arms, and head to the life of the laurel, these beautiful (if idealized) women show us a fusion of forms, where nature and the feminine offer an integrated, self-determined persona.

This essay will engage the three themes central to the curators of this show: art nouveau, the female form, and the incorporation of the digital graphic techniques—a medium shared by many of these artists.

I. A Tale of Two Centuries

There are significant connections between the artists and artworks included in this exhibition and the mega-movement that was Art Nouveau. Most obvious is the shared focus on two-dimensionality and the curved line. The significance of the line as energetic force cannot be underestimated. Belgian theorist and designer Henry van de Velde argued that this "vitality" or energy of the line—what he called *line force*—was "at the basis of ornamental activity." [3] The line holds the energy of the person making it, van de Velde claimed. It is not "simply a 'decorative' line…but a vital, creative carrier of human energy." [4] From Hermann Obrist's needlework *Whiplash*, 1895, to Hector Guimard's 1899 Paris Métro Entrance, the sinuous, organic lines of Art Nouveau were a testament to the power of design. We can see an excellent example of line force in Pomme Chan's site-specific columns. Chan covers freestanding columns with looping, high-contrast designs, which transform a simple white pillar into a pulsing, abstract surface. The line in motion changes solid structures into living gardens—this is Art Nouveau's essence.

Indeed, the power of line force can be seen throughout this collective body of work. From Deanne Cheuk's gorgeous outlines and watercolor drips in her *Mushroom Girls Virus Book* series to Alberto Seveso's sperm-shaped vectors in his sensual *The Three Graces* (which, of course, carry additional symbology), the sinuous energy of the line fuses nature and the human. "Decorative," that oft-maligned descriptive, is rearticulated by these twenty-first-century artists much as it was at the end of the nineteenth century: as a fundamental human activity. We create our environment through the act of ornamentation. To embrace the decorative is to "embrace all branches of art equally." [5]

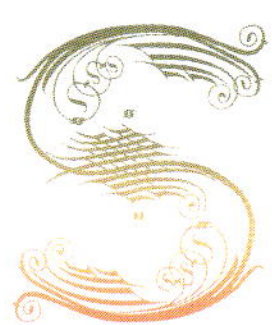

ignificantly, *Redefining the Line* shares the international character of the movement that was variably known as "Art Nouveau," "Modernismo," "New Style," "Jugendstil," etc. (Interestingly, the French liked to use the English term "New Style," while the English and Americans preferred the French "Art Nouveau.") The sheer plethora of names for the movement was an indication of its international popularity. In this exhibition, artists hailing from/working in no fewer than eight countries are represented. While we are (fortunately) less nationalistically inclined in today's "global" culture than were our nineteenth-century forebears, the spirit of internationalism in the arts is wonderfully demonstrated by this exhibition: Australia, Denmark, England, France, Italy, Japan, Russia, U.S.A.

The importance of periodicals for the distribution of forms and designs is another important link between then and now. In the United

States alone, more than 7,000 new periodicals were published between 1885 and 1905.[6] Magazines such as *The Studio, The Yellow Book, Harper's, Lippincott's,* and *Jugend* featured works of up-and-coming artists much as today's magazines, exhibition catalogues, and "zines" are important venues for emerging artists. Eveline Tarunadjaja's exquisite drawings have been published in *Vogue Girl, Elle,* and *Frankie*; prolific artist Deanne Cheuk worked as art director (*Tokion*) and a designer, illustrator, and publisher (*Neomu*); Yoshi Tajima publishes his multimedia collages in *Vogue*—these are just a few examples among this highly published group of young artists.

II. Liberating the Line

Does "redefinition" precede "liberation"? I think they are part of the same project. Key to this exhibition is the representation of the feminine *into and out of* a static—and singular—notion of the feminine. Many of us trained in the last decade/s to analyze interconnections of gender, sexuality, and representation would assume a contemporary woman artist's representation of a female body would be at odds with the traditional, hegemonic aesthetics of pleasure (back to Apollo chasing Daphne). But nipples are powerful. The representation of women by women—and the power of self-determination—is a strong current throughout this show, exemplified by Marguerite Sauvage's *Pudeur*, 2007, Aya Kato's *Cinderella (Metamorphosis)*, 2006, Sonya Suhariyan's *Seasons*, and Naja Conrad-Hansen's *Don't Call Me Girl*, 2009.

Pudeur offers contemporary viewers a rethinking of the eroticism of vintage pinups. Gaze averted in a daydream of the boudoir, Sauvage's woman in pink would appear to be the passive object of our gaze, but her doubled figure shows us there is more than meets the eye. She is both introspective and layered with saucy pink nudes who cavort across the composition and play with the nostalgic mood, activating the scene with their indiscretions. The artist doesn't allow us to slip into the simple admiration of an objectified female body; she and her women mess with us—just enough.

ya Kato's elongated, geometric forms in *Cinderella (Metamorphosis)* remind me of another brilliant illustrator: Erté (Romain de Tirtoff), famous for his Art Deco covers for *Harper's Bazaar* of the late 1920-30s. Far from being the beleaguered heroine, Kato's Cinderella shows us a process of self-transformation, morphing before our eyes from lifeless to alive. Sonya Suhariyan's stunning ink-and-watercolor series of the seasons borrows from the popular nineteenth-century practice of using women to represent the four seasons;

but unlike Art Nouveau's pale muses (with their seasonal shades of hair and garb), her *Autumn*, 2005, is African and her *Spring*, 1999, is Asian—they are proud and elegant, far from the idly voluptuous muses of Mucha.

A fascination with fashion, black and white, and psychologically complex women are at the core of Naja Conrad-Hansen's dynamic conception of the feminine. This aesthetic links her to that "decadent" bad boy of British Art Nouveau, Aubrey Beardsley. In today's world, where male muses are as useful as female muses have always been, Beardsley is huge. He defied the hierarchies of "fine art" and "illustration" with designs that pushed the moral and artistic limits of his day, creating works that parodied the stodgier Medievalism of William Morris. Conrad-Hansen's women are slender, groomed, and defiant—twenty-first century *femmes fatales* of Salomé-esque force, who clearly acknowledge the visual grace of Japanese art and culture, as do many of these artists—and their Art Nouveau kin.

It is their combination of artistic innovation alongside creative reuse/rethinking of Art Nouveau's subject matter that distinguishes these contemporary (male and female) artists; they go well beyond appropriation or imitation to redefinition and even...liberation.

III. Playing with the Digital/Final Thoughts

The effort to break down longstanding academic hierarchies in the arts, such as the opposition between "crafts" and "art" or (more recently) "applied" and "fine art," has been going on for well over a century. William Morris, founder of the Arts and Crafts movement (1860s-early 1890s), promoted the belief that "craft" was an art form on equal footing with painting or sculpture. Morris's efforts did awaken society to the idea that objects of everyday use were worthy of careful and innovative design. However, his rejection of industrialization on the moral grounds that it separated the worker from the products of his/her labor was at odds with that century's trajectory toward mass production. Mass-produced goods were, simply put, more affordable and available to a growing middle class than the costly handcrafted goods of the Arts and Crafts guild system. The "new art for the new age" (Art Nouveau) distanced itself from the small-scale production mindset of the utopian Arts and Crafts movement. Though both movements believed in the equality of the arts and celebrated the decorative arts in particular, Art Nouveau embraced industrialism, with its tantalizing abundance of new materials and revolutionary manufacturing methods, such as iron and glass casting and, key to this comparison, chromolithography (color lithography).[7]

Chromolithography was the mechanical process responsible for the explosion of the poster as *the* nineteenth-century vehicle for advertisement. Scores of artists, including Jules Chéret, Alphonse Mucha, and Henri de Toulouse-Lautrec, adopted and transformed this relatively new technology to publicize the many entertainments and commodities available to the urban populace, from Sarah Bernhardt to beer. The use of digital technology by many of the artists of *Redefining the Line*, a number of whom are also creating work for commercial venues, echoes the *fin-de-siècle's* fascination with new technology and its application to the popular arts. The glittering, floral layers of Aya Kato's *Rapunzel,* 2004, or Yoshi Tajima's evocative collages, *6 a.m., 7 a.m., 8 a.m.*, 2006, incorporate digital technology much as the Parisian poster artists employed chromolithography. Refined drawing skills are still key. We could say that while the line is handmade, the technical processes of Photoshop, Illustrator, and other software permit the line to be *played*.

I have long loved Ovid's story of Daphne, perhaps because of the poignant image of a young woman transformed into a tree. The bond between nature and the feminine is an ancient one that can be traced in the folklore and legends of many peoples. As I have touched upon in these brief pages, artists of our present moment are very much absorbed in this ongoing story, in ways that echo the past while they redefine it. Pandarosa, the Melbourne-based collaborative, in their epic vinyl installation for the Main Gallery's front window, offers a new Daphne, one capable of thoughts and dreams. While Ovid's figure must surrender her selfhood to escape, Pandarosa's heroine looks out at us, identity intact, branches extending from her hair like so many ideas. We are greeted here, and repeatedly within the walls of *Redefining the Line*, by a vision of the feminine in which "her grace, her shining" is not lost but continually rediscovered within the female form. ✿

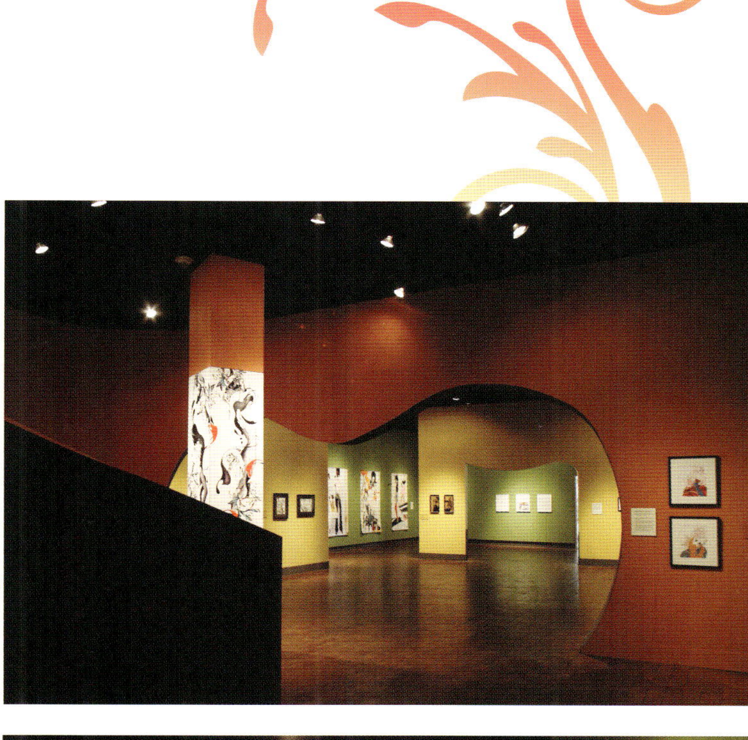

Joanna Roche
Roche is a professor of Art History at Cal State Fullerton, specializing in 20th century and contemporary art history and theory. She has published on a range of 20th and 21st century artists, notably Joseph Cornell and Goat Island.

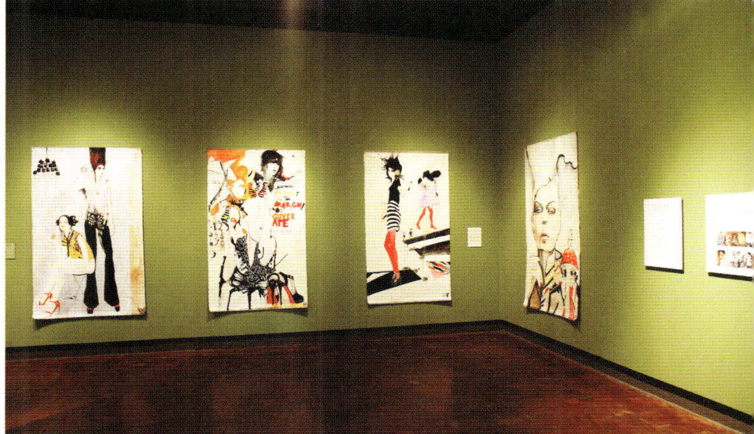

1. Stephen Eskilson, *Graphic Design: A New History* (New Haven: Yale University Press, 2007): 98.

2. Ovid, *Metamorphoses*, trans. Rolfe Humphries (Bloomington & London: Indiana University Press, 1955): 19-20.

3. Elie Haddad, "On Henry van de Velde's *Manuscript on Ornament*," *Journal of Design History* 16, no 2 (2003): 135.

4. Ibid.

5. Bradford Collins, "The Poster as Art: Jules Chéret and the Struggle for Equality of the Arts in Late Nineteenth-Century France," *Design Issues 2* (spring 1985); reprint, *Design History: An Anthology*, ed. Dennis Doordan, Cambridge, Mass. & London: MIT Press, 1995), 24 (page citation is to the reprint edition).

6. Eskilson, 52.

7. Although this process was discovered in the mid 1900s, it came into wide use in the 1890s, especially with the technical innovations of Jules Chéret, whose large-format color posters were of an unprecedented "hue, value and intensity." Eskilson, 36. See Collins article for detailed discussion of Chéret's innovations.

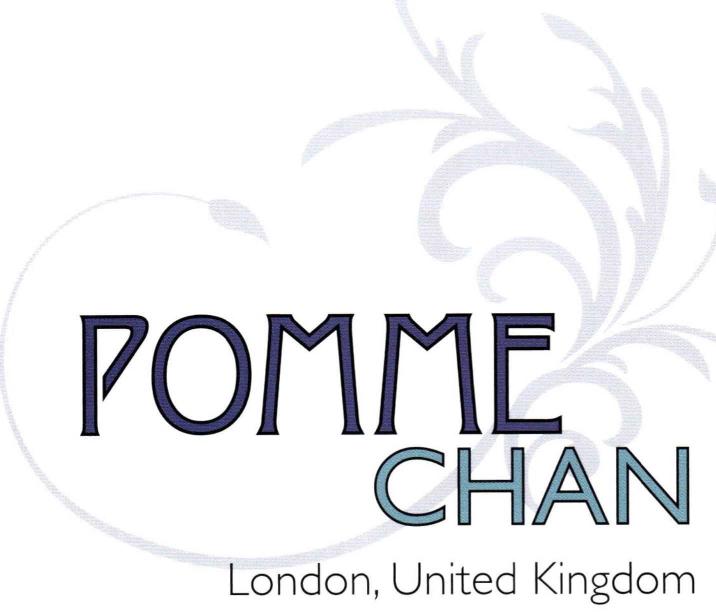

London, United Kingdom

"Carefully and sensitively constructed, each illustration is bursting at the seams with thoughtful and delicate detail. It is such precision that [gives] Chan's work a floating, three-dimensional feel."

~ Grafik Magazine, March 2006

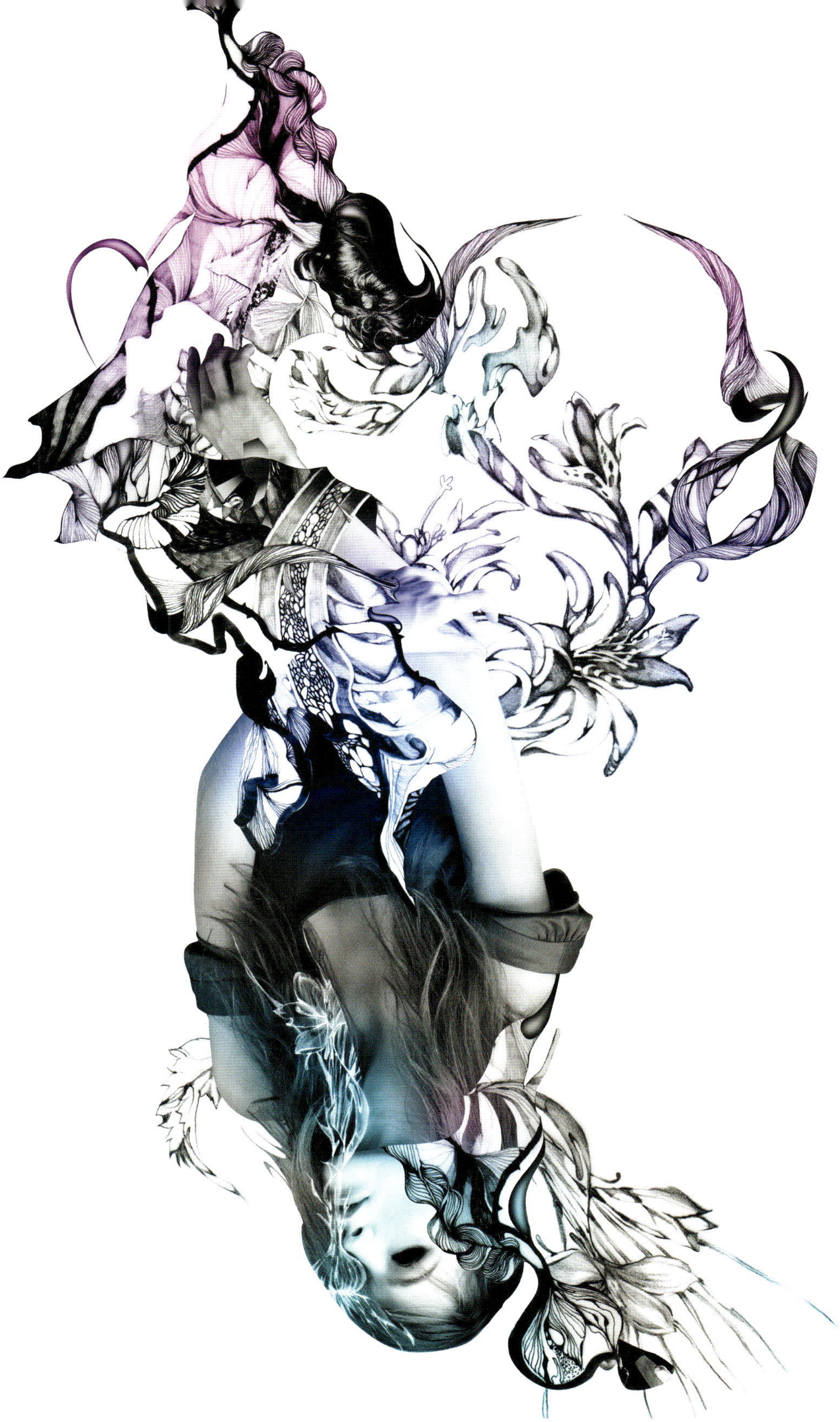

Pomme Chan | *Lust*, 2009 | Created specifically for *Redefining the Line* | Print on canvas (original hand-drawn + photo collage + computer finish) | 30 × 25 inches | Courtesy of the artist

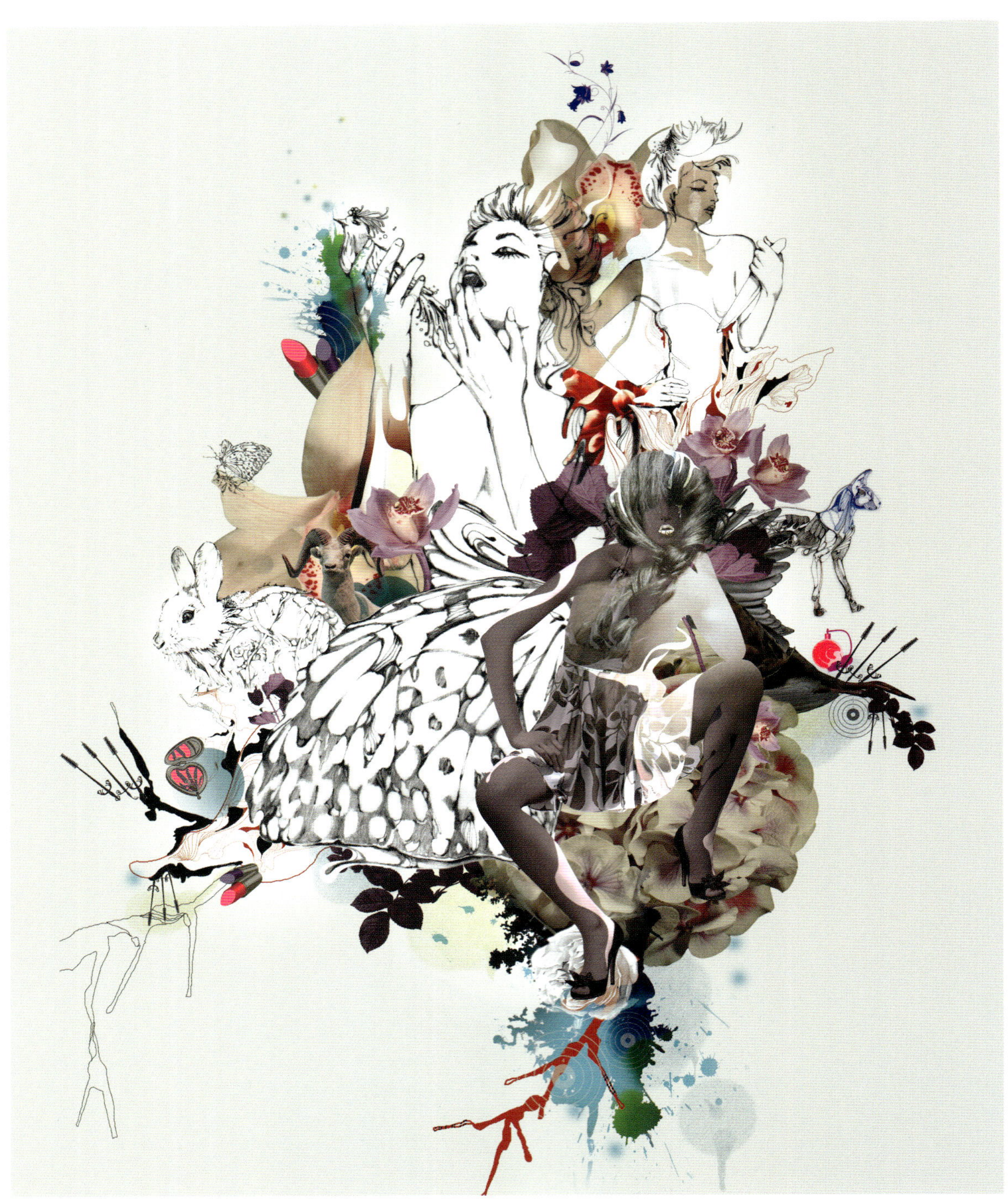

Pomme Chan | *H.Un.t Project Image #1*, 2007 | Print on canvas (original hand-drawn + photo collage + computer finish)
30 × 25 inches | Courtesy of the artist

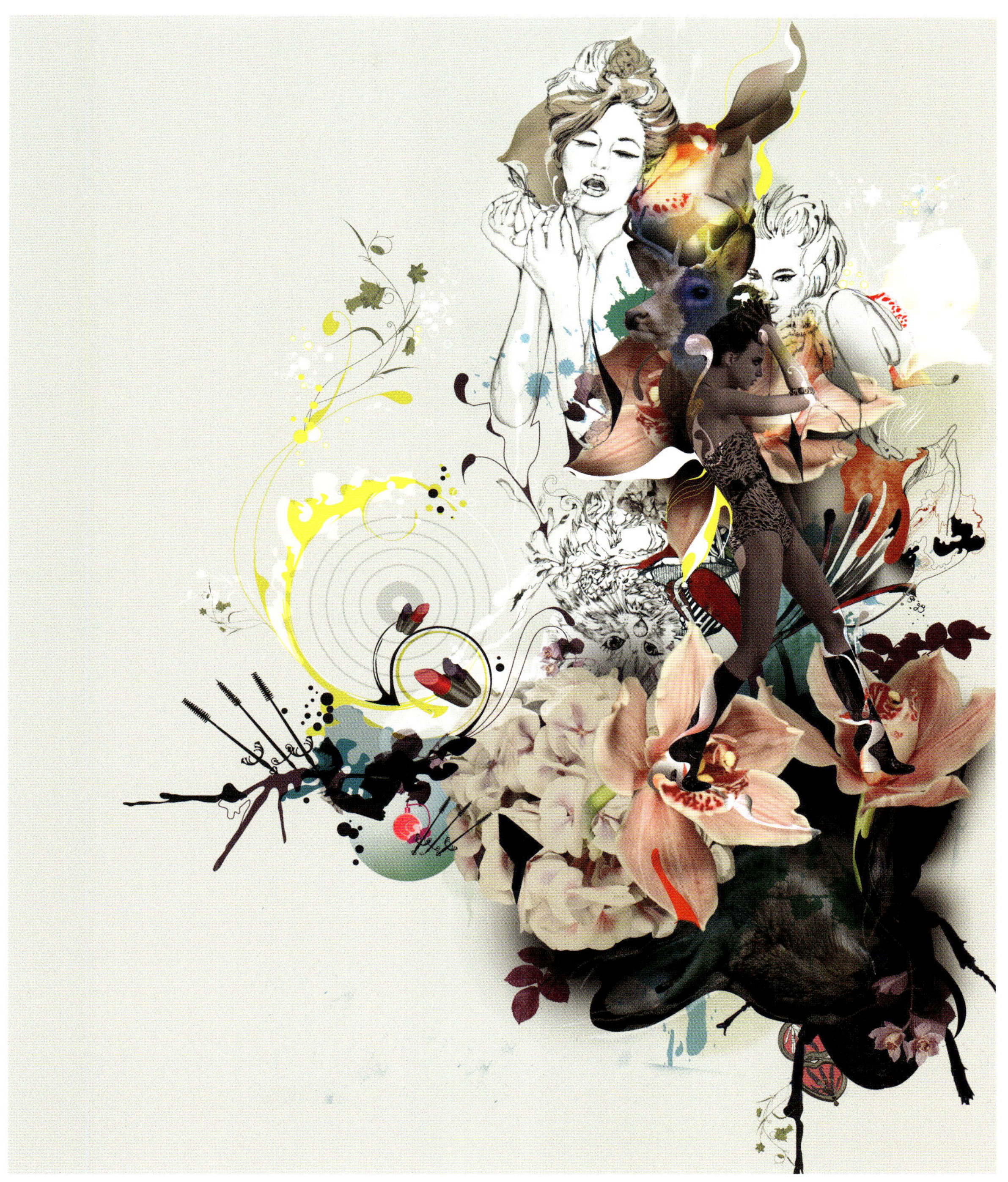

Pomme Chan | *H.Un.t Project Image #2*, 2007 | Print on canvas (original hand-drawn + photo collage + computer finish)
30 × 25 inches | Courtesy of the artist

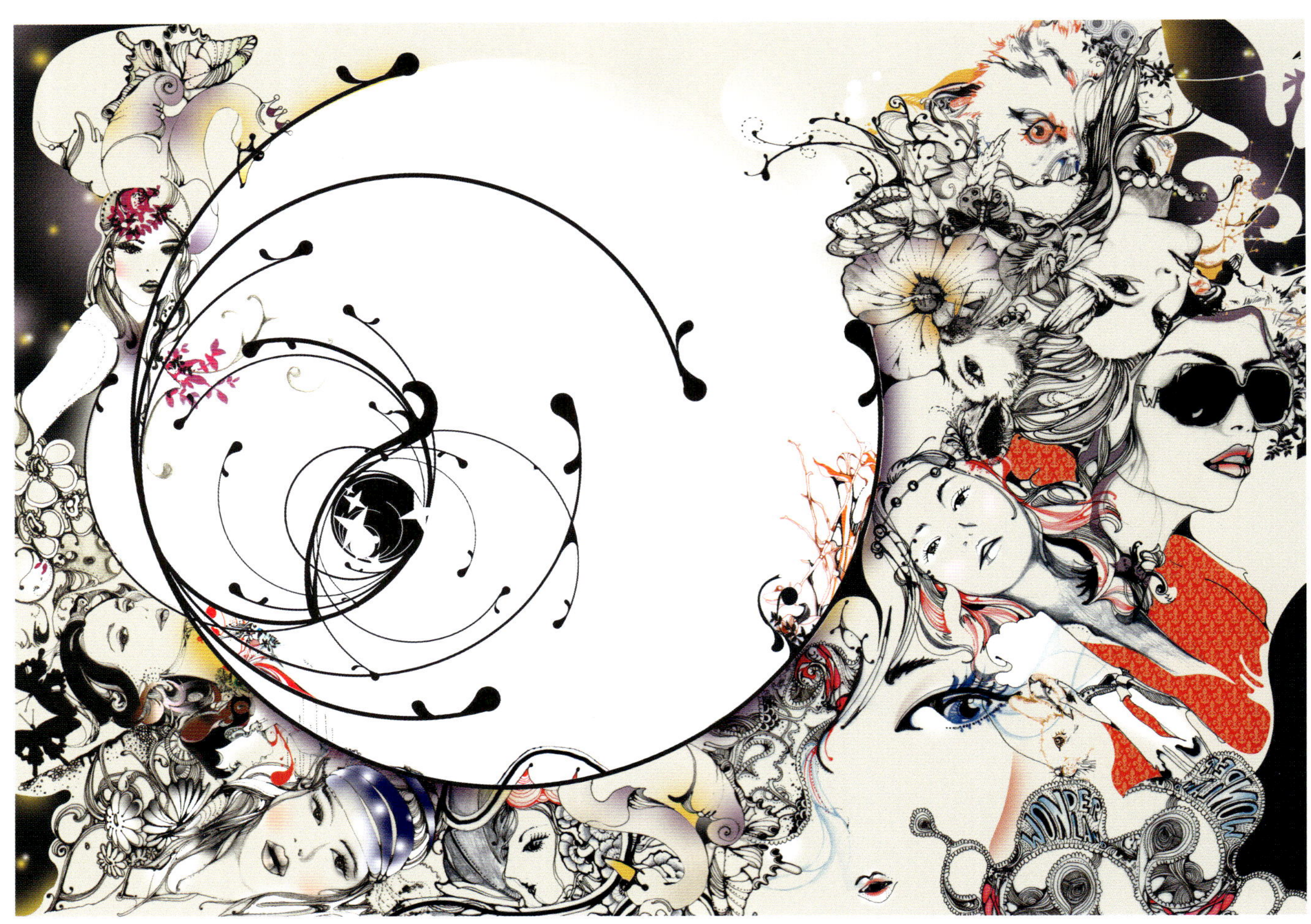

Pomme Chan | *Wonder*, 2006 | Print on canvas (original hand-drawn + photo collage + computer finish)
20 × 30 inches | Courtesy of the artist

(opposite) **Pomme Chan** | *She*, 2009 | Created specifically for *Redefining the Line* | Print on canvas (original hand-drawn with watercolors + computer finish) | 23½ × 16½ inches | Courtesy of the artist

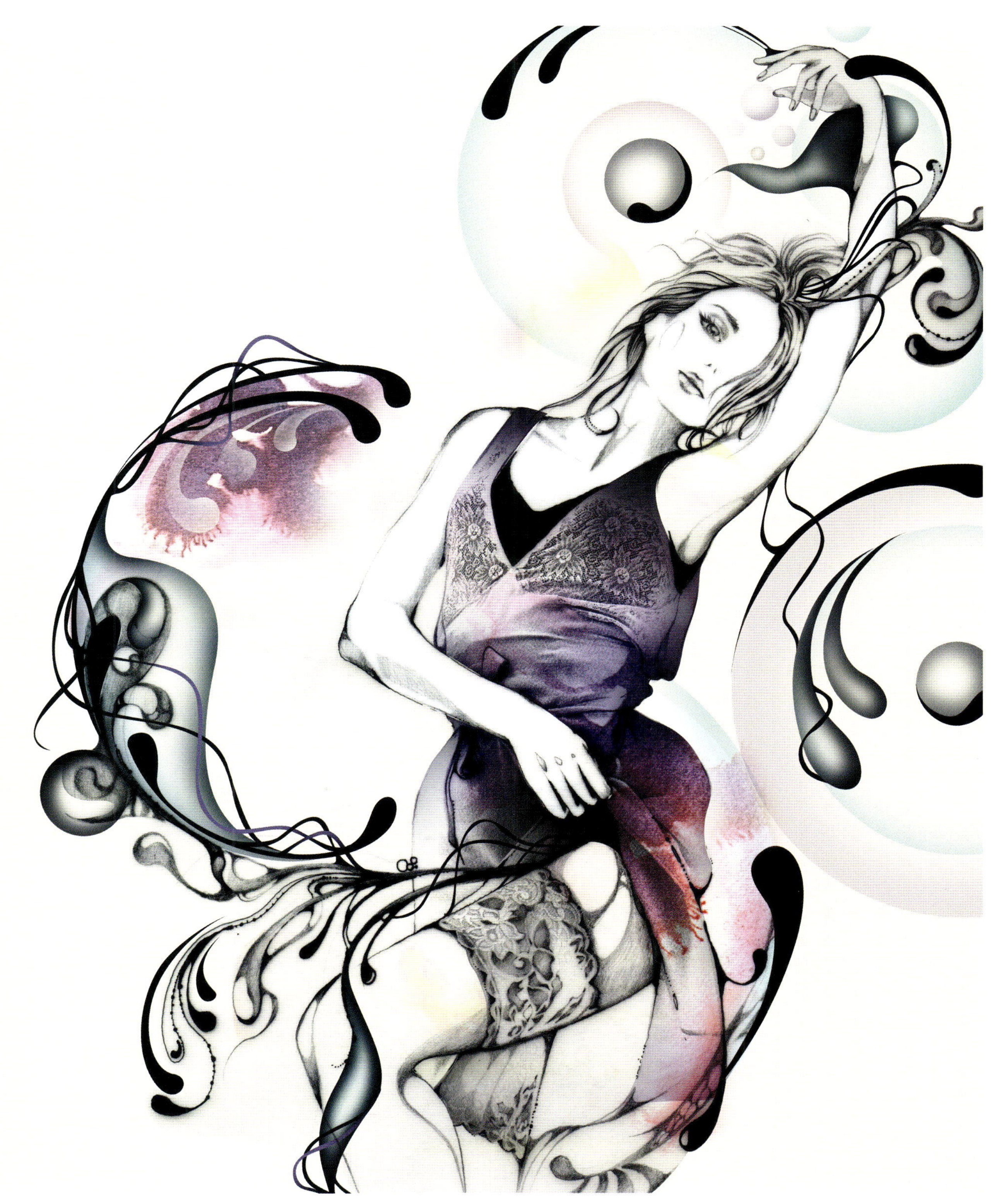

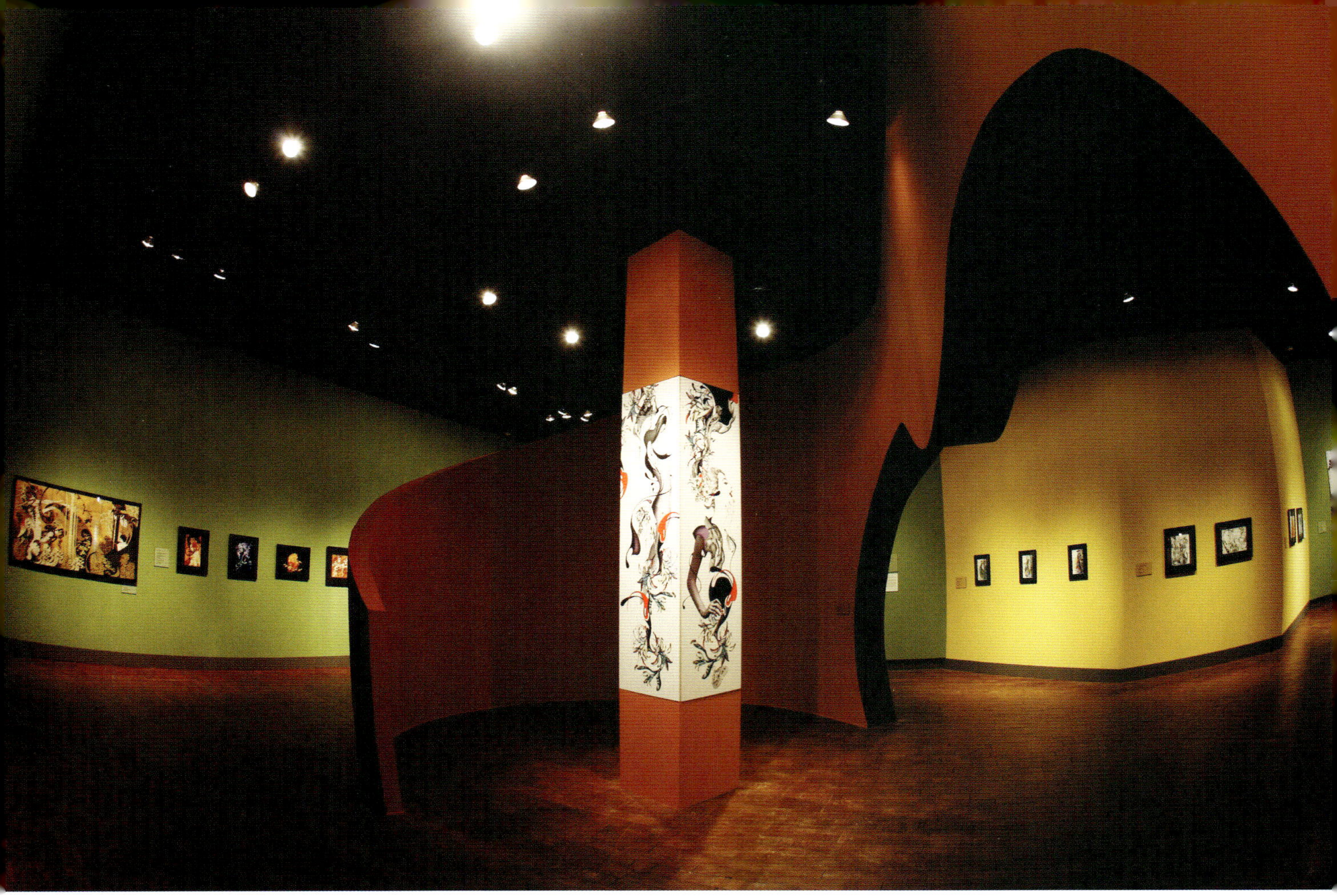

Pomme Chan | *Secret World*, 2009 | Site-specific installation | Print on canvas (original hand-drawn with watercolors + computer finish)
4 parts, 86½ × 23½ inches each | Courtesy of the artist

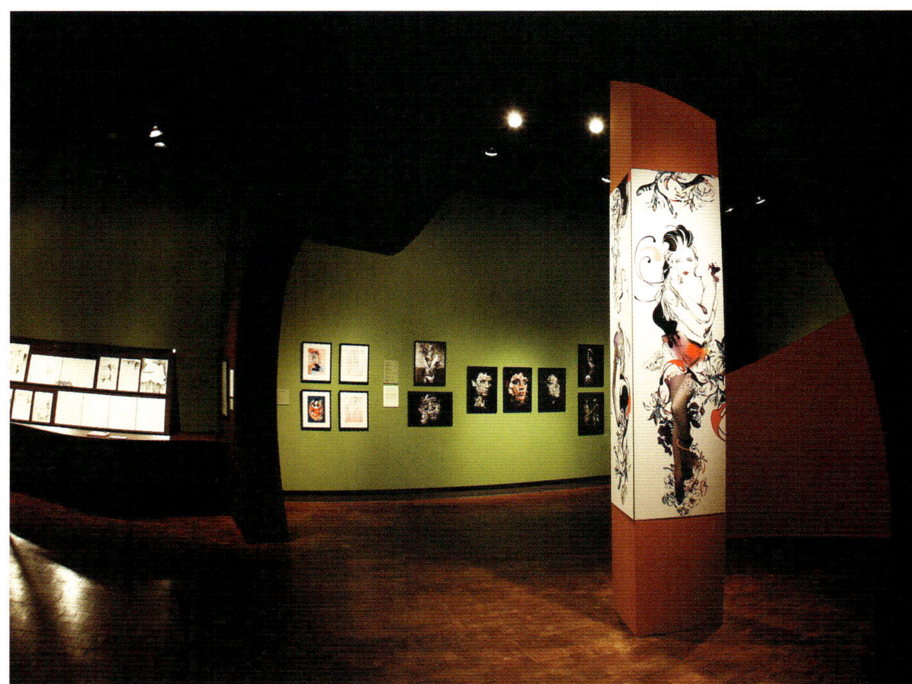

POMME
CHAN

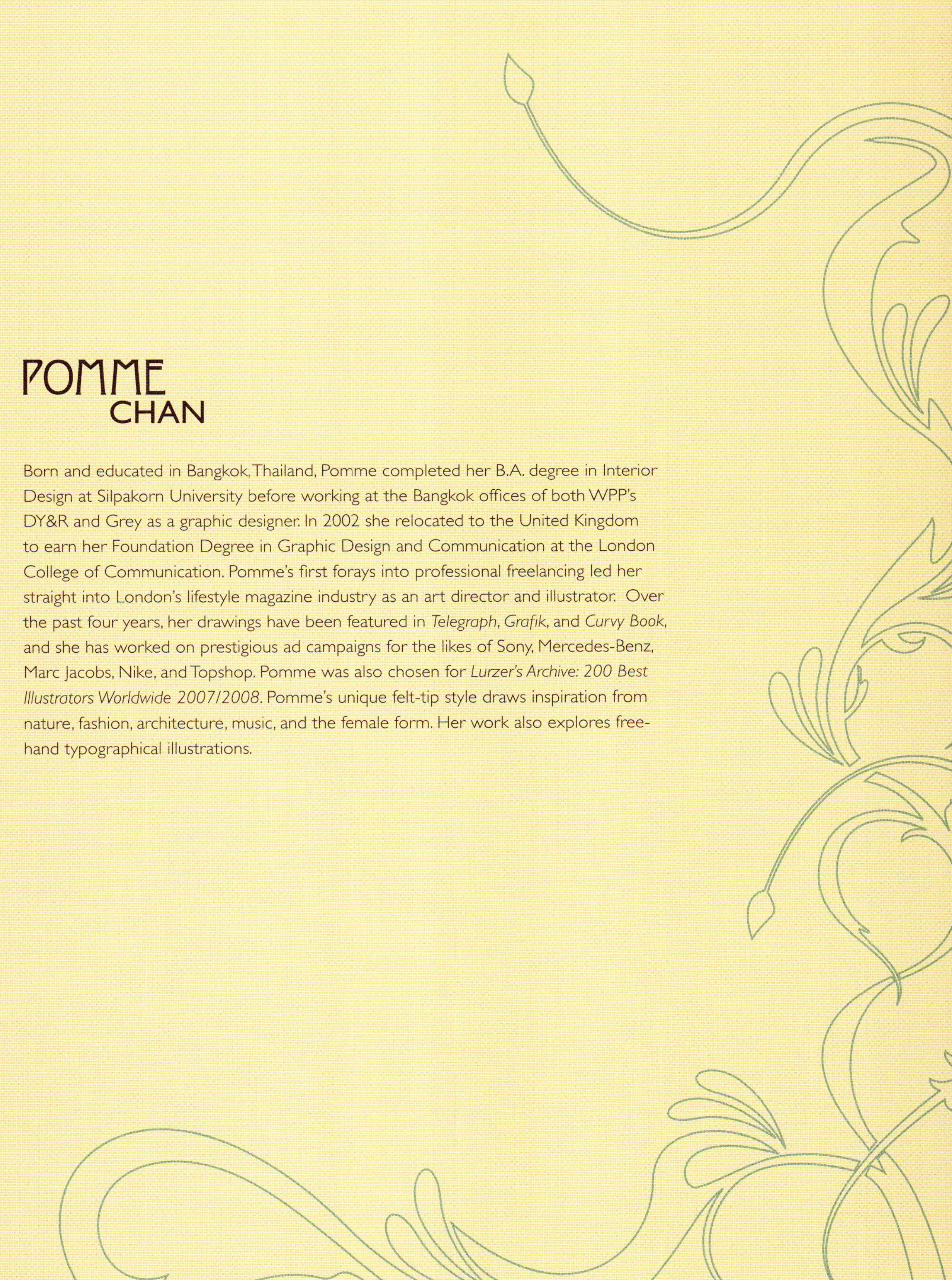

Born and educated in Bangkok, Thailand, Pomme completed her B.A. degree in Interior
Design at Silpakorn University before working at the Bangkok offices of both WPP's
DY&R and Grey as a graphic designer. In 2002 she relocated to the United Kingdom
to earn her Foundation Degree in Graphic Design and Communication at the London
College of Communication. Pomme's first forays into professional freelancing led her
straight into London's lifestyle magazine industry as an art director and illustrator. Over
the past four years, her drawings have been featured in *Telegraph*, *Grafik*, and *Curvy Book*,
and she has worked on prestigious ad campaigns for the likes of Sony, Mercedes-Benz,
Marc Jacobs, Nike, and Topshop. Pomme was also chosen for *Lurzer's Archive: 200 Best
Illustrators Worldwide 2007/2008*. Pomme's unique felt-tip style draws inspiration from
nature, fashion, architecture, music, and the female form. Her work also explores free-
hand typographical illustrations.

DEANNE CHEUK

New York, USA

"My work is many-layered and laborious. I believe that we are the sum of all of our experiences and that we are all connected. In that way, I try to impart some of this knowledge into each piece of my work."

~ Deanne Cheuk

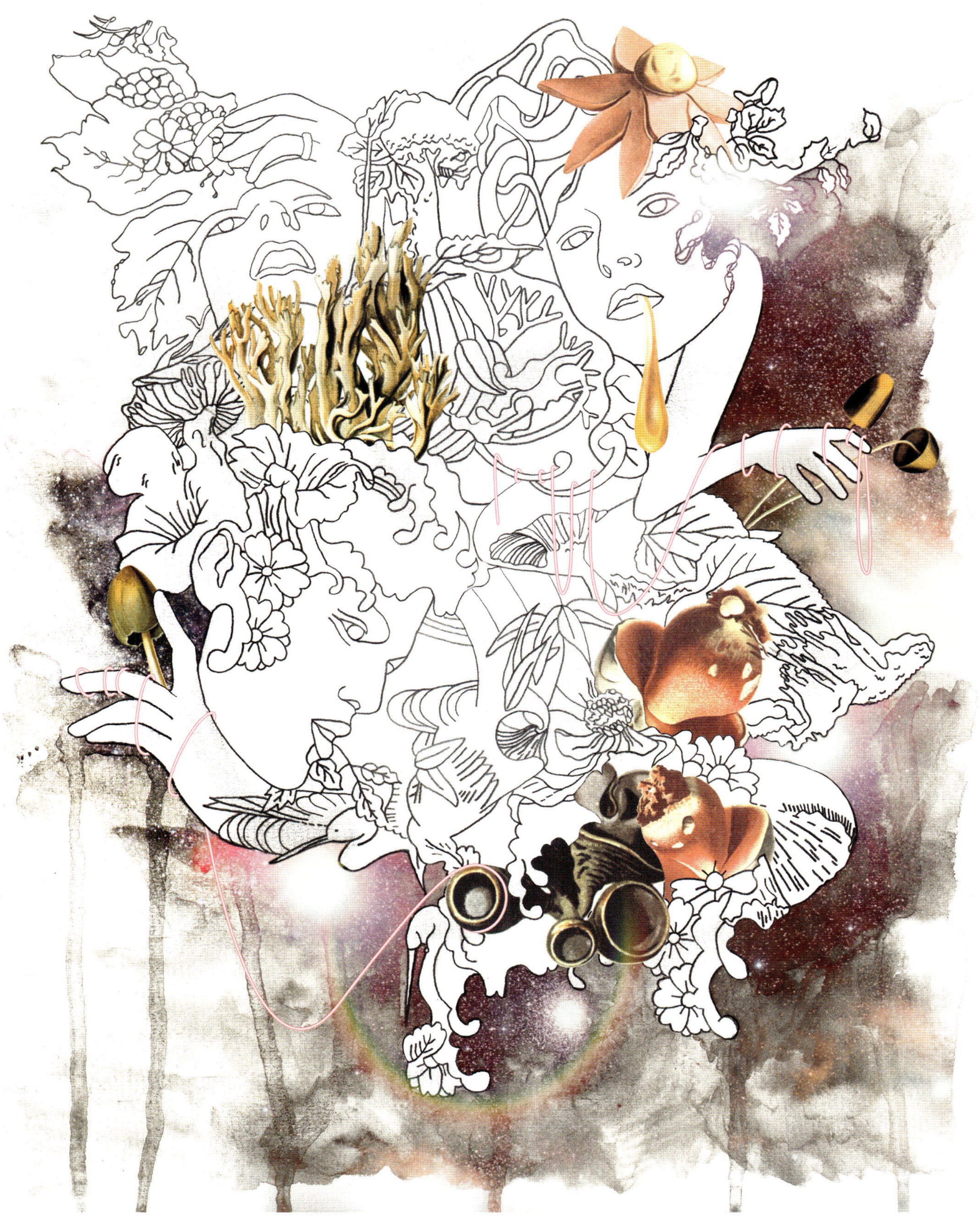

Deanne Cheuk | *Elegance Bizarre, Part 3*, 2003 | Digital print on archival paper | 27 × 21 inches | Courtesy of the artist

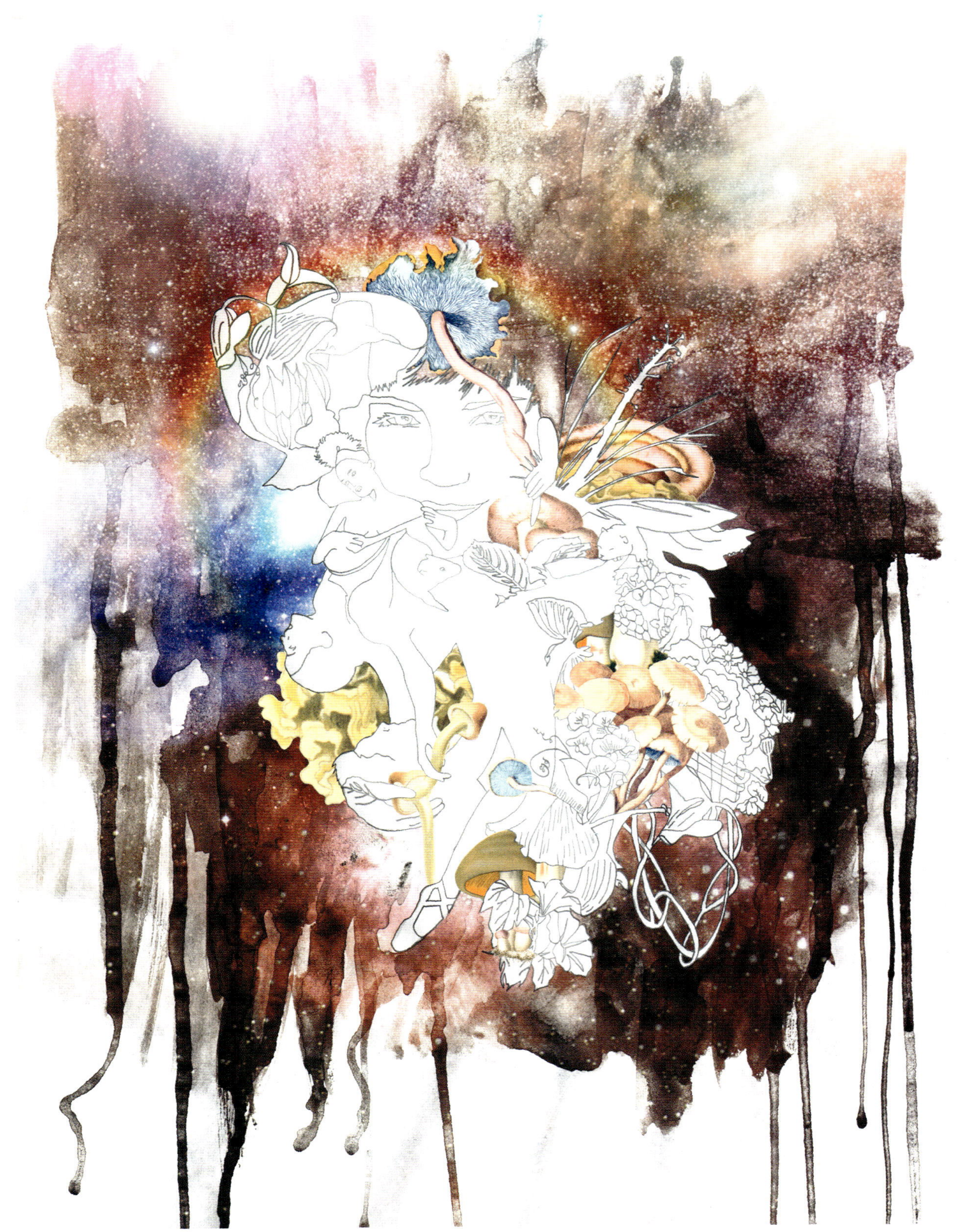

Deanne Cheuk | *Mushroom Girls Mandolin, on Decayed Wood,* 2003 | Digital print on archival paper | 24 × 19 inches | Courtesy of the artist

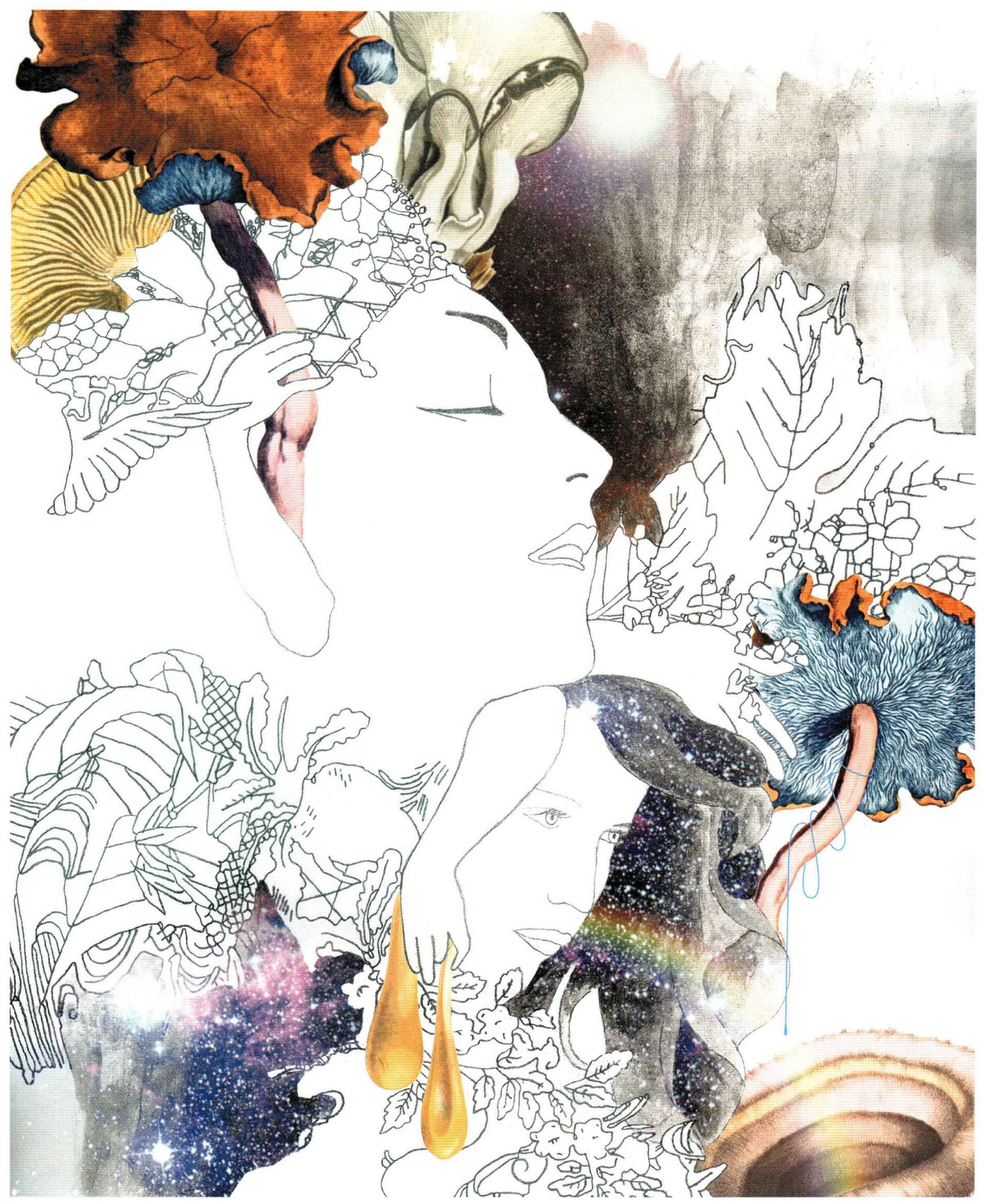

Deanne Cheuk | *Psyc Girl*, 2002 | Digital print on archival paper | 12½ × 10 inches | Courtesy of the artist

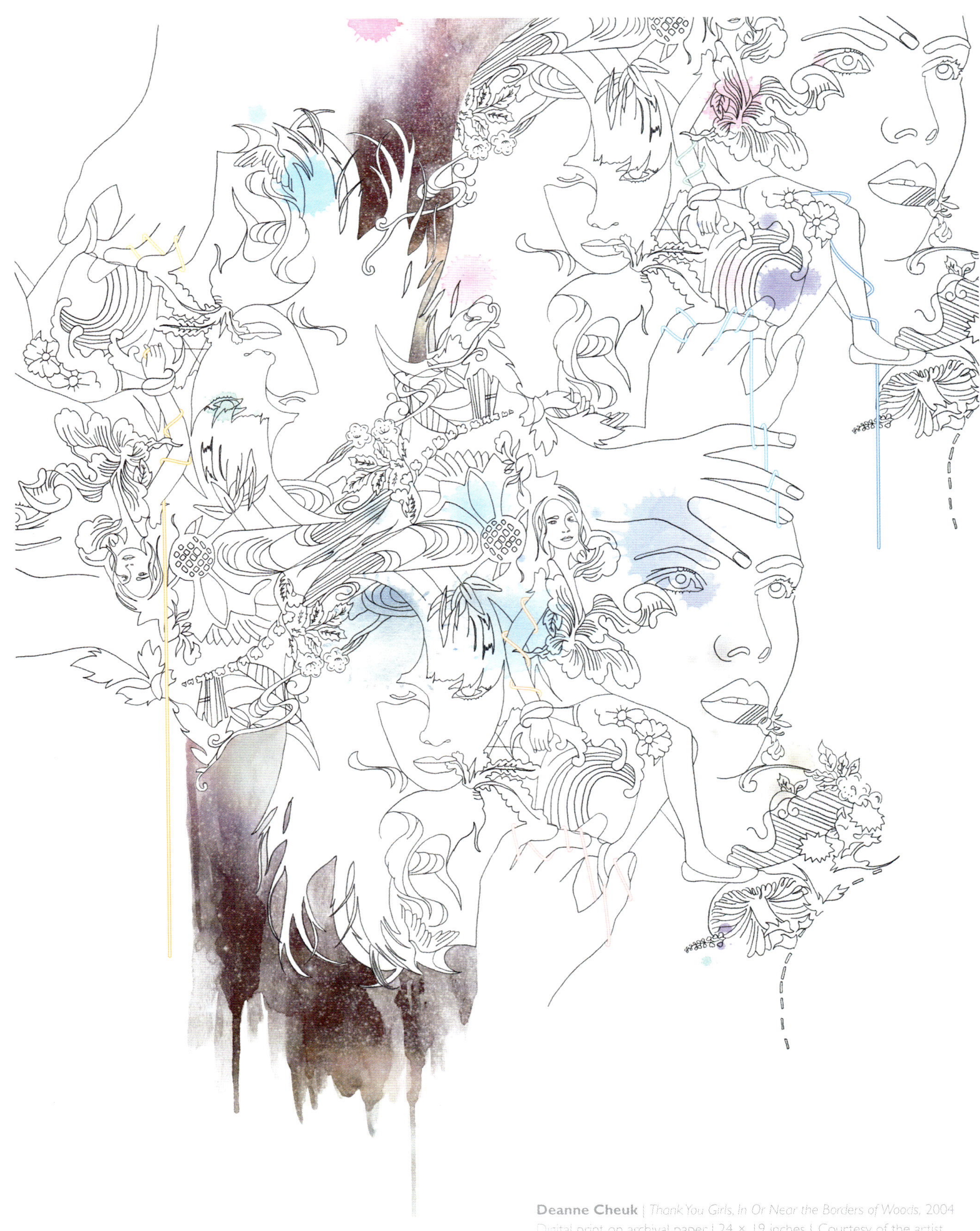

Deanne Cheuk | Thank You Girls, In Or Near the Borders of Woods, 2004
Digital print on archival paper | 24 × 19 inches | Courtesy of the artist

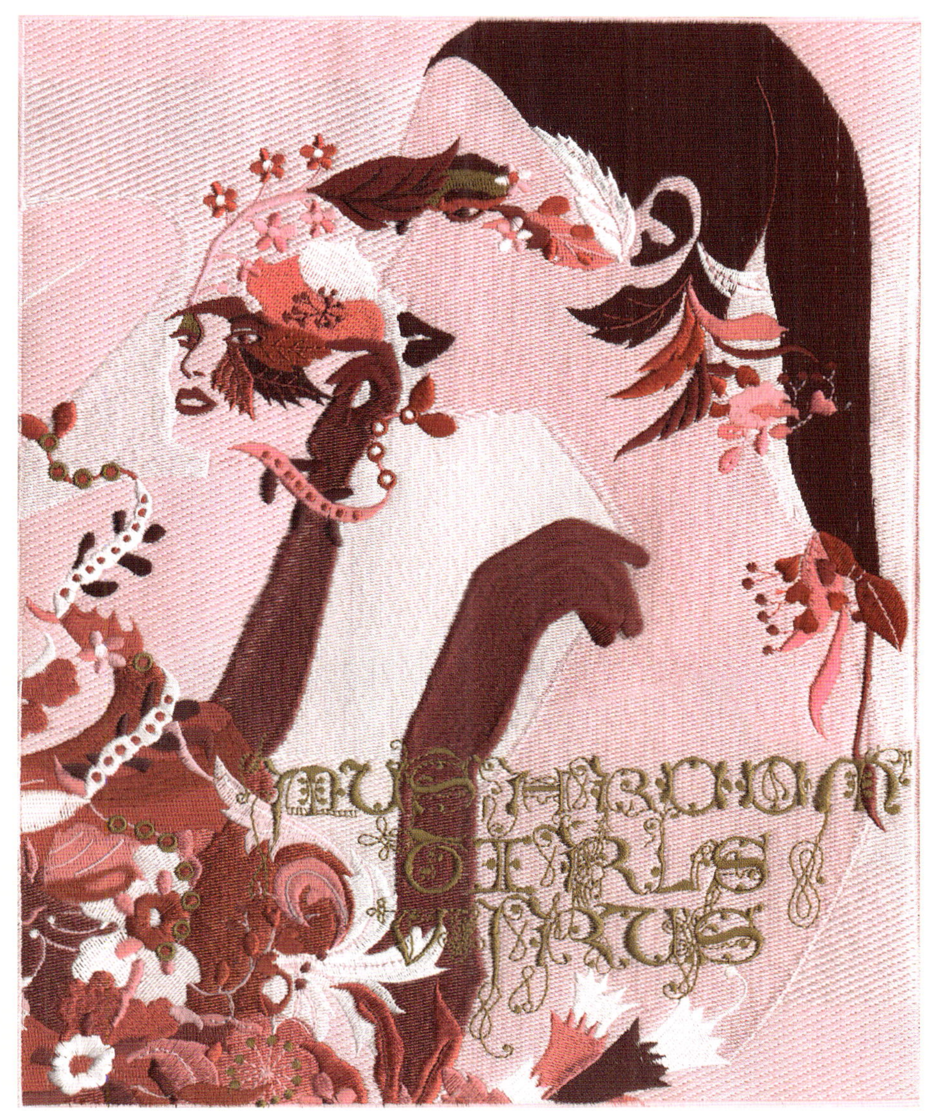

Deanne Cheuk | *Mushroom Girls Virus*, 2005 | Artist book with embroidered cloth cover | 64 pages, printed offset | edition 3,000 (out of print) | 11 × 9 × ½ inches | Courtesy of the artist

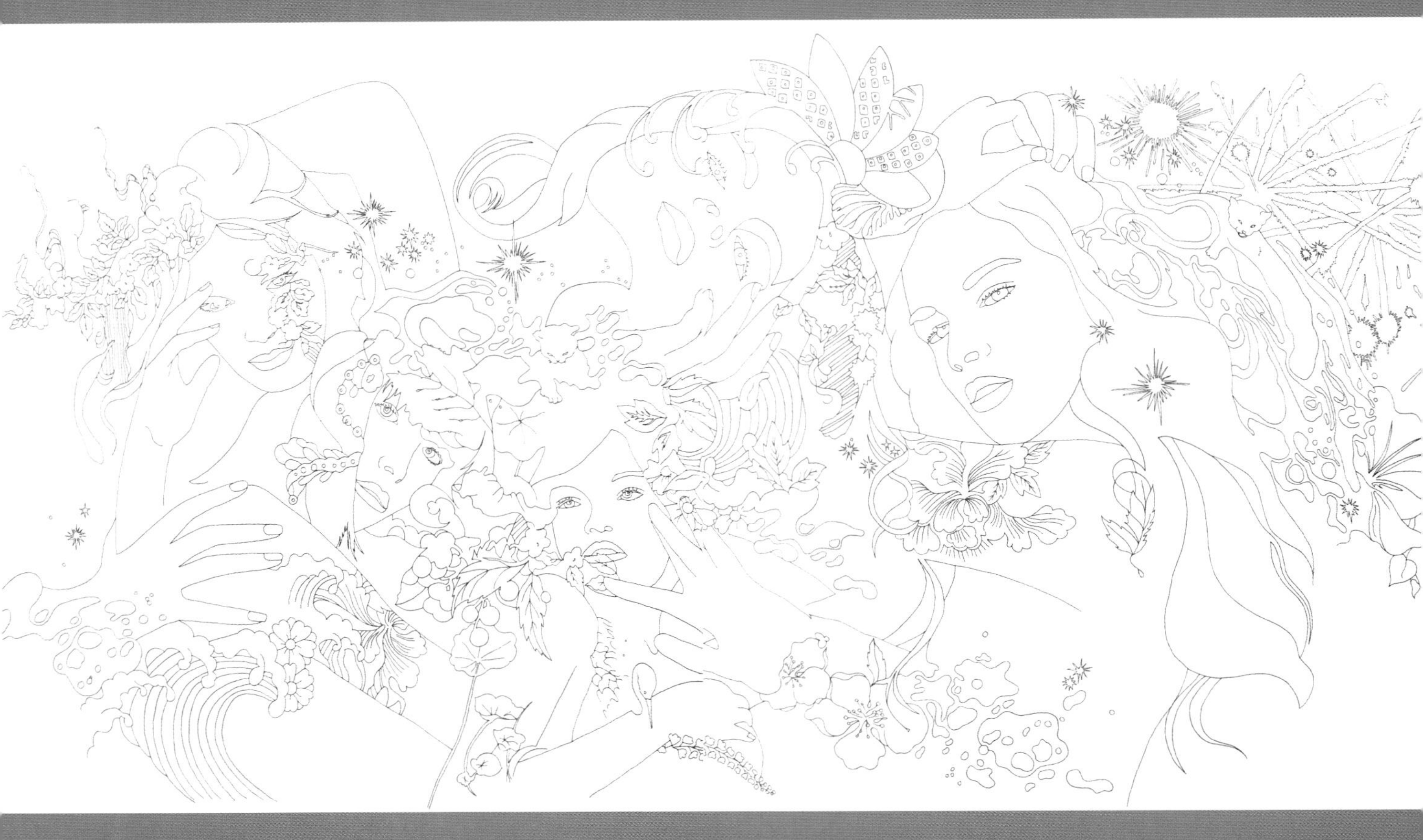

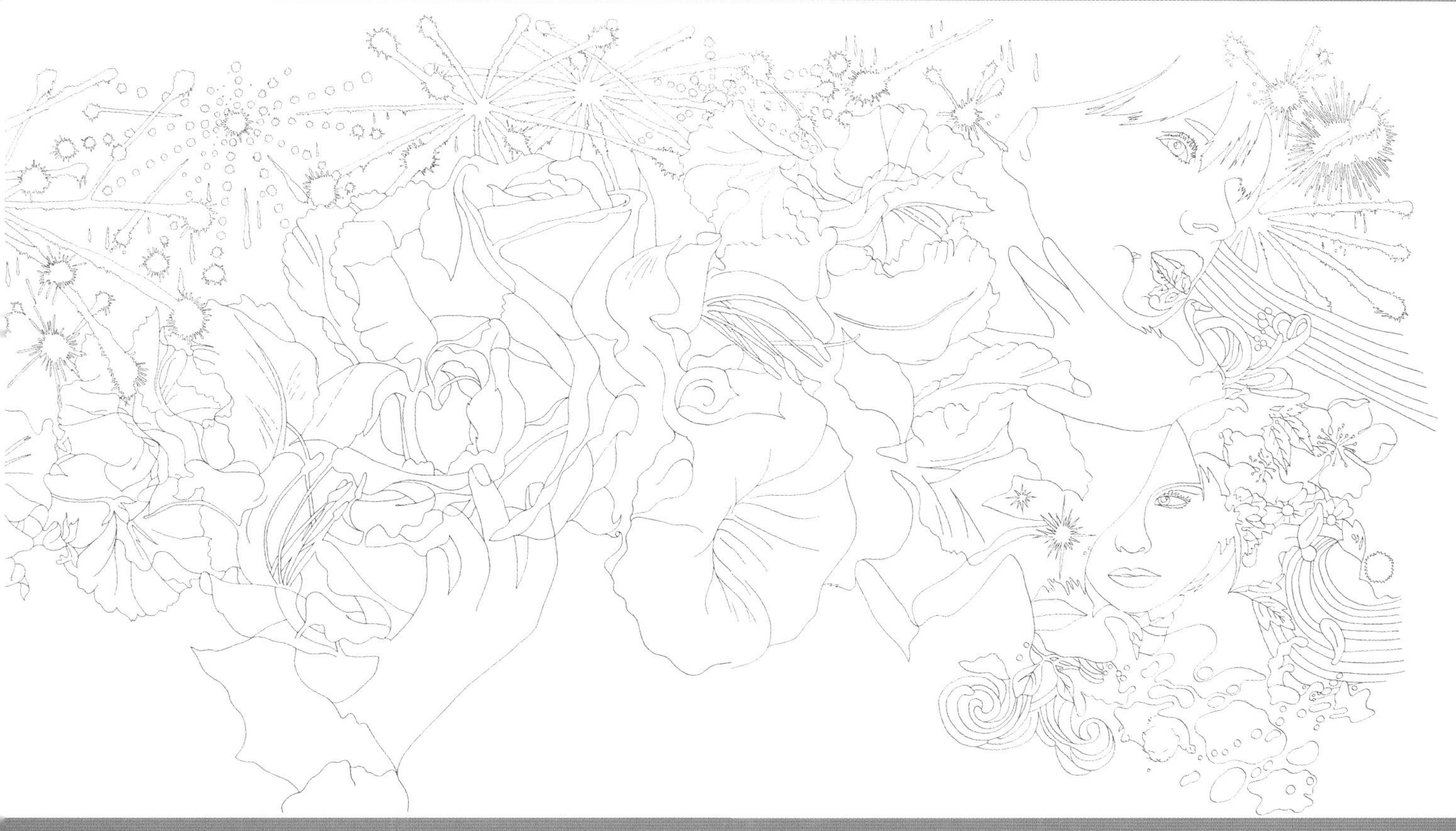

Deanne Cheuk | *Fireworks Girls*, 2004 | Pen on paper | 4 parts, 16½ × 15 inches each | Courtesy of the artist

Cheuk's twenty-four drawings, created in preparation for her *Mushroom Girls Virus* book, were first exhibited in *Redefining the Line*.

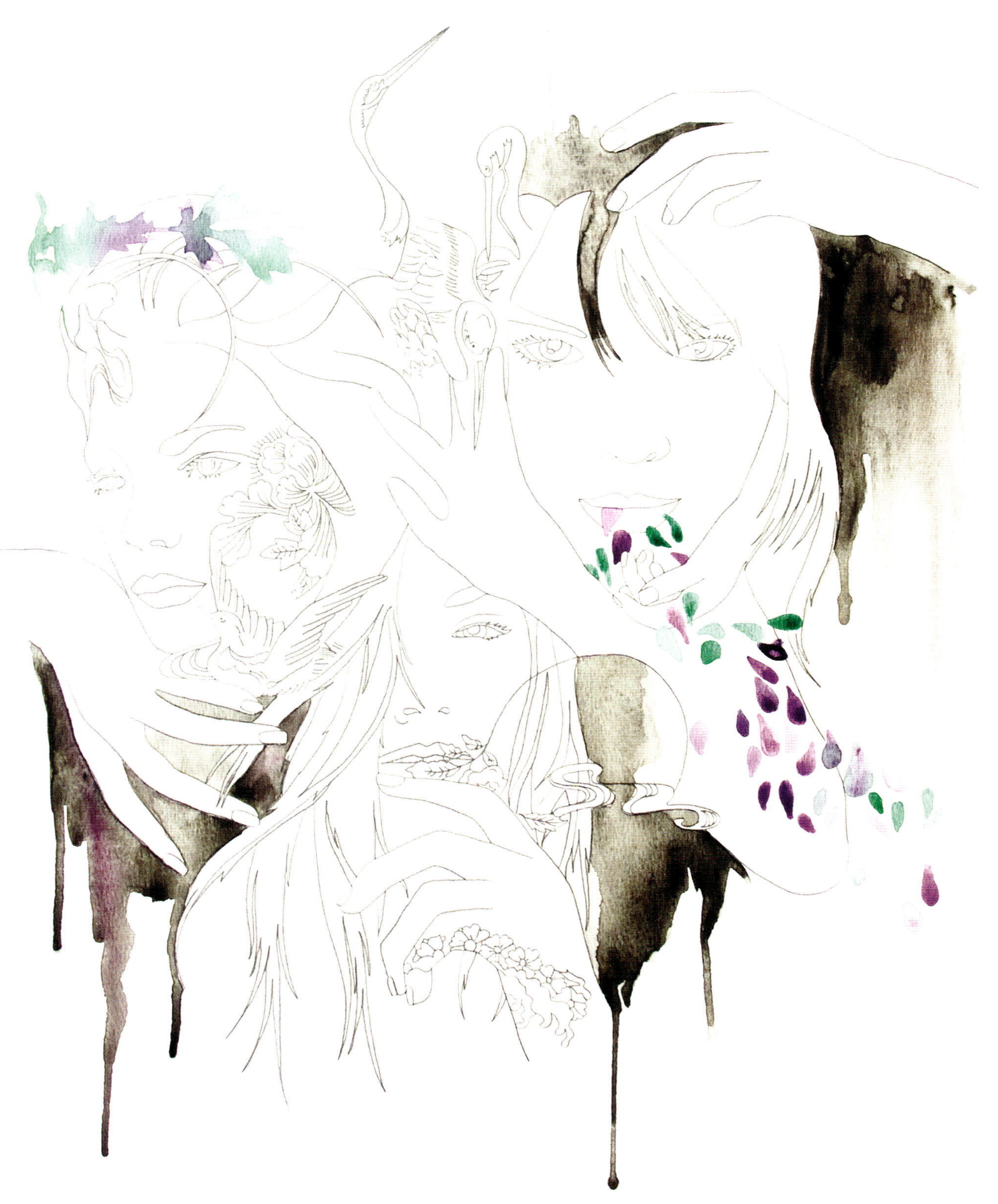

Deanne Cheuk | *Triplets of Mushroomville*, 2004 | Pencil and watercolor on paper | 20 × 15 inches | Courtesy of the artist

DEANNE CHEUK

Deanne Cheuk was born in Perth, Australia, in 1974. She graduated with a B.A. degree in Graphic Design from Curtin University. That same year she received her first design job as the art director for one of only two magazines that were produced in Perth. Cheuk relocated to New York in 2000, and taught herself to be an illustrator. She exhibited her celebrated *Mushroom Girls Virus* series in 2004 at 222 Gallery in Philadelphia and published a book of that same series in 2005.

Cheuk's extensive design and illustration experience includes her work as art director for *Tokion* and publisher of her own zine, *Neomu*. Her work is influenced by Art Nouveau, psychedelia, and nature, and is often imbued with touches of surrealism. Cheuk's art has been exhibited around the world, most recently in Beijing, Berlin, Hong Kong, the Czech Republic, Sydney, and New York.

NAJA
CONRAD-HANSEN

Copenhagen, Denmark

"Conrad likes to challenge herself as well as her audience. In her work, she strives to fabricate a fictive universe around her subjects, always eager to bare their very soul."

~ Gabor Menor, *AdvancedMinority.com*, October 2008

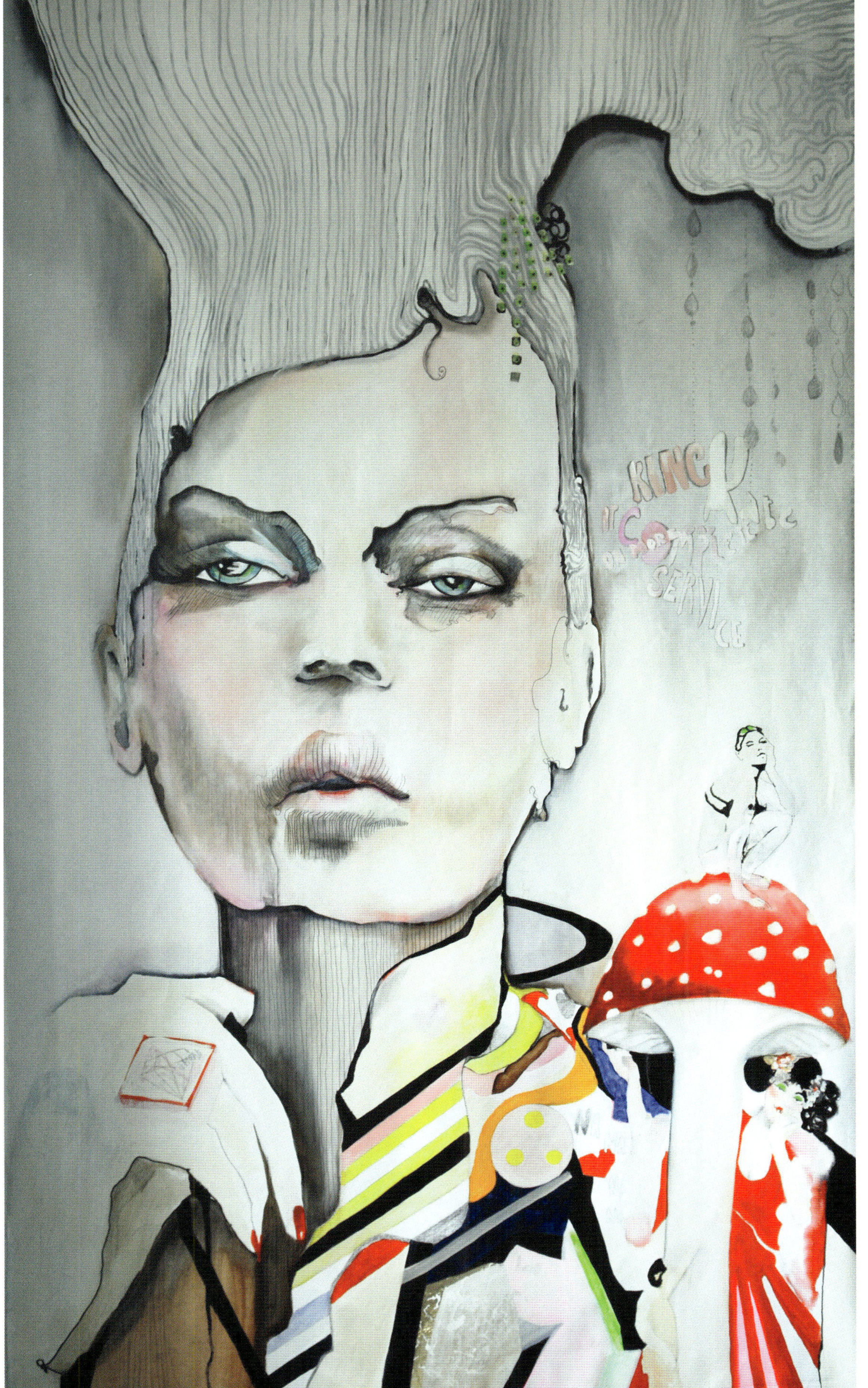

Naja Conrad-Hansen | *Is It Real or Am I Confused?*, 2009 | Created specifically for Redefining the Line | Oil and mixed media on linen | 83½ × 51 inches | Courtesy of the artist

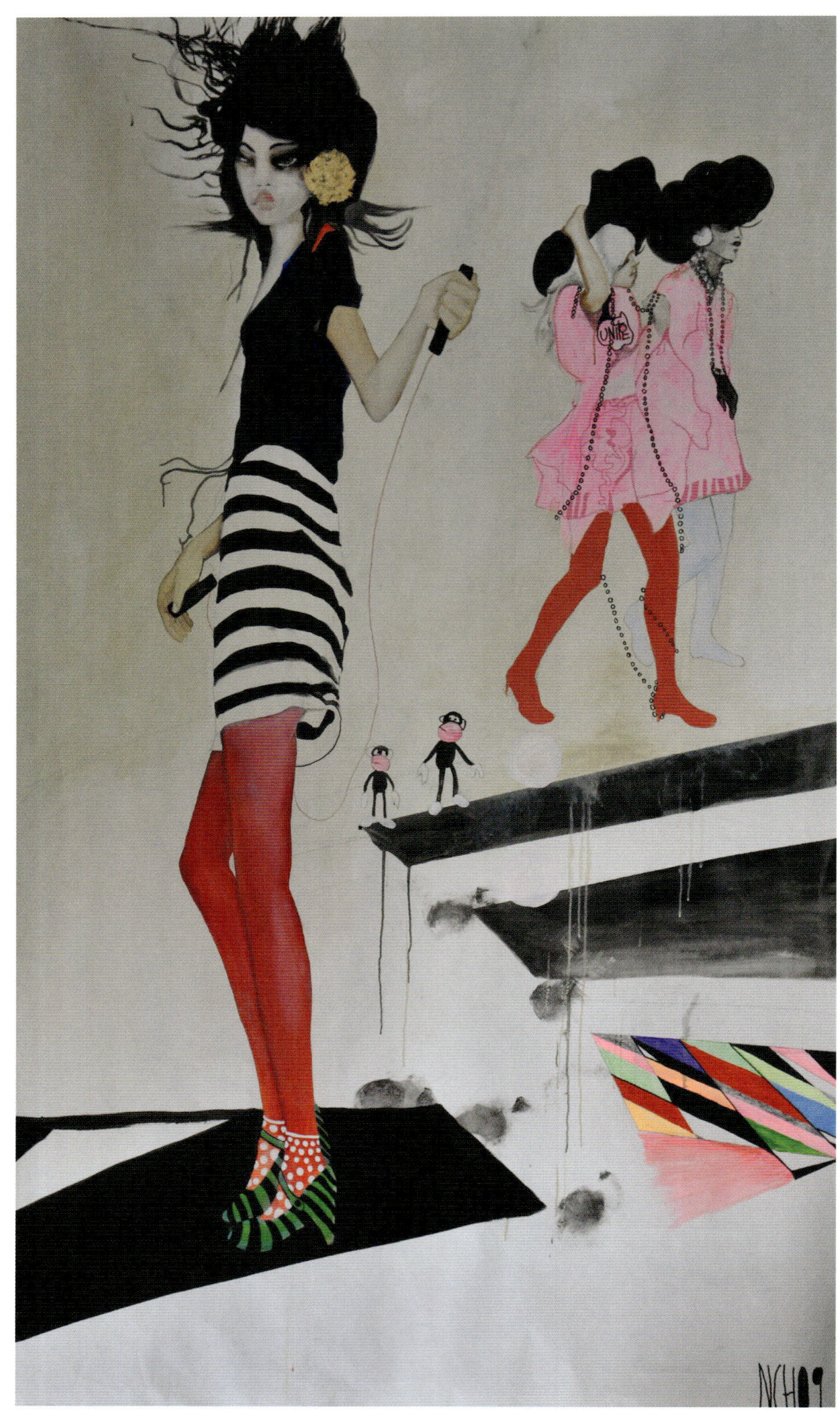

Naja Conrad-Hansen | *Making Filthy Footprints*, 2009 | Created specifically for *Redefining the Line*
Oil and mixed media on linen | 83 ½ × 48 inches | Courtesy of the artist

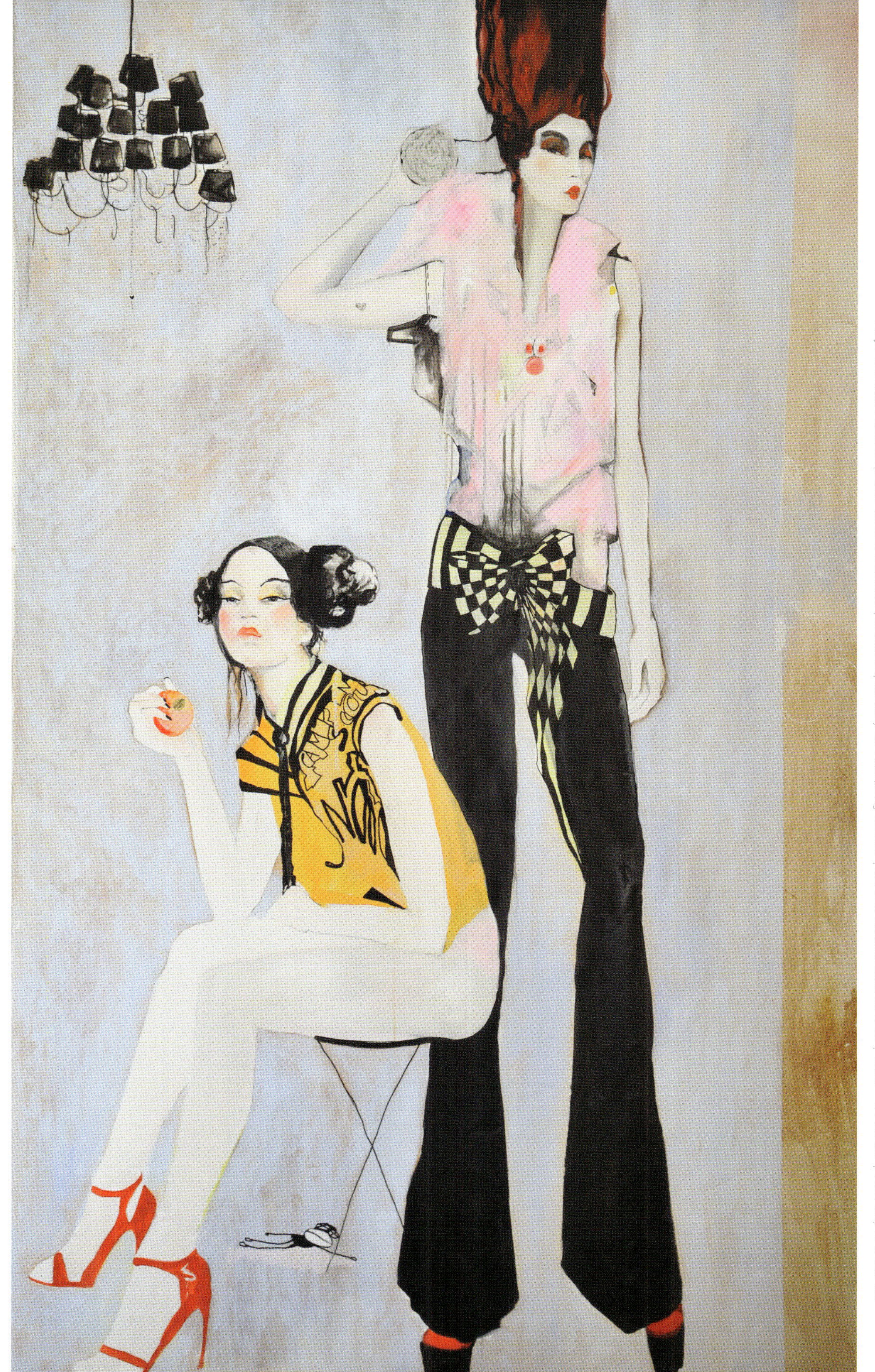

Naja Conrad-Hansen | Don't Call Me Girl, 2009 | Created specifically for Redefining the Line | Oil and mixed media on linen | 83½ × 51 inches | Courtesy of the artist

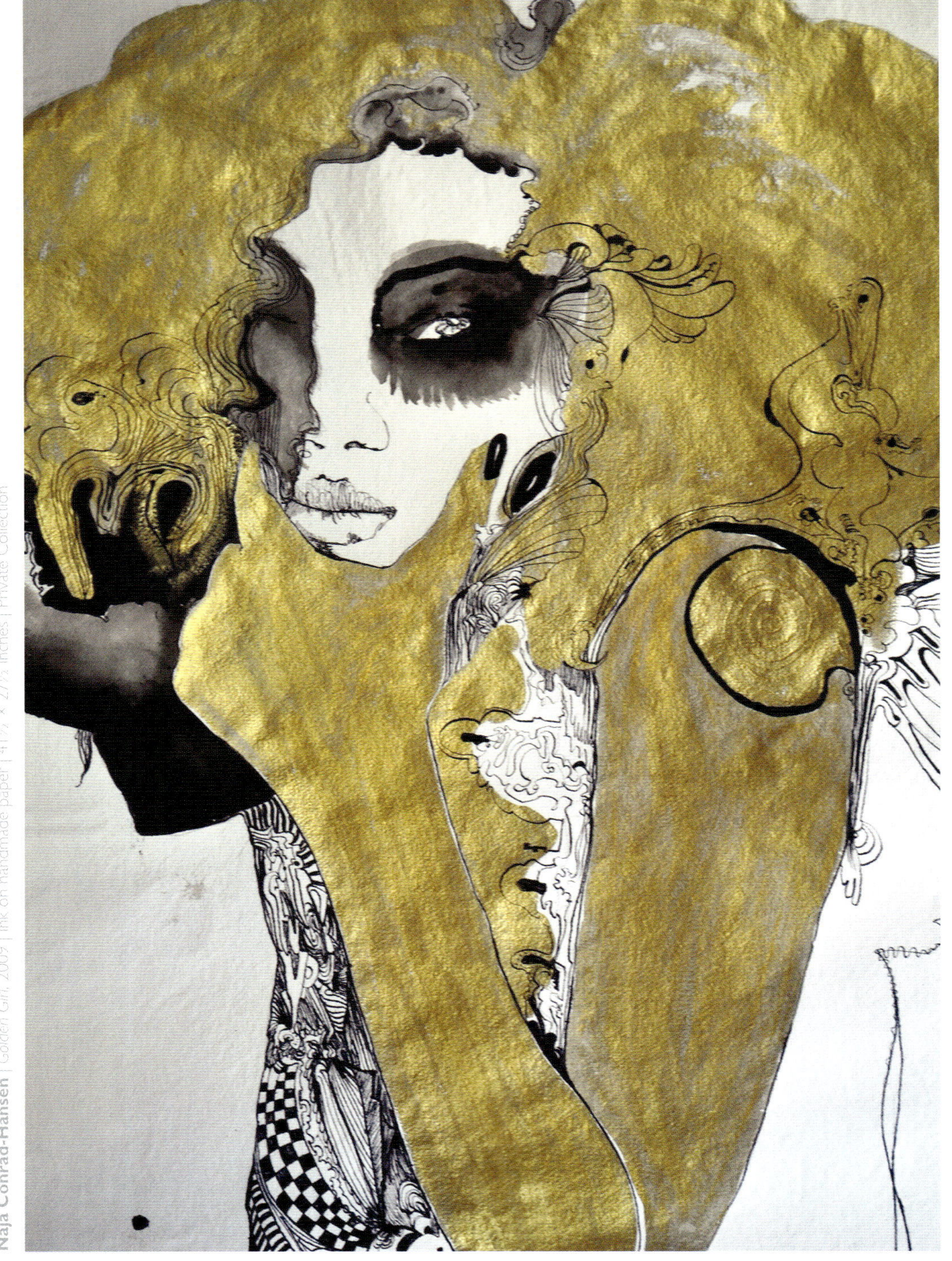

Naja Conrad-Hansen | Golden Girl, 2009 | Ink on handmade paper | 41½ × 27½ inches | Private Collection

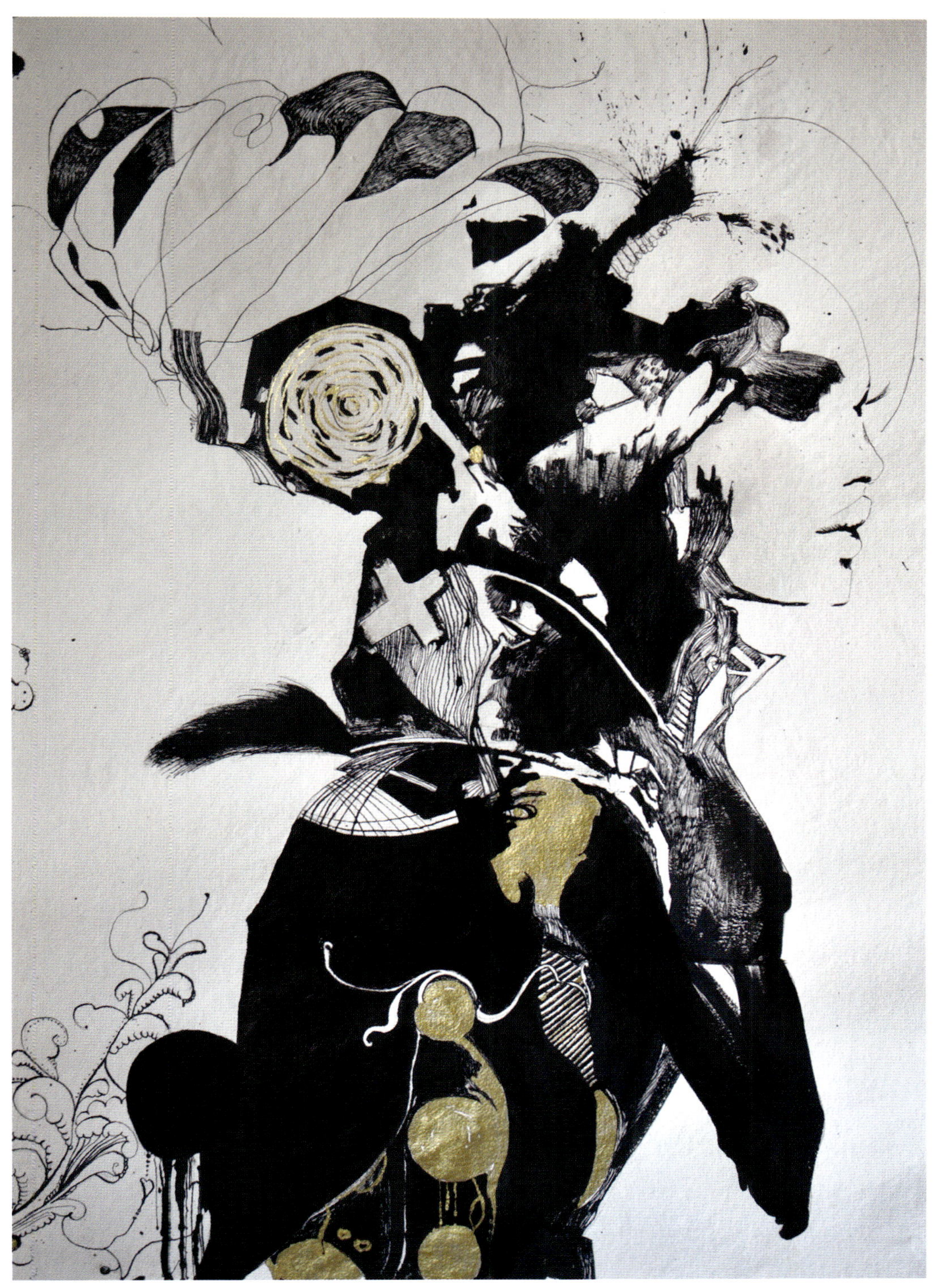

Naja Conrad-Hansen | *Is it Dark Yet?*, 2009 | Ink on handmade paper
41½ × 27½ inches | Courtesy of the artist

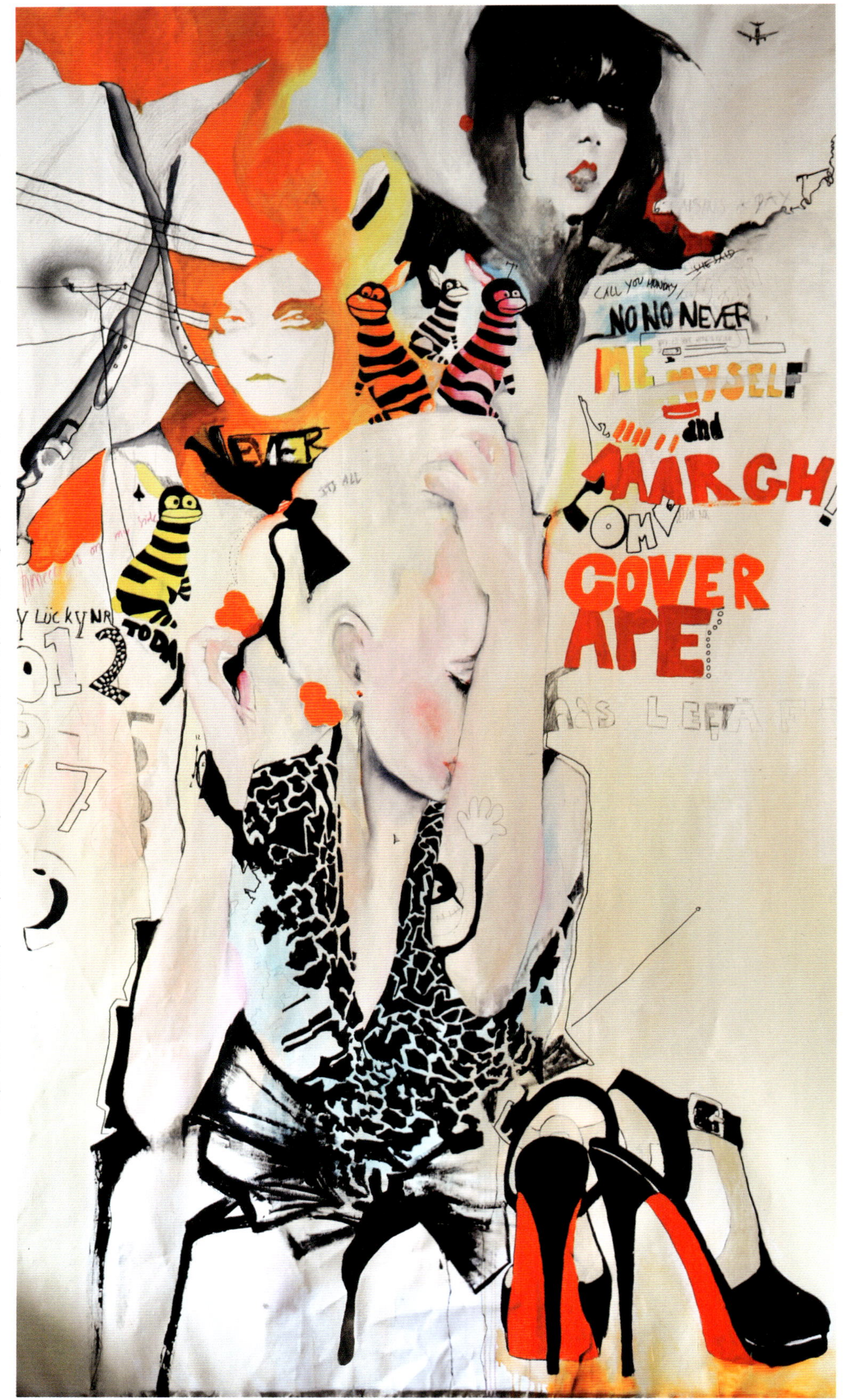

Naja Conrad-Hansen | *Me, Myself, and Aarg*, 2009 | Created specifically for *Redefining the Line* | Oil and mixed media on linen | 83½ × 51 inches | Courtesy of the artist

NAJA CONRAD-HANSEN

Naja Conrad-Hansen was born, lives, and works in Copenhagen, Denmark. She graduated from The Danish Design School in 2003 with an M.A. degree in Visual Communication. She began her profession as a freelance designer and artist in 2003.

Conrad-Hansen's practice embraces illustration, painting, graphic design, art direction, making silk-screen prints and more. Her inspiration comes equally from the worlds of fashion, hardcore music, traditional art and design, and in the general observation of the world around her. She describes the goal of her illustration style as "finding some untouched areas of the mind and stimulating the eye and imagination."

Her artworks have been included in a wide variety of fashion and graphic publications including *Lurzer's Archive: 200 Best Illustrators Worldwide 2007/2008* and *The Age of Feminine Drawing*, 2006. Conrad-Hansen's own fashion collection, Meannorth, showcases her print and pattern designs.

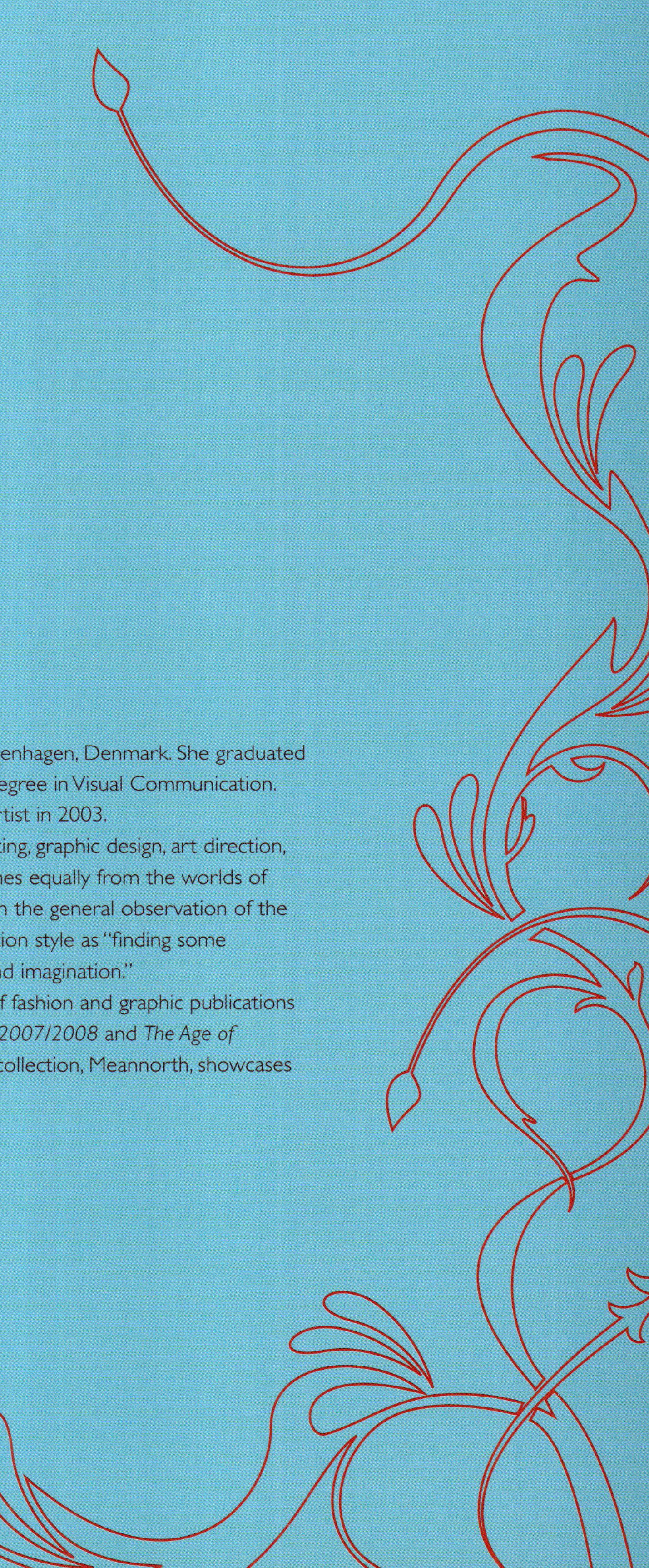

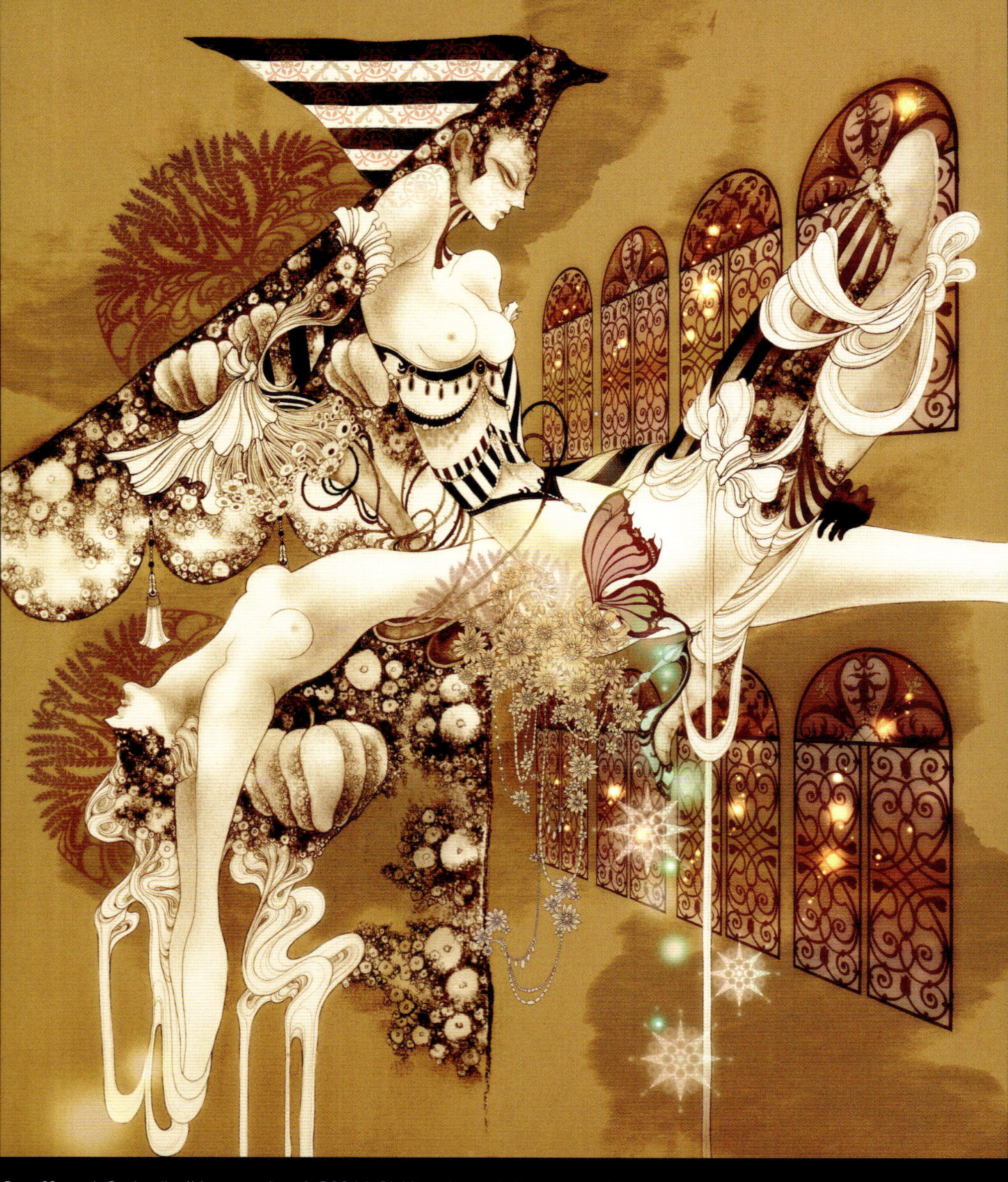

Aya Kato | *Cinderella (Metamorphosis)*, 2006 | Giclée print and silkscreen print on paper

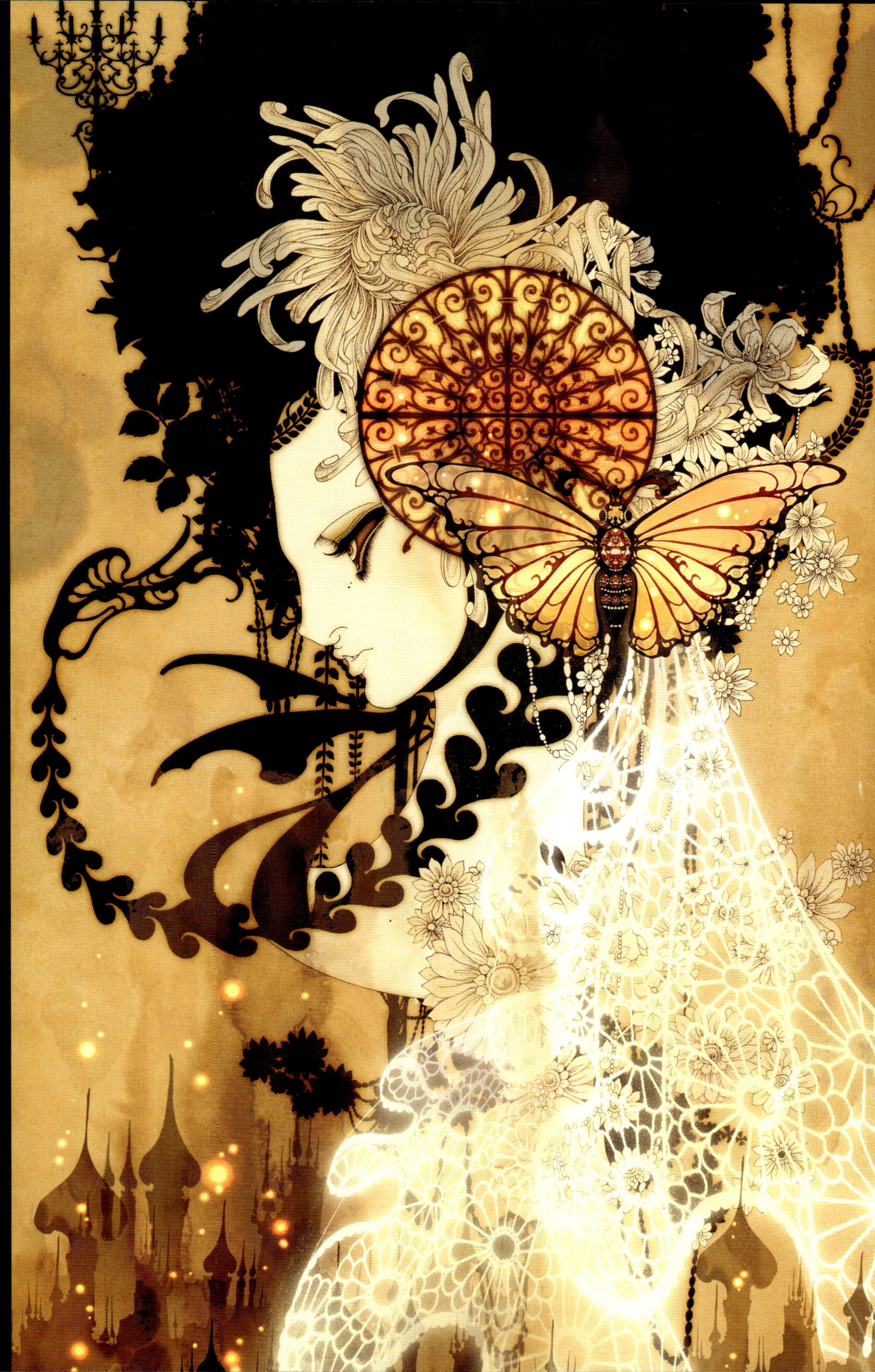

Aya Kato | Snow White (Sweet Enchantment), 2005 | Giclée print and silkscreen print on paper | 22 × 18 inches | Courtesy of the artist

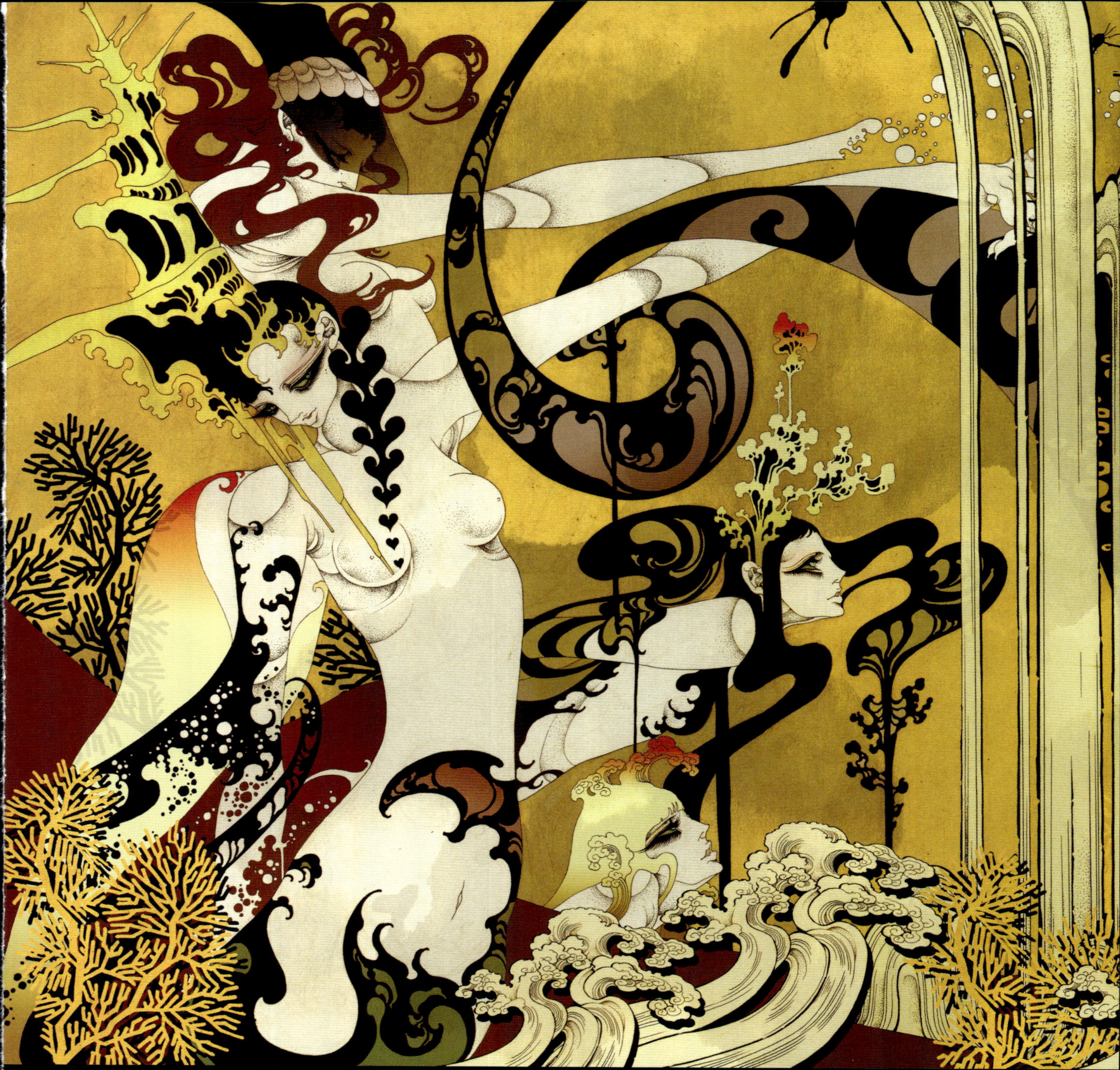

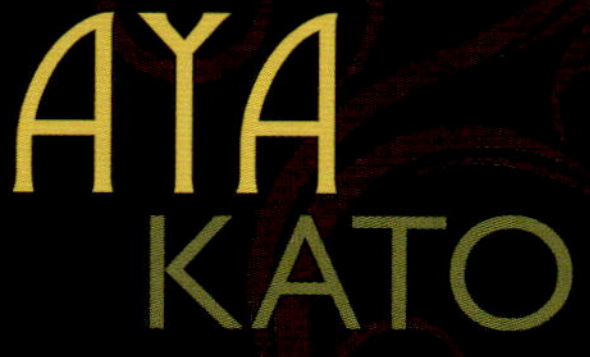

AYA
KATO

Tokyo, Japan

"Her visually stunning artwork incorporates imagery ranging from bold dreamscapes, striking scenery filled with fluid architecture, enticing women and supremely detailed foliage."

~ *Beautiful/Decay Blog*, December 2007

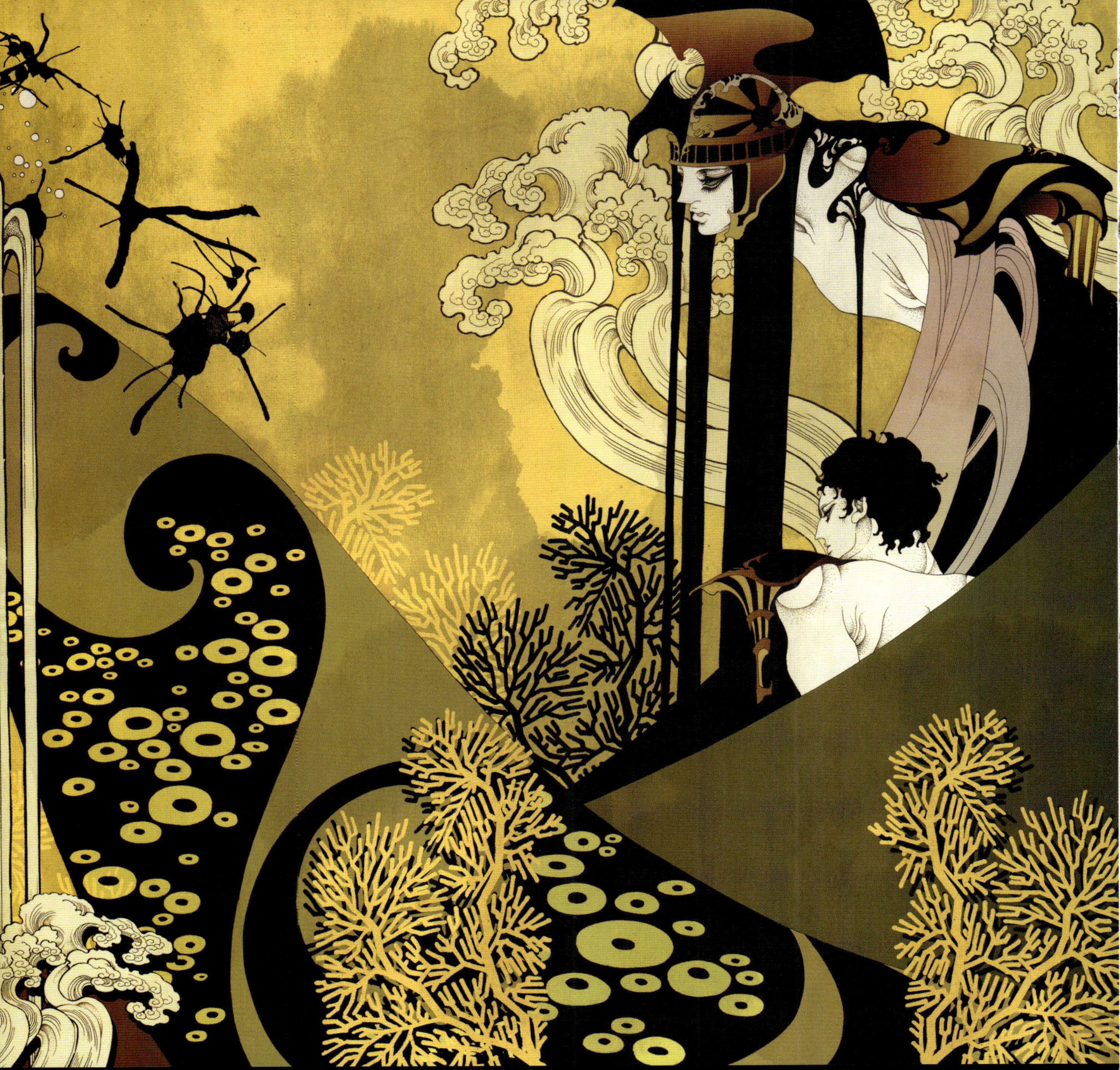

Aya Kato | *The Witch's Love (Hero)*, 2006 | Giclée print on paper | 35½ × 71 inches | Courtesy of the artist

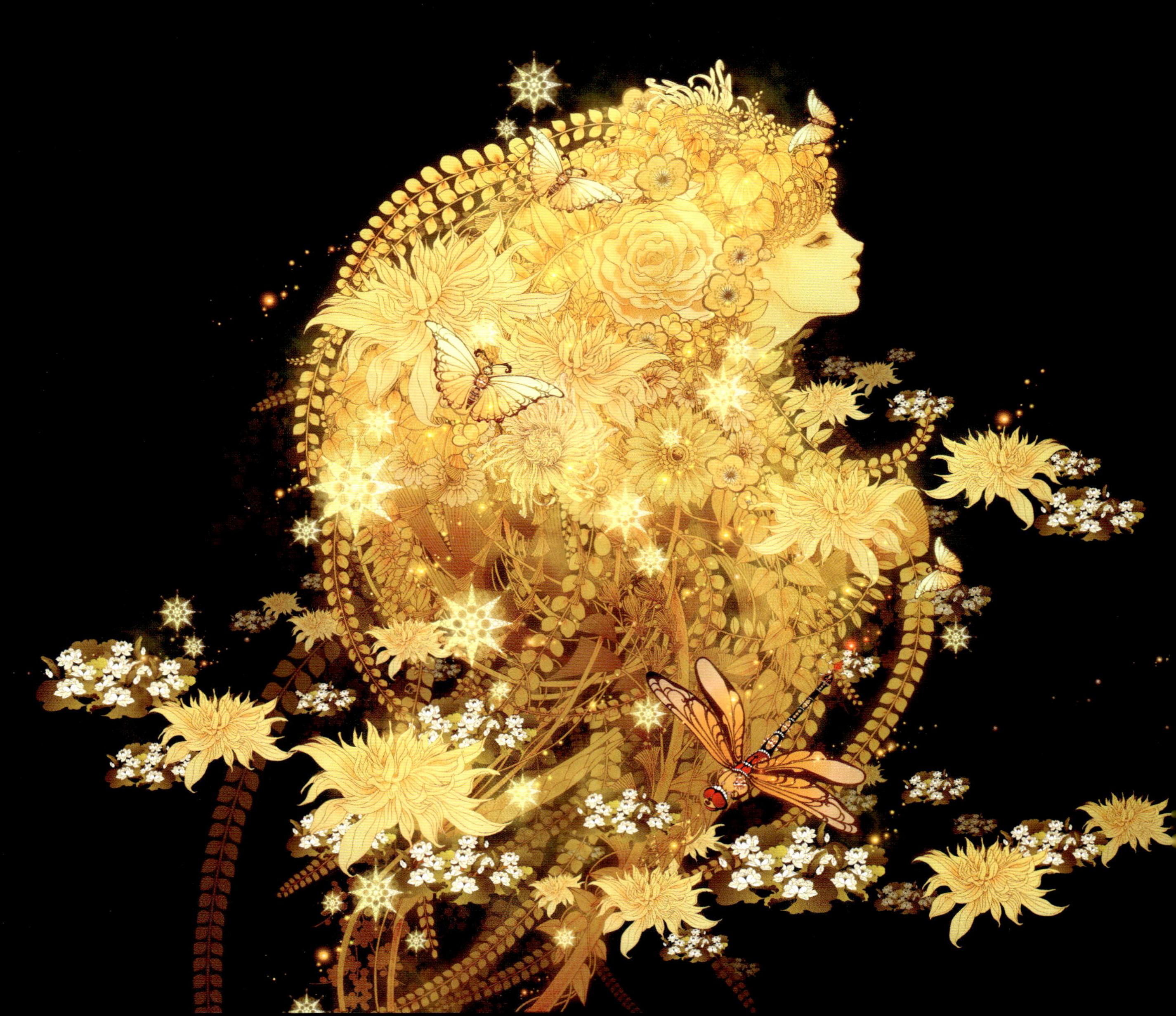

Aya Kato | *Rapunzel*, 2004 | Giclée print and silkscreen print on paper | 22 × 18 inches | Courtesy of the artist

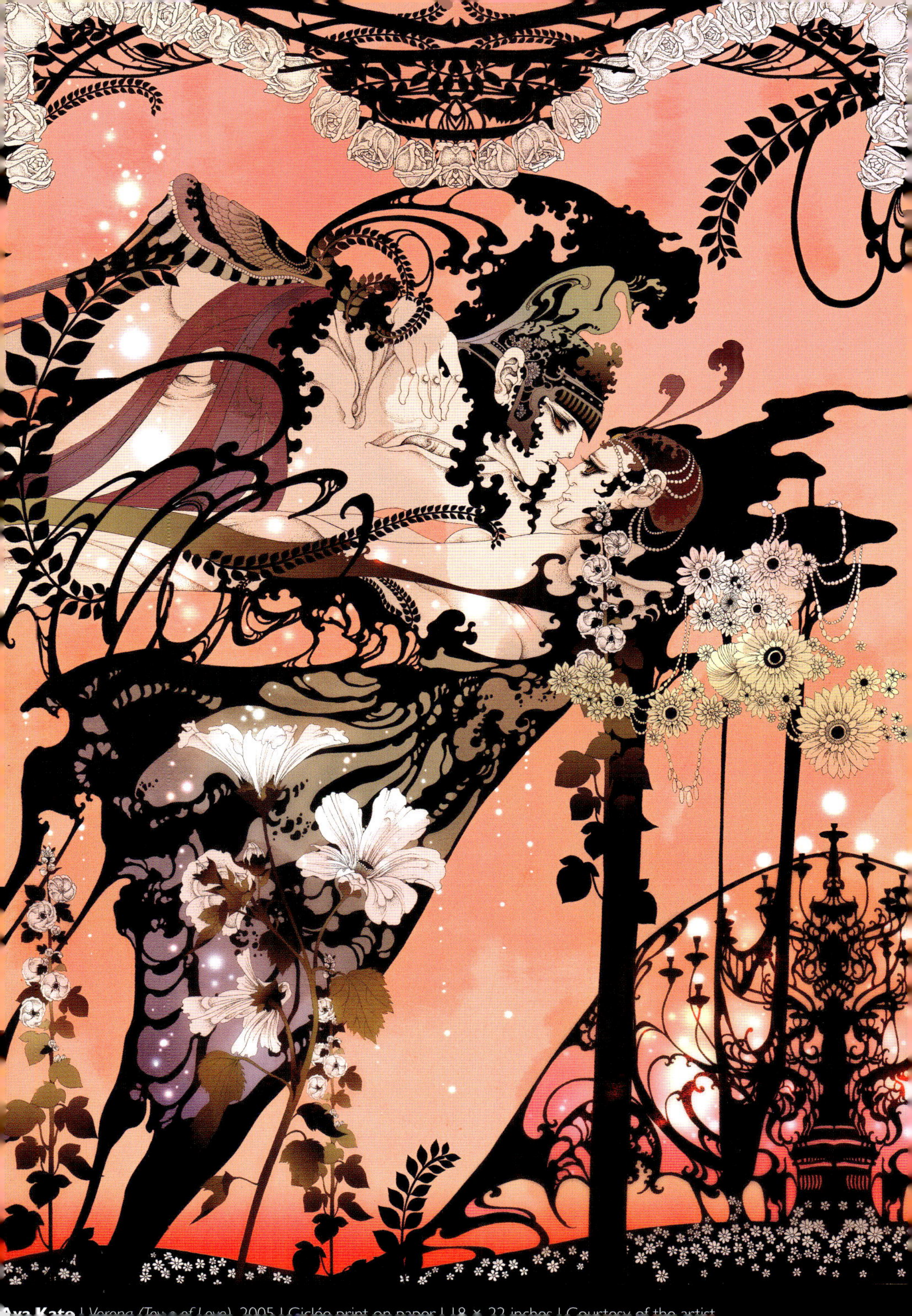

Aya Kato | *Verona (Toys of Love)*, 2005 | Giclée print on paper | 18 × 22 inches | Courtesy of the artist

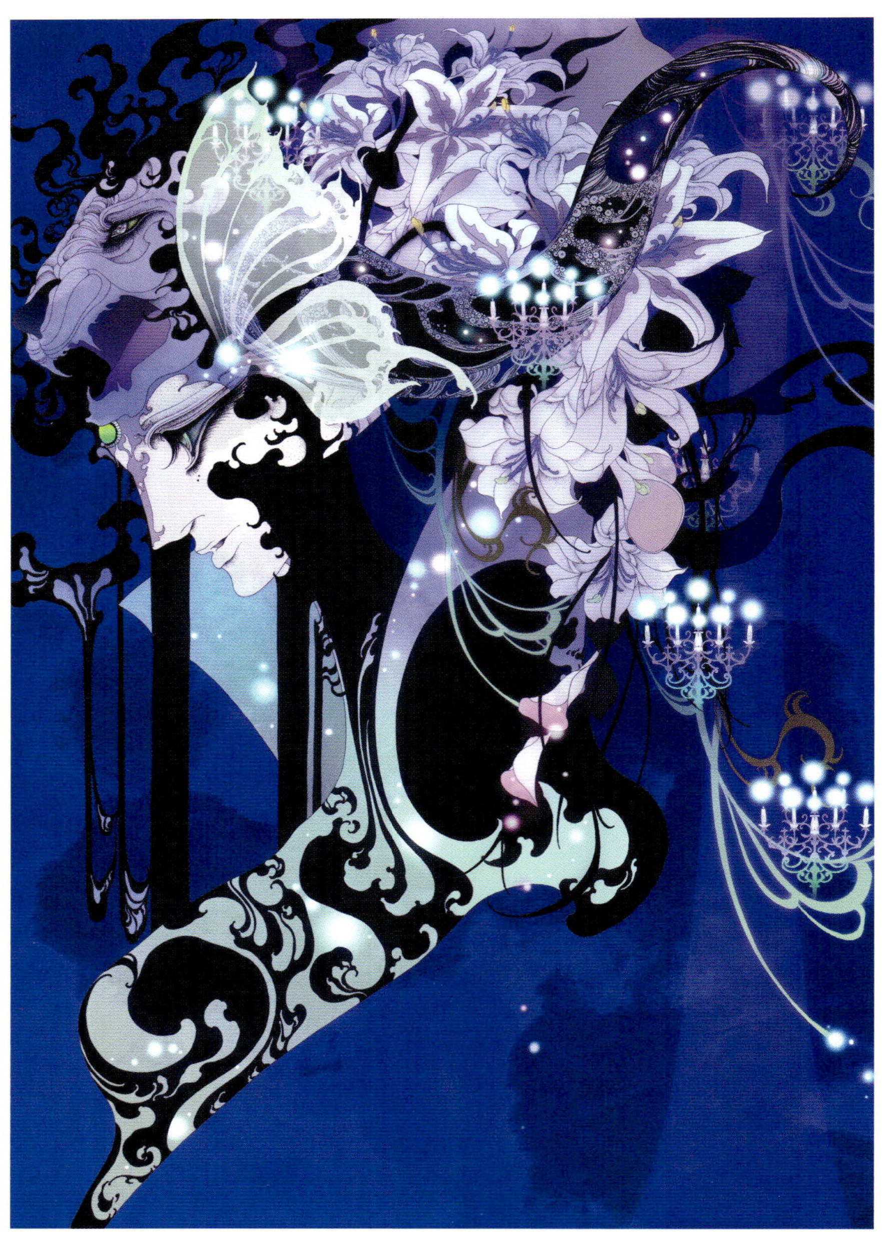

Aya Kato | *The Witch's Love (Secret Desire)*, 2006 | Giclée print and silkscreen print on paper
22 × 18 inches | Courtesy of the artist

AYA
KATO

Aya Kato was born in Seto, Aichi, Japan in 1982. She studied Visual Art Education and Graphic Design at the Aichi University of Education. Kato combines hand-drawn and digitally created elements to express what she describes as the "female image in a new age."

Aya Kato's wish is that her passion for her work inspires an awakening of the soul, which she believes can lie dormant in all human beings. She also hopes that her artwork reminds audiences of their own histories, roots, and true wishes.

Kato's recent solo exhibitions include: *Earth Dreaming*, March 2009 at the National Gallery of Malaysia and *Flower of Memory*, April 2008 in Bucharest, Romania. Her work was also exhibited in Barcelona, Milan, and Sao Paulo in collaboration with the international arts organization ROJO. Her extensive list of clients includes Microsoft, Shu Uemura, and Tori Amos for her music video *Sleeps with Butterflies*.

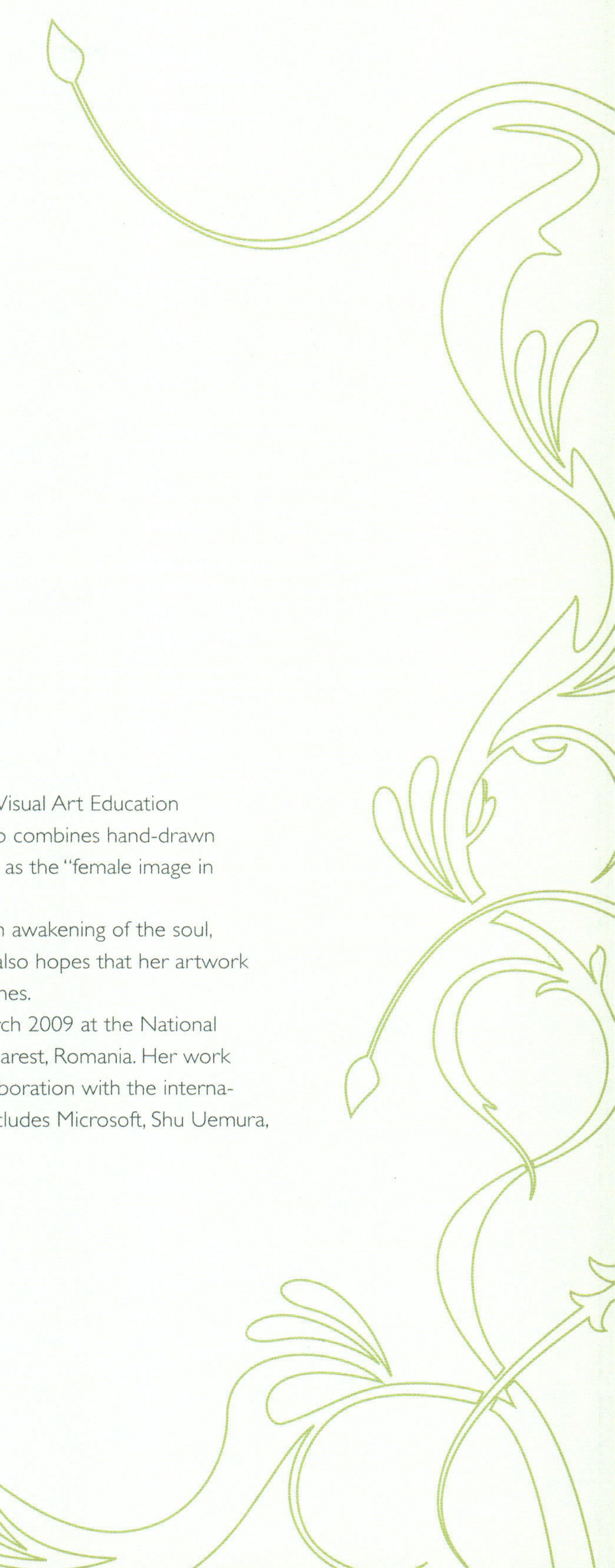

PANDAROSA

Melbourne, Australia

"We've always been drawn towards organic fluid forms in nature and the female figure. This flowing curvaceous subject matter is a constant point of reference and inspiration which visually allows for abstraction, re-interpretation, decoration and intricacy."

~ Pandarosa

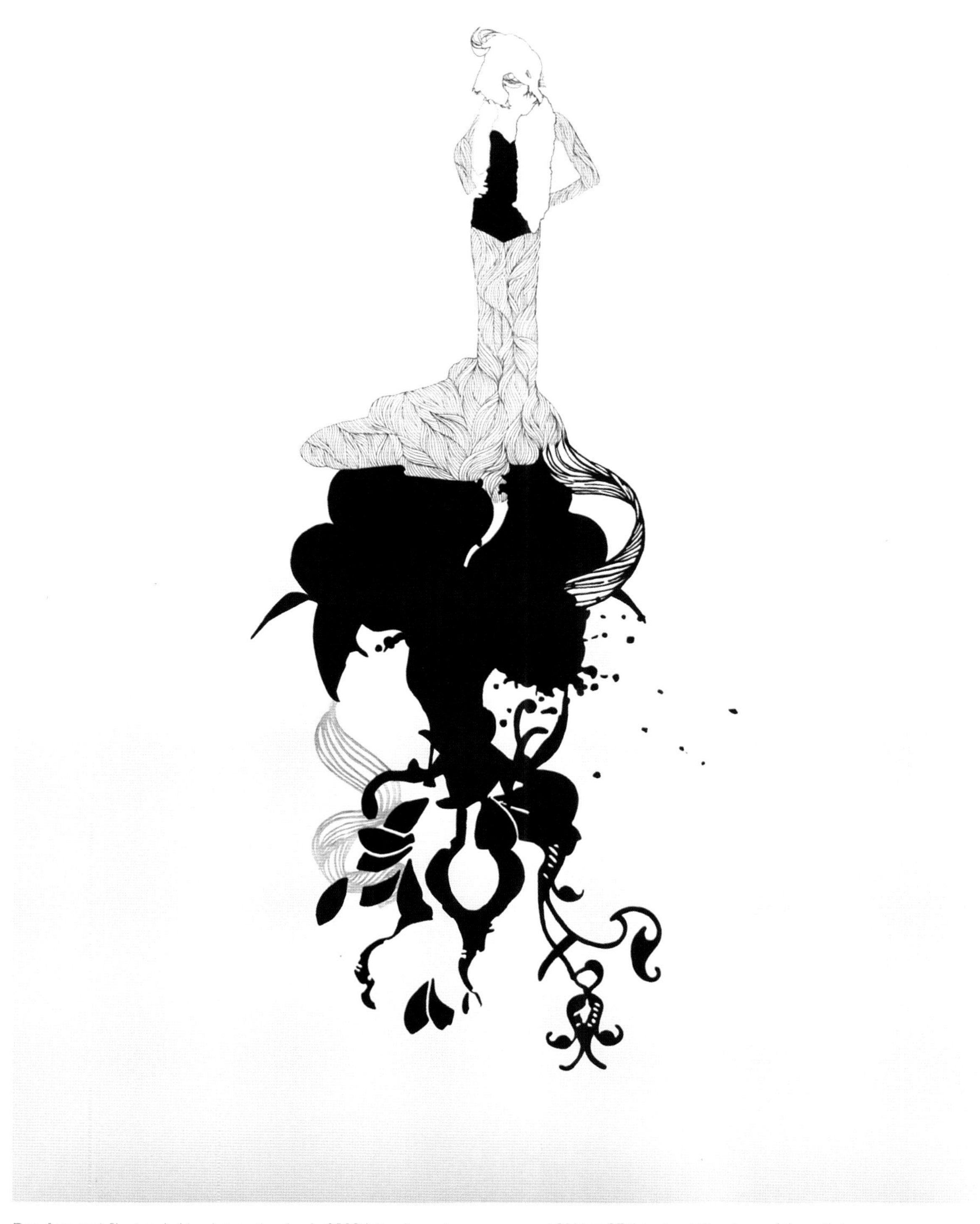

Pandarosa | *She tangled her hair in the clouds,* 2009 | Acrylic and pen on paper | 35½ × 27½ inches | Courtesy of the artists

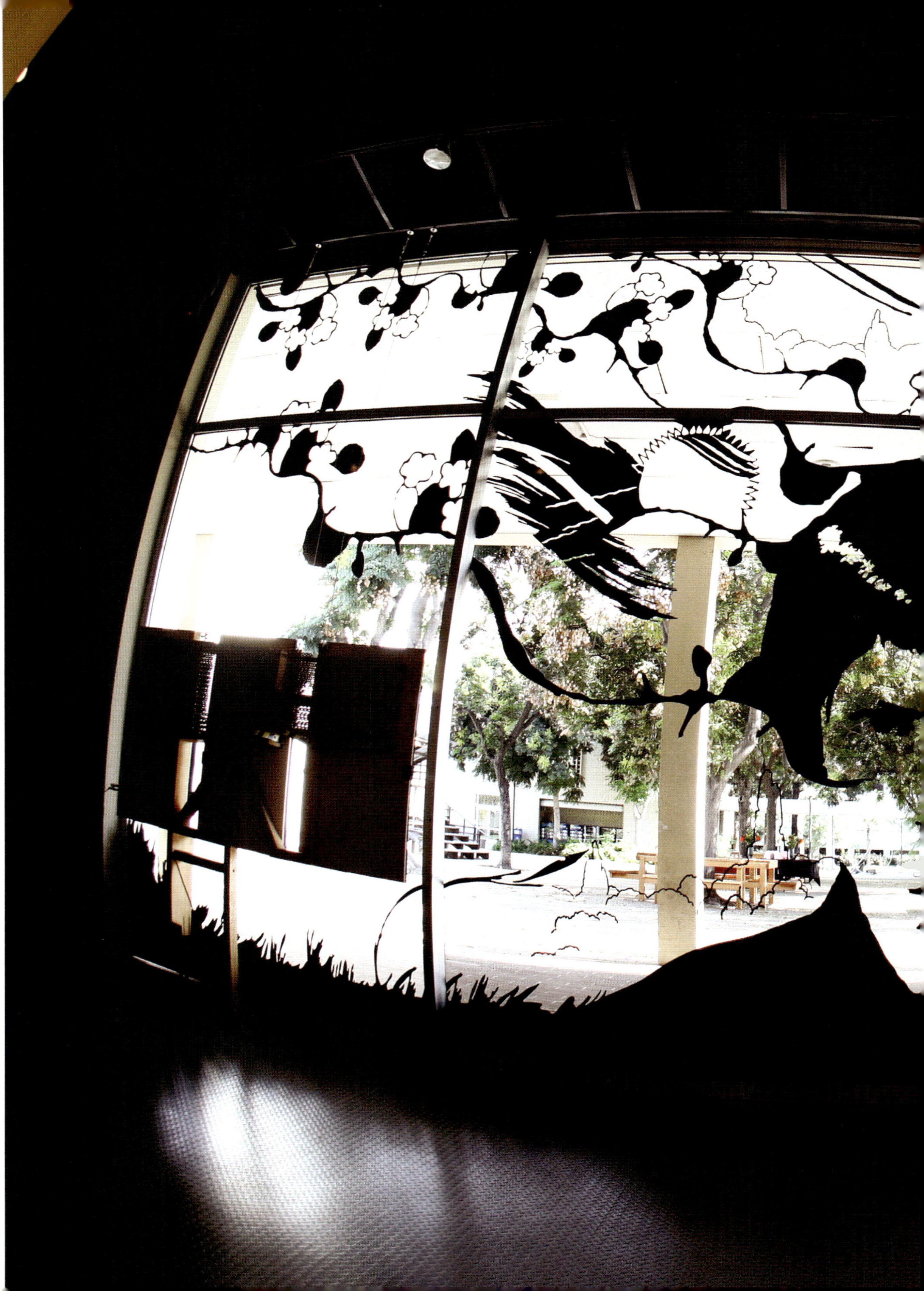

Pandarosa | *Noir Sunshine*, 2009 | Site-specific vinyl installation | 6 feet 4½ inches × 10 feet 3½ inches | Courtesy of the artists

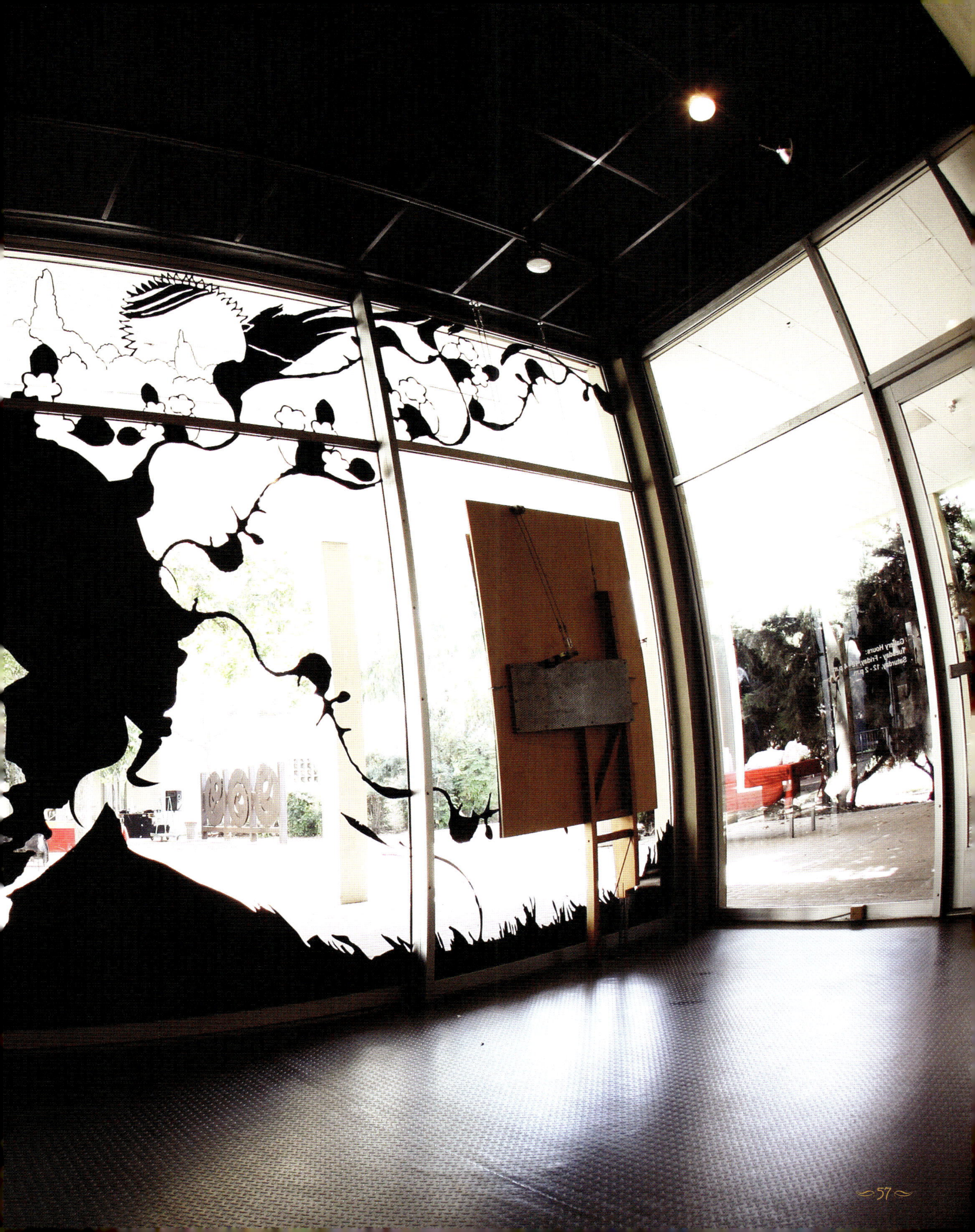

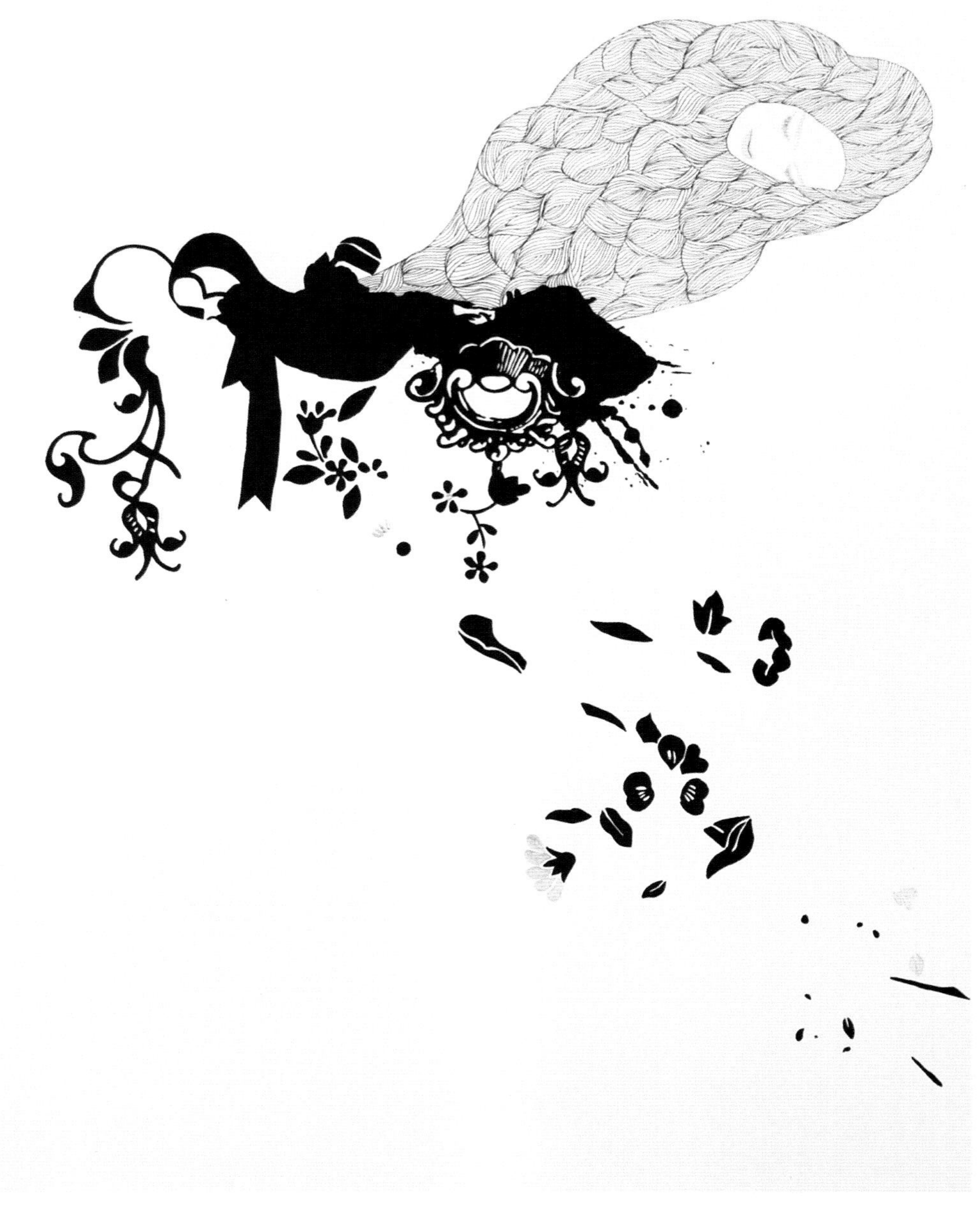

Pandarosa | *somewhere between Sunset and Sunrise*, 2009
Acrylic and pen on paper | 35½ × 27½ inches
Courtesy of the artists

PANDAROSA

Pandarosa is the brainchild of artists Ariel Aguilera and Andrea Benyi. Originally hailing from Chile and Hungary, they joined forces in Melbourne and are currently based in Berlin, Germany. Their work expands a wide range of approaches, including figurative illustration, abstract dreamscapes, bold iconic designs, detailed hand-drawn lines, nature-inspired organic forms, and pattern-based imagery.

The duo's large-scale murals adorn the walls of Copenhagen's Hotel Fox and the Salon International de la Lingerie, Paris. Their illustrations have decorated the pages of *Frame*, *Icon*, *Tokion*, and *Poster*. Clients such as Volkswagon and Adidas have also commissioned their graphic talents.

The pair exhibits regularly and has been involved in numerous exhibitions across Melbourne, Hamburg, Madrid, Berlin, Barcelona, Tokyo, and Los Angeles.

The artists behind Pandarosa have a commitment toward developing their own perspectives of thinking, feeling, and researching in their works, and through them aim to not only describe but also stimulate the imagination, thus showing the possibility of a tight coexistence between design and art.

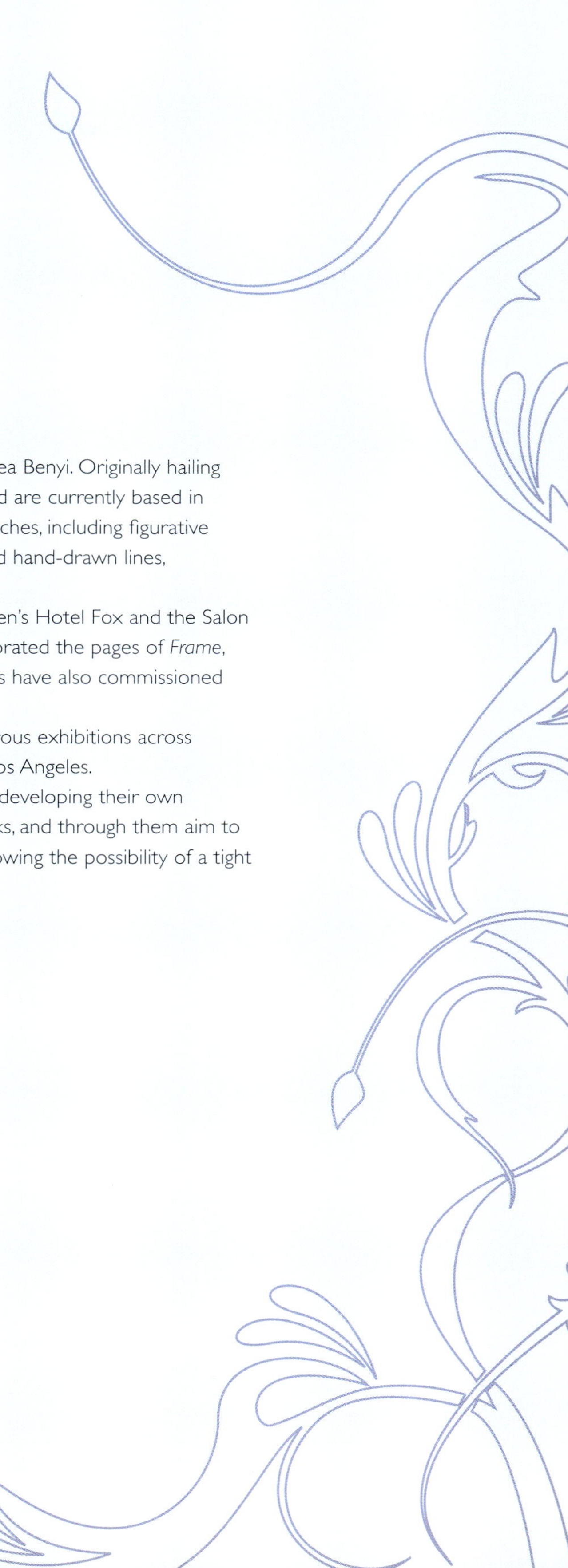

MARGUERITE SAUVAGE

Paris, France

"She can capture character with just a few simple lines, and her eye for clever graphic elements is exemplary – no wonder French illustrator Marguerite Sauvage is in demand with the ever-restless fashion world."

~ *Computer Arts Magazine*, August 2007

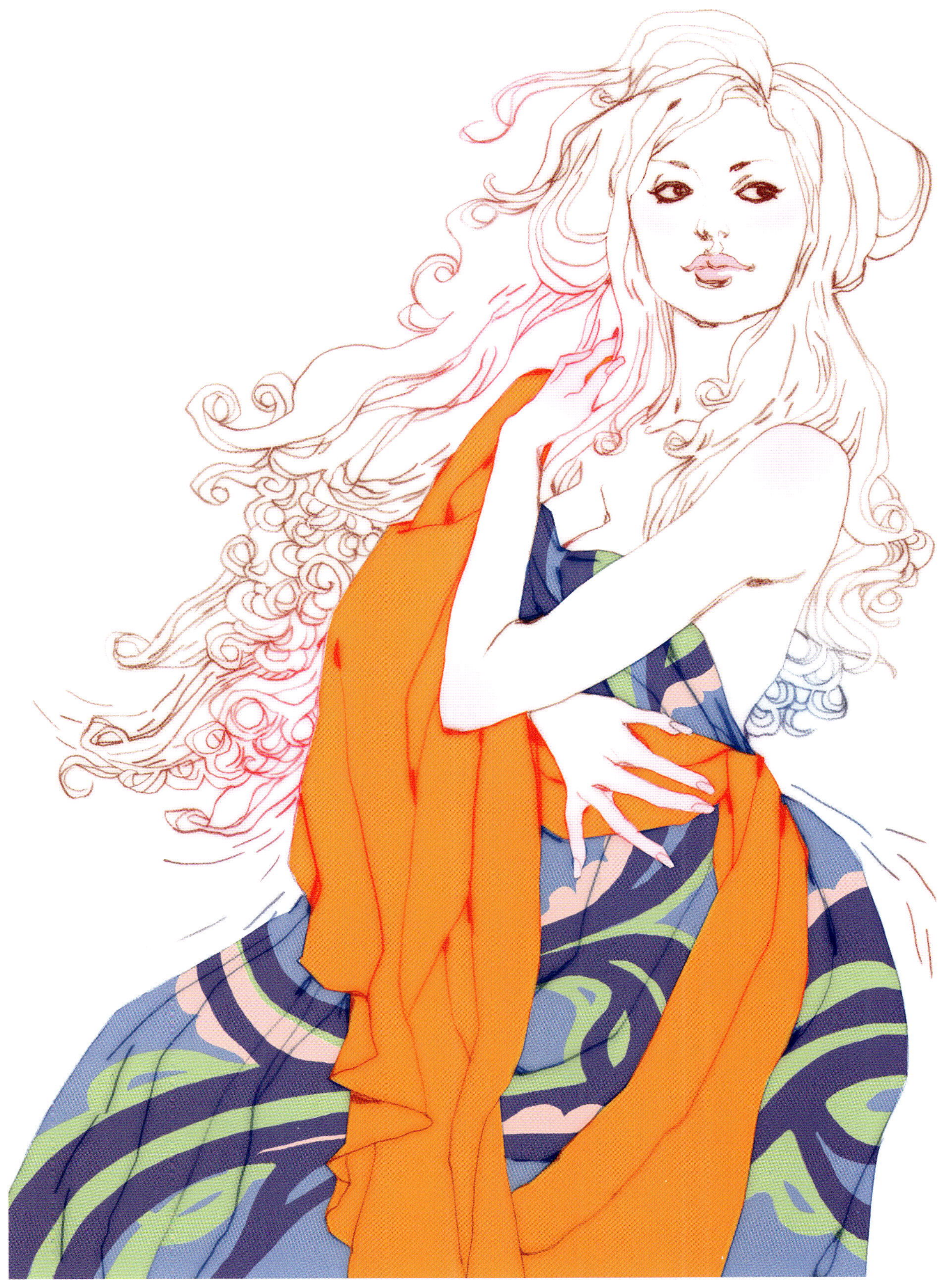

Marguerite Sauvage | *Dress and Hair (01)*, 2008 | Drawing on paper, colors on computer | 16½ × 11½ inches | Courtesy of the artist

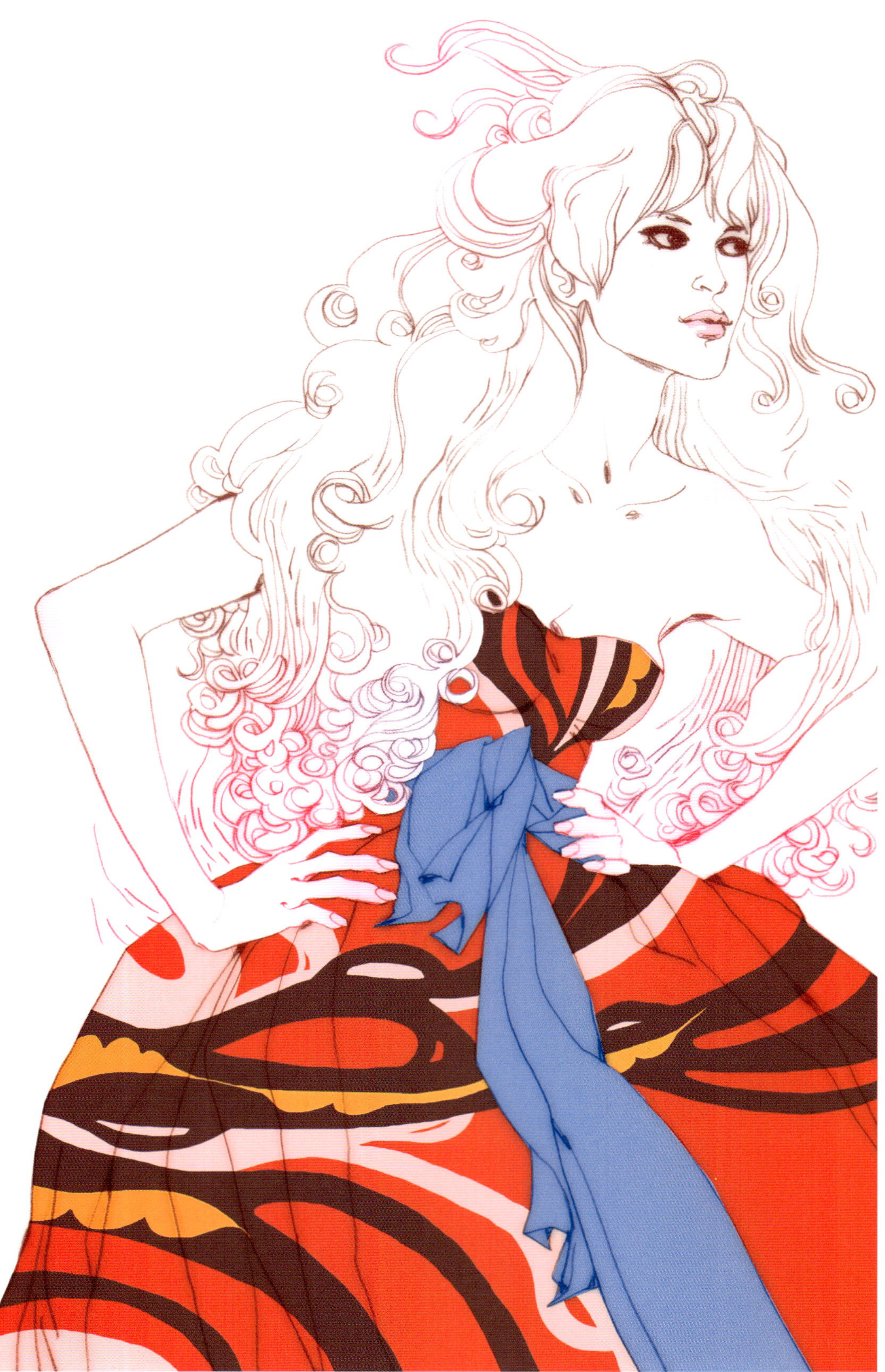

Marguerite Sauvage | *Dress and Hair (02),* 2008 | Drawing on paper, colors on computer | 16½ × 11¾ inches | Courtesy of the artist

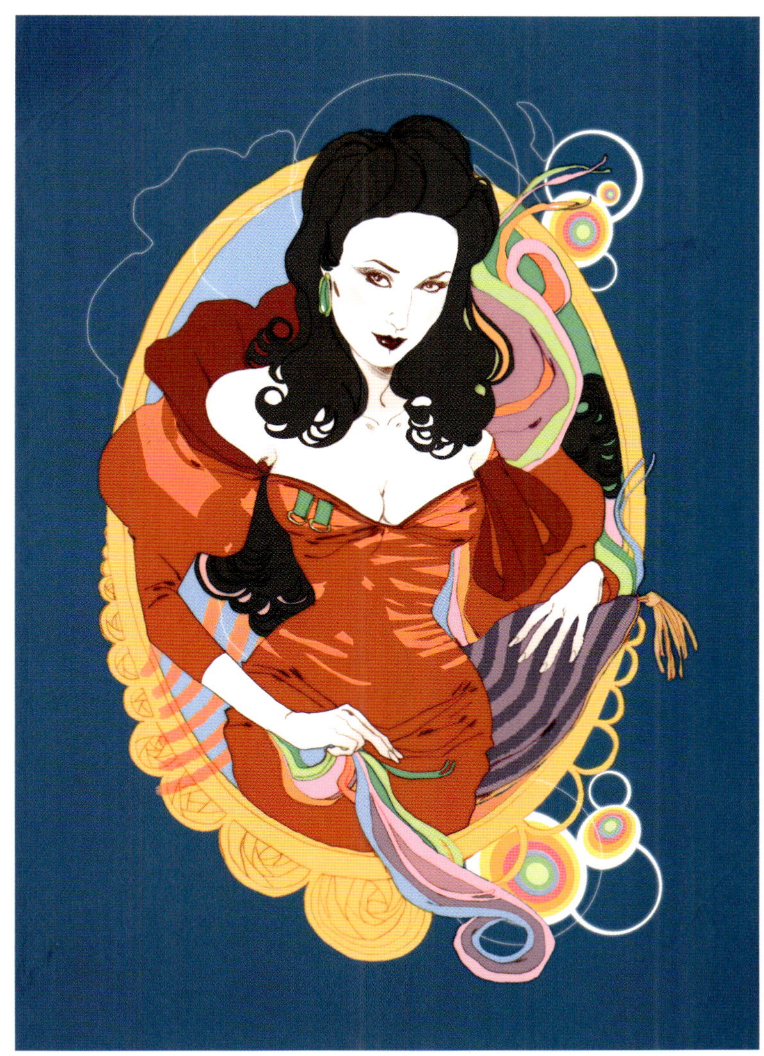

Marguerite Sauvage | *Dita*, 2008 | Drawing on paper, colors on computer
16½ × 11½ inches | Courtesy of the artist

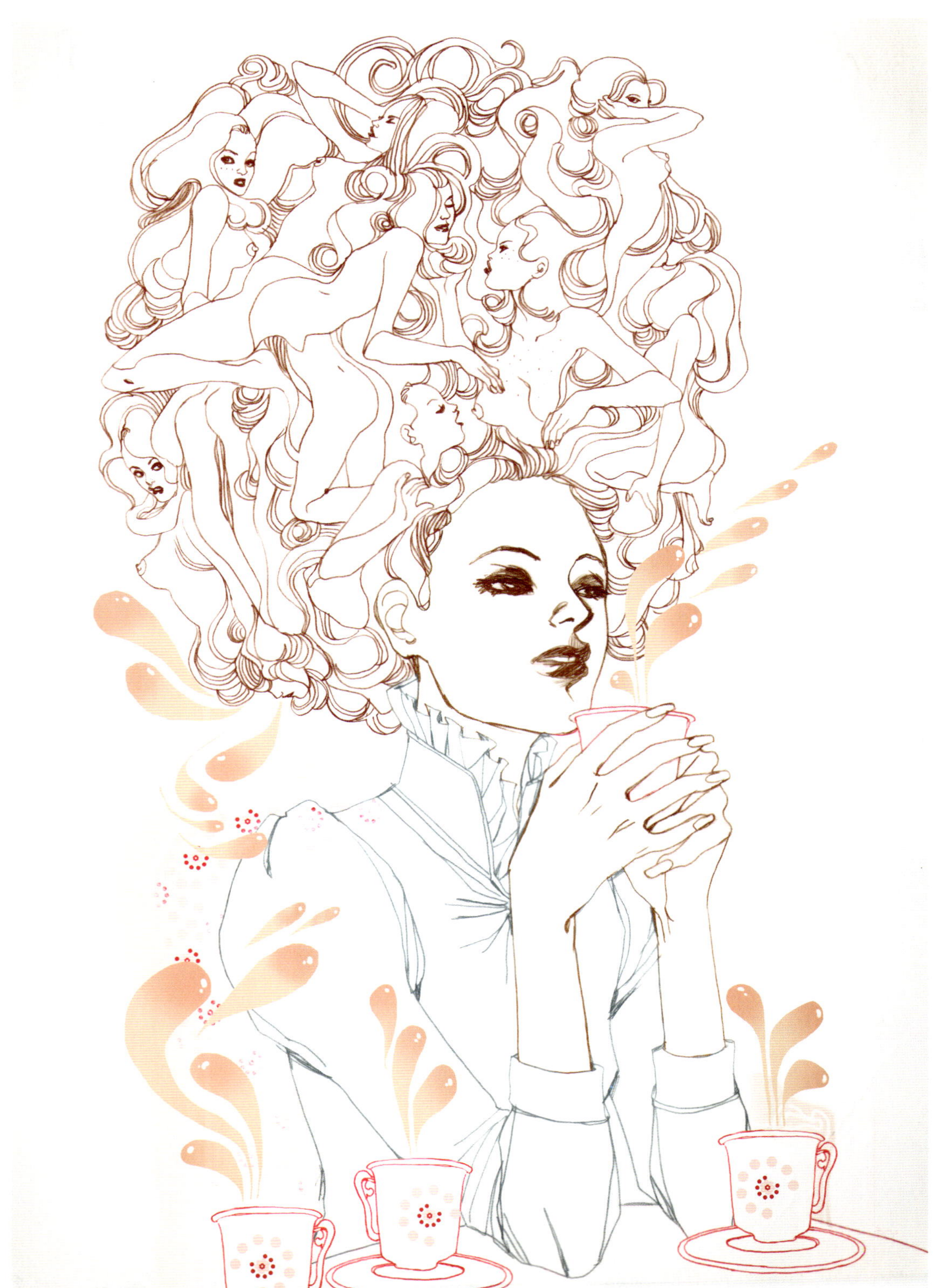

Marguerite Sauvage | *Cups of Tea*, 2007 | Drawing on paper, colors on computer | 16½ × 11½ inches | Courtesy of the artist

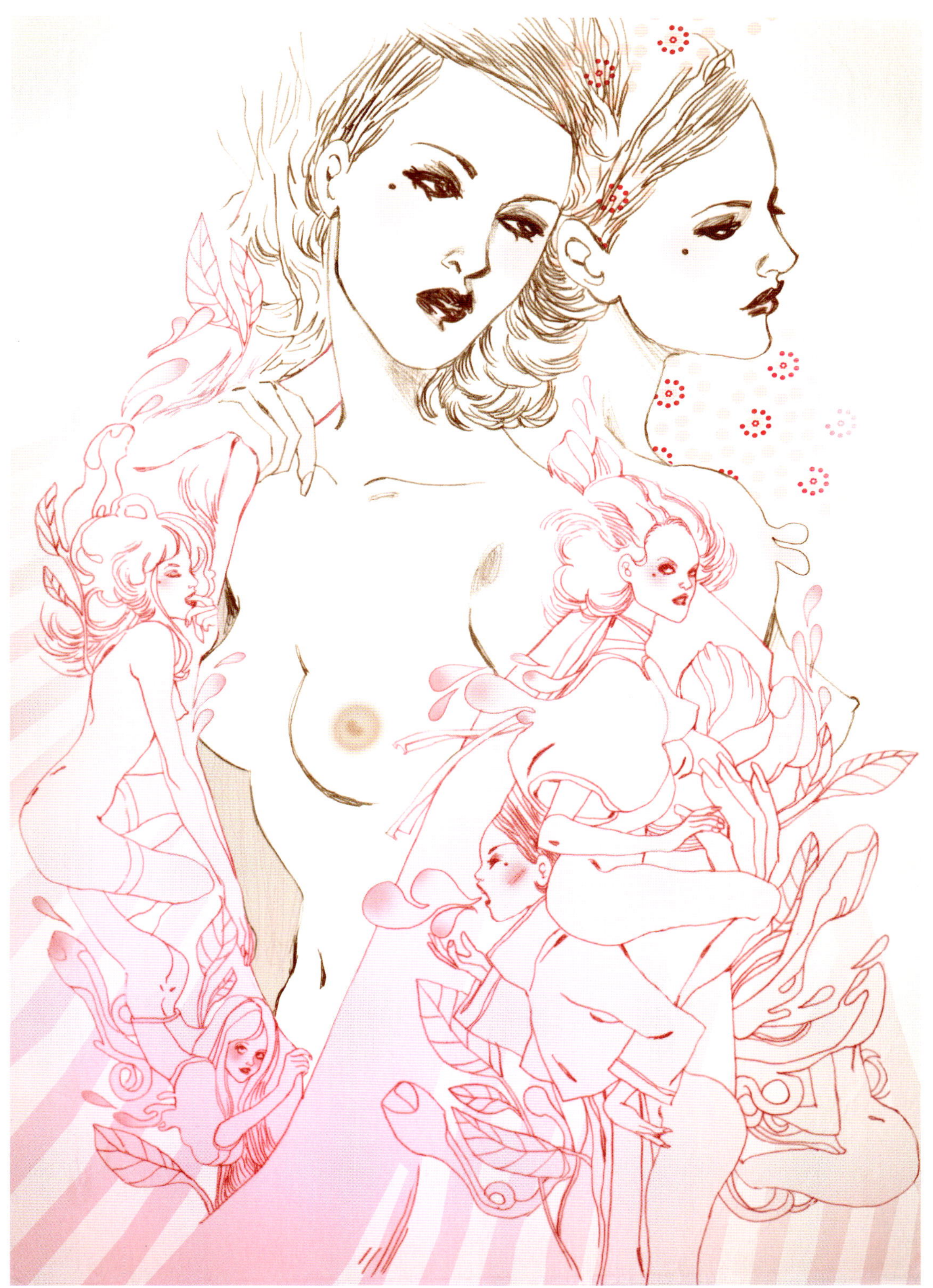

Marguerite Sauvage | *Pudeur, 2007* | Drawing on paper, colors on computer | 16½ × 11½ inches | Courtesy of the artist

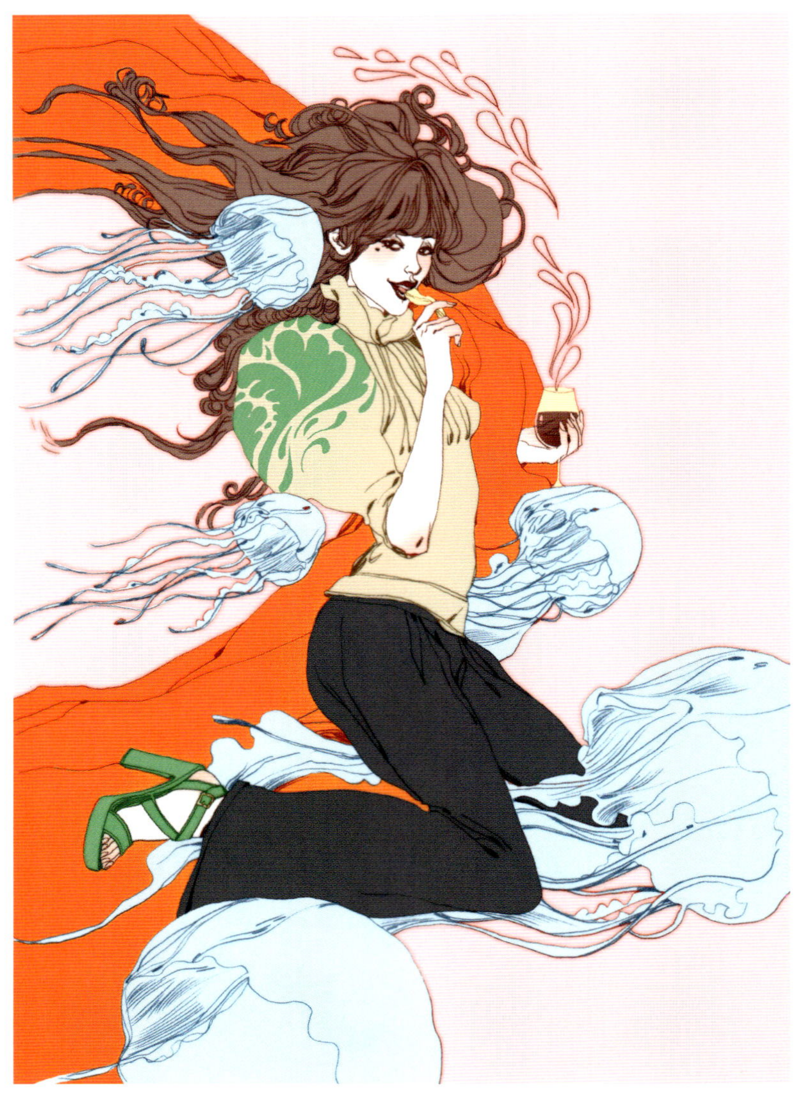

Marguerite Sauvage | *Jelly Fish*, 2008 | Drawing on paper, colors on computer
16½ × 11½ inches | Courtesy of the artist

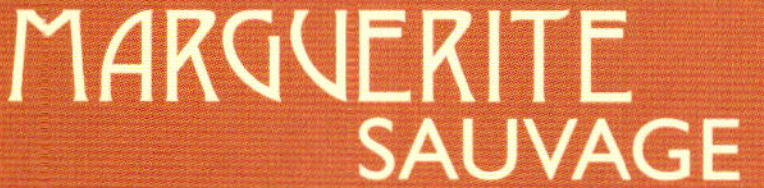

MARGUERITE
SAUVAGE

Based in Paris, France, self-taught artist Marguerite Sauvage has worked since 2001 as an illustrator, art director, and animator creating chic modern illustrations that capture the lifestyle of today's trendsetters.

Sauvage begins her illustrations with pencil sketches and transfers her drawings to the computer, where she manipulates the composition in Photoshop before applying color digitally. Her work combines sophisticated European sensibilities with line-work inspired by both traditional Japanese art and contemporary Japanese culture.

Marguerite Sauvage's work is hailed as stylish yet accessible, and is in demand with prominent advertising and corporate clients including Apple, Mattel, and L'Oreal/Garnier (France). Her work has seduced publications such as *Elle*, *InStyle*, and *Glamour* among many others. Sauvage was recently chosen for *Lurzer's Archive: 200 Best Illustrators Worldwide 2007/2008*.

Sauvage admires the strong, beautiful, and feminine aspects of life. She cites her travels, everyday life, and Japanese artist and animator Rumiko Takahashi as additional sources of inspiration.

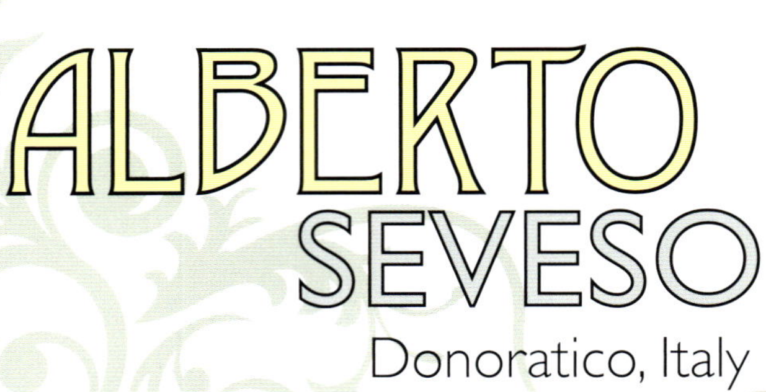

ALBERTO SEVESO

Donoratico, Italy

"Does not really matter who I am or where I come from, the world has no borders. My illustrations speak for me..."

~ Alberto Seveso

(opposite) **Alberto Seveso** | Non Perderne Uno, 2007 | Illustrator and Photoshop on paper | 23¼ × 16½ inches | Courtesy of the artist

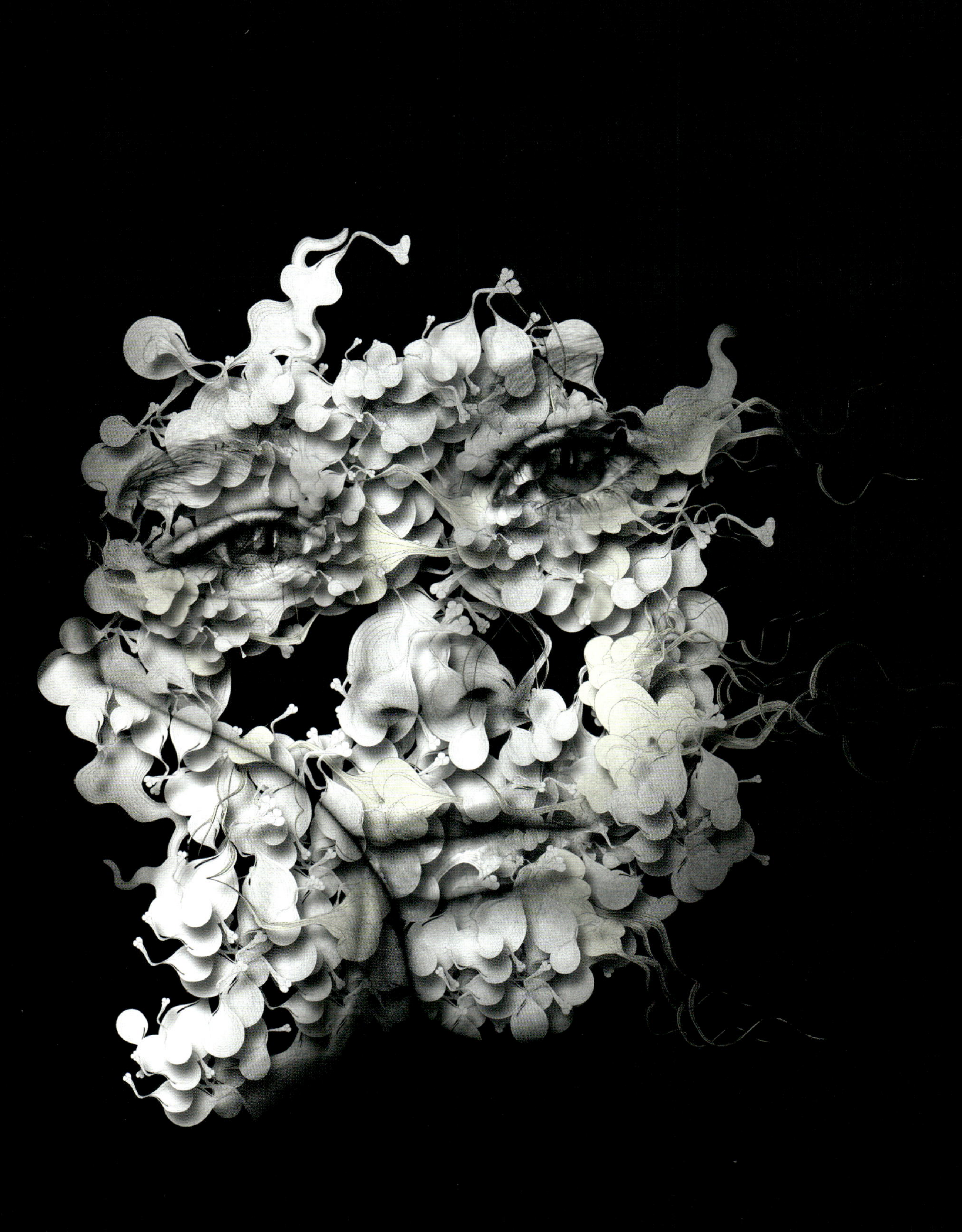

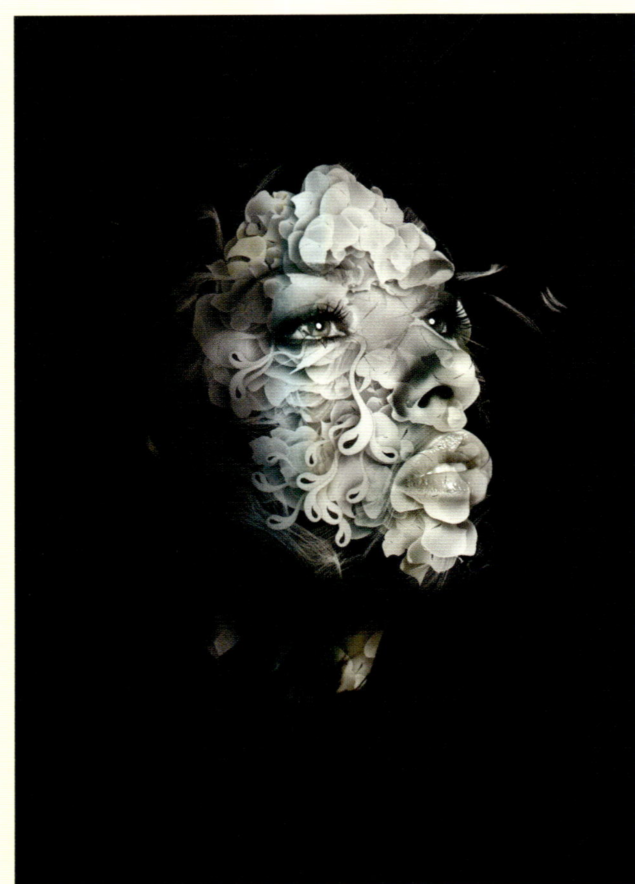

Grazia

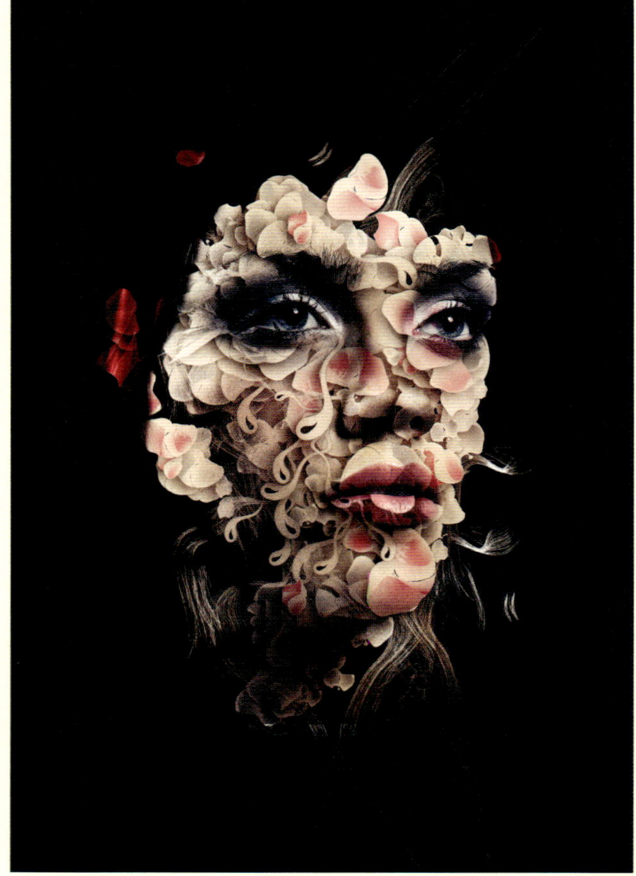

Graziella

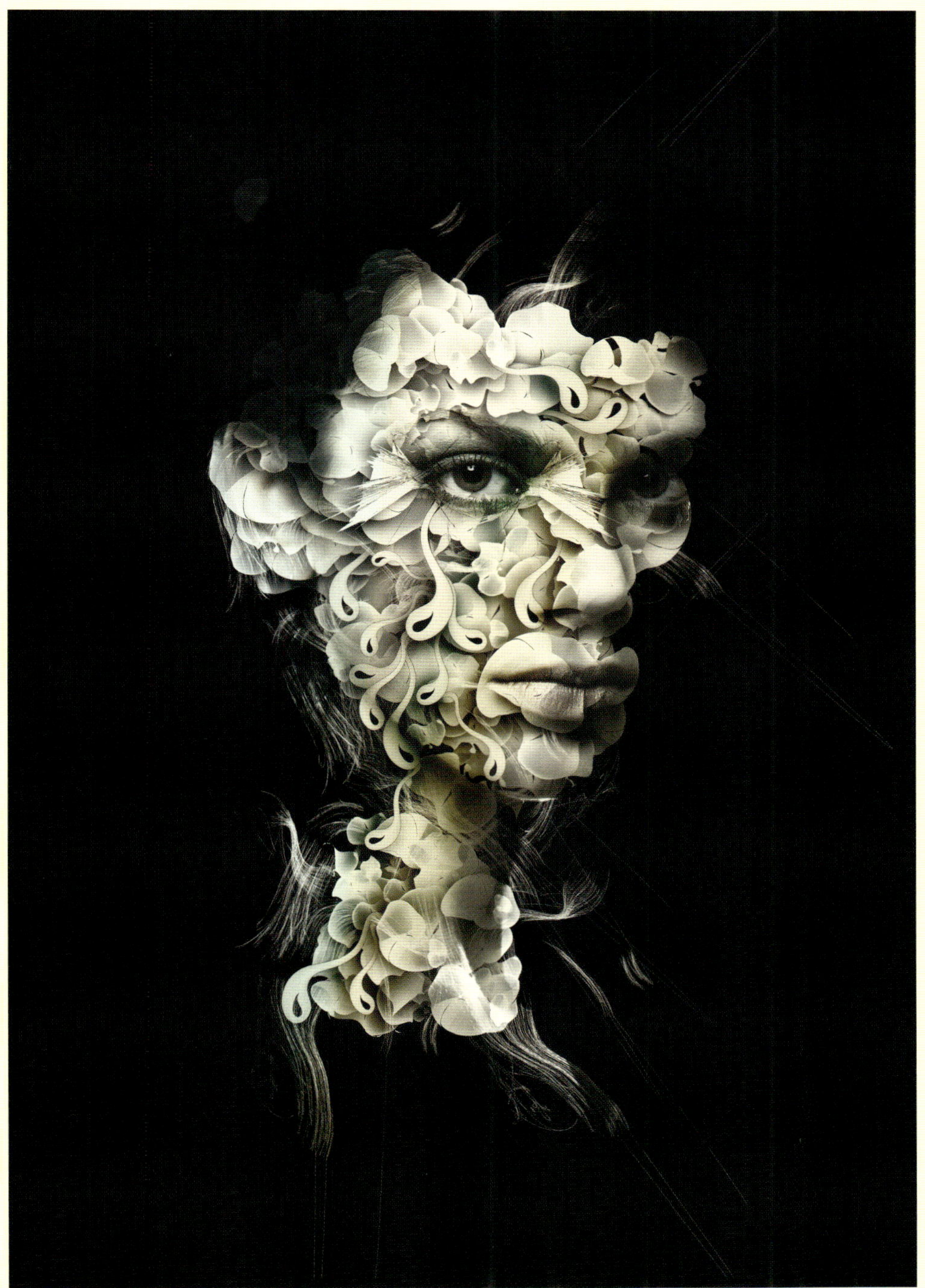

Alberto Seveso | *The Three Graces (Grazia, Graziella e Grazie al Cazzo!)*, 2008
Illustrator and Photoshop on paper | 23¼ × 16½ inches each | Courtesy of the artist

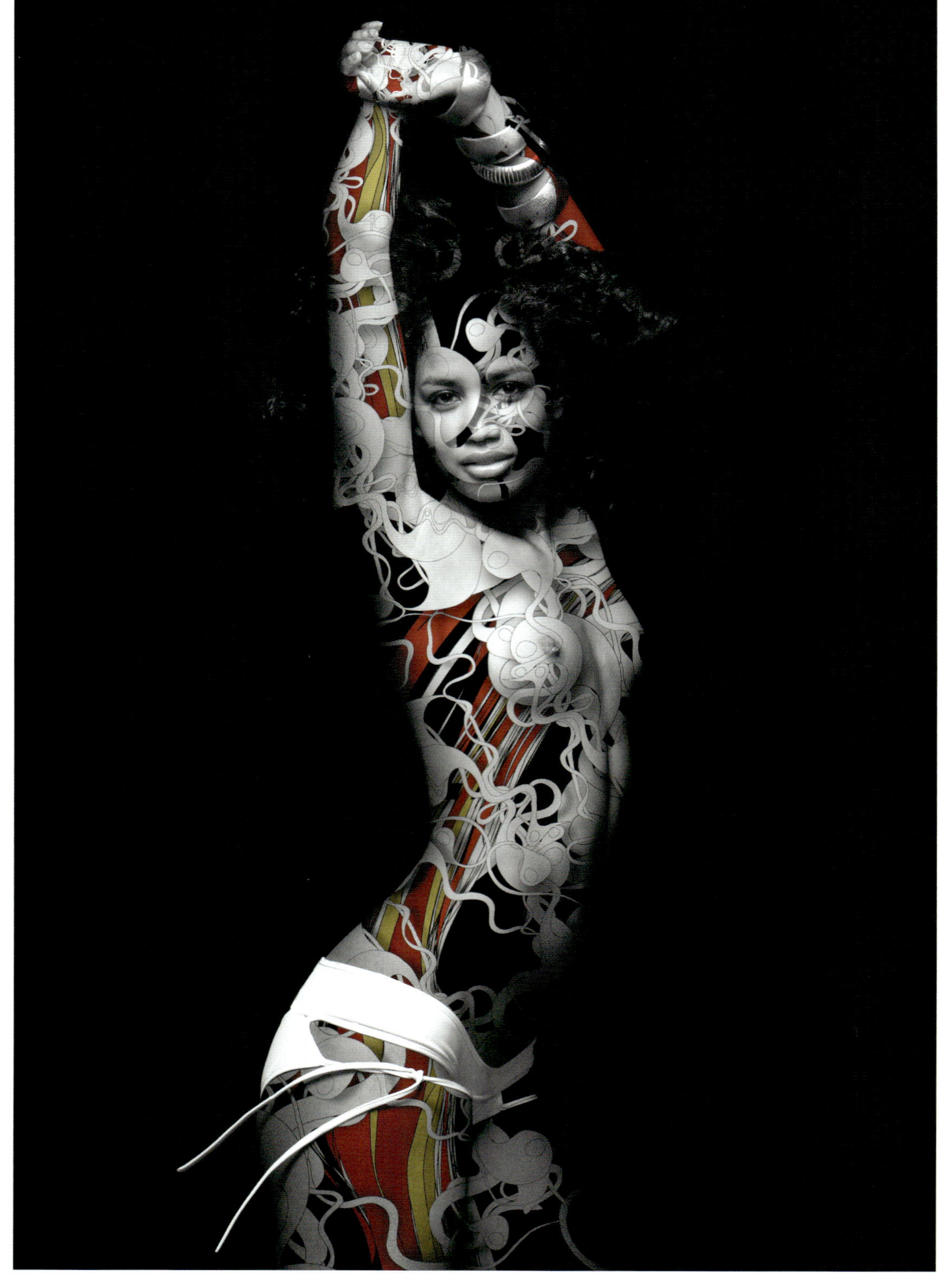

Alberto Seveso | *Firiyal*, 2007 | Illustrator and Photoshop on paper | 23¼ × 16½ inches | Courtesy of the artist

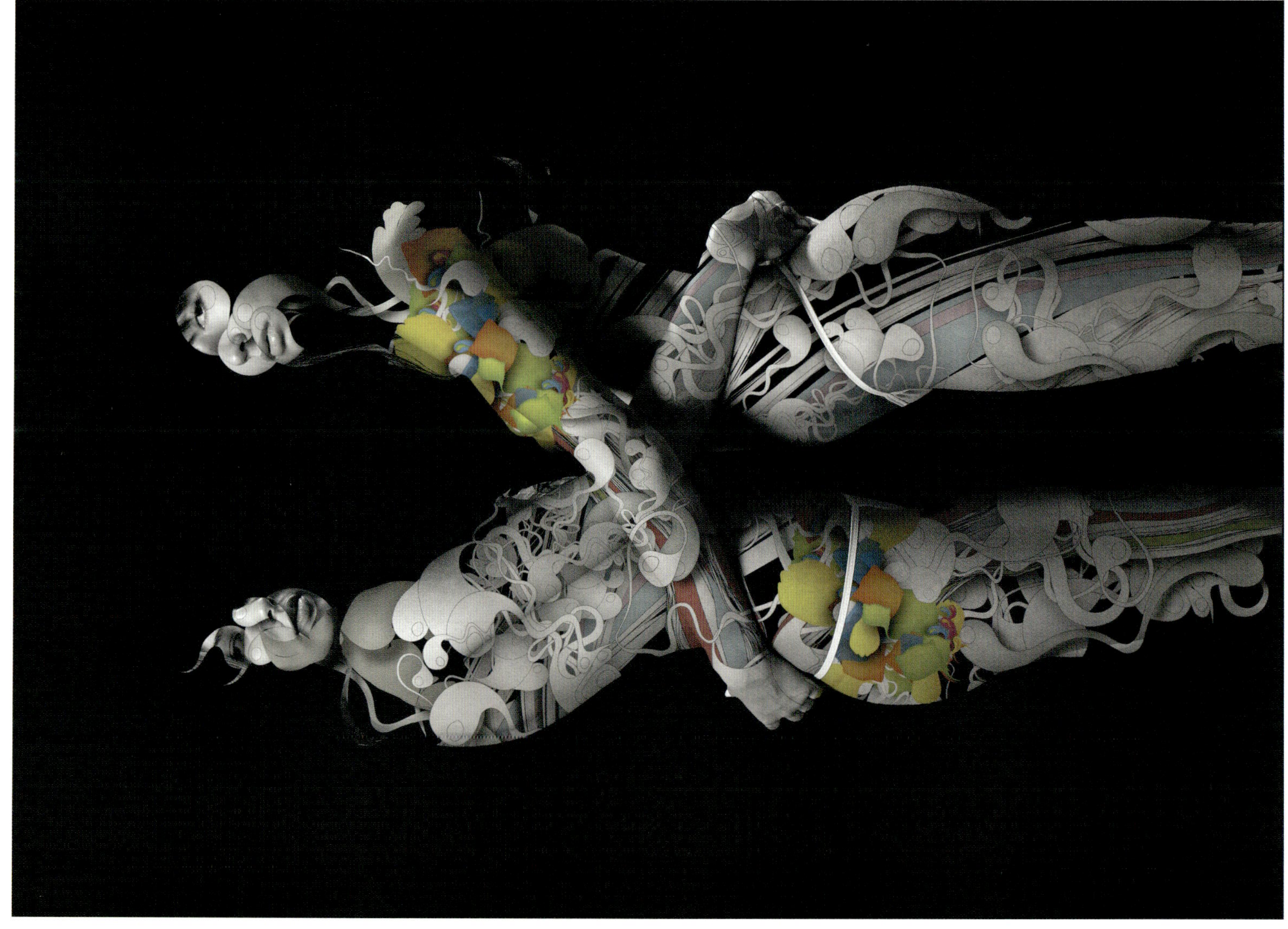

Alberto Seveso | *Coppia di Bagasce (Incostituzionale)*, 2009 (Remake of 2007) | Illustrator and Photoshop on paper | 23¼ × 16½ inches | Courtesy of the artist

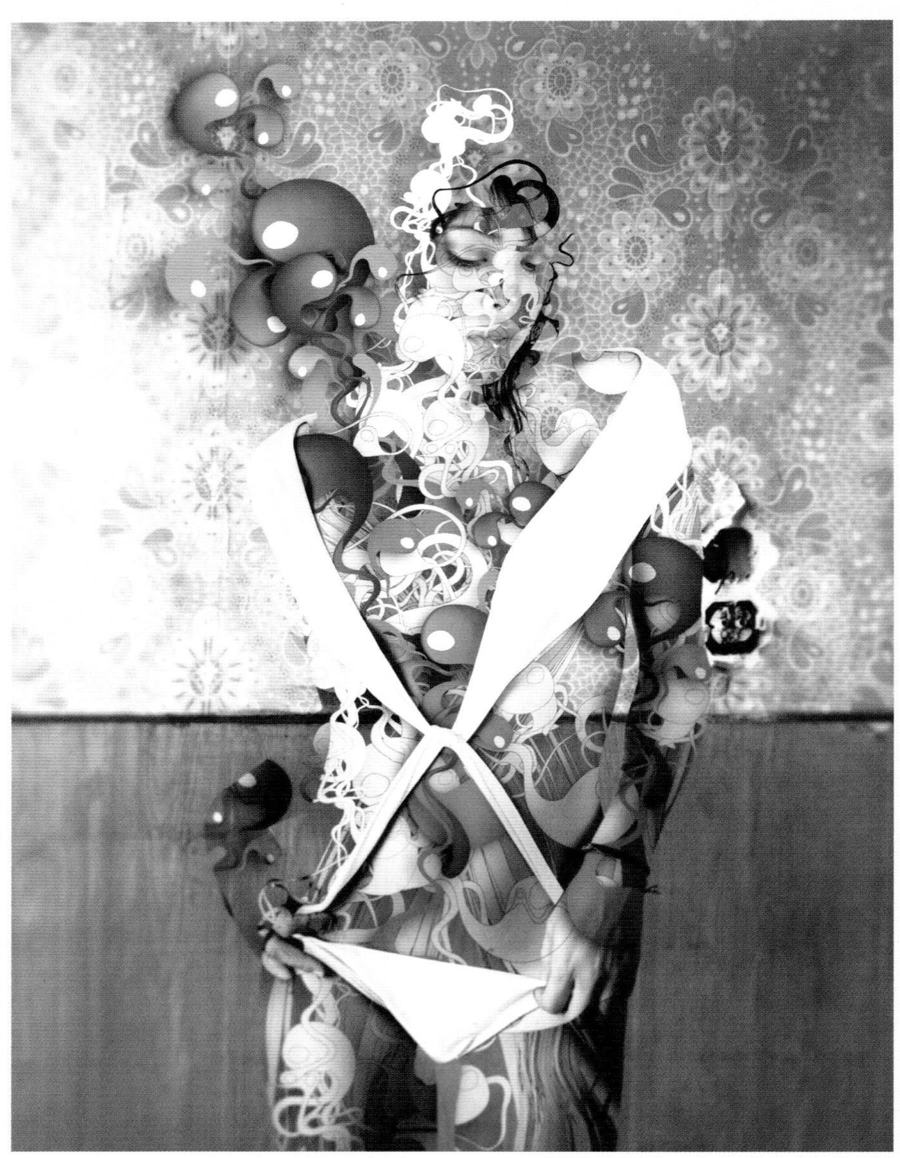

Alberto Seveso | *Camera Con Vista*, 2007 | Illustrator and Photoshop on paper
23¼ × 16½ inches | Courtesy of the artist

ALBERTO
SEVESO

Based in Rome, Italy, graphic designer and illustrator Alberto Seveso uses Illustrator and Photoshop to create multilayered images of the female figure. Seveso's technique or "sperm shaping" as Fabio Sasso, author of the design blog *Abduzeedo.com* describes it, combines "colorful vectors with black-and-white photos." His sensual designs were featured in Nucleus Gallery's *Grafik 3* exhibition and publication. In addition to his work with a female focus, Seveso's design work has also transformed images of male faces and bodies, including Michael Phelps, as seen on the December 2008 cover of *ESPN Magazine*; Kelly Slater for his October 2008 *RelentlessEnergy.com* interview; and David Lynch and Ice Cube for Seveso's work with international design agency Factory 311.

Seveso recently created artwork for the exhibition *Run, Jump and Throw - Athletics in International Contemporary Art* for the IAAF World Championships in Athletics, Berlin 2009™.

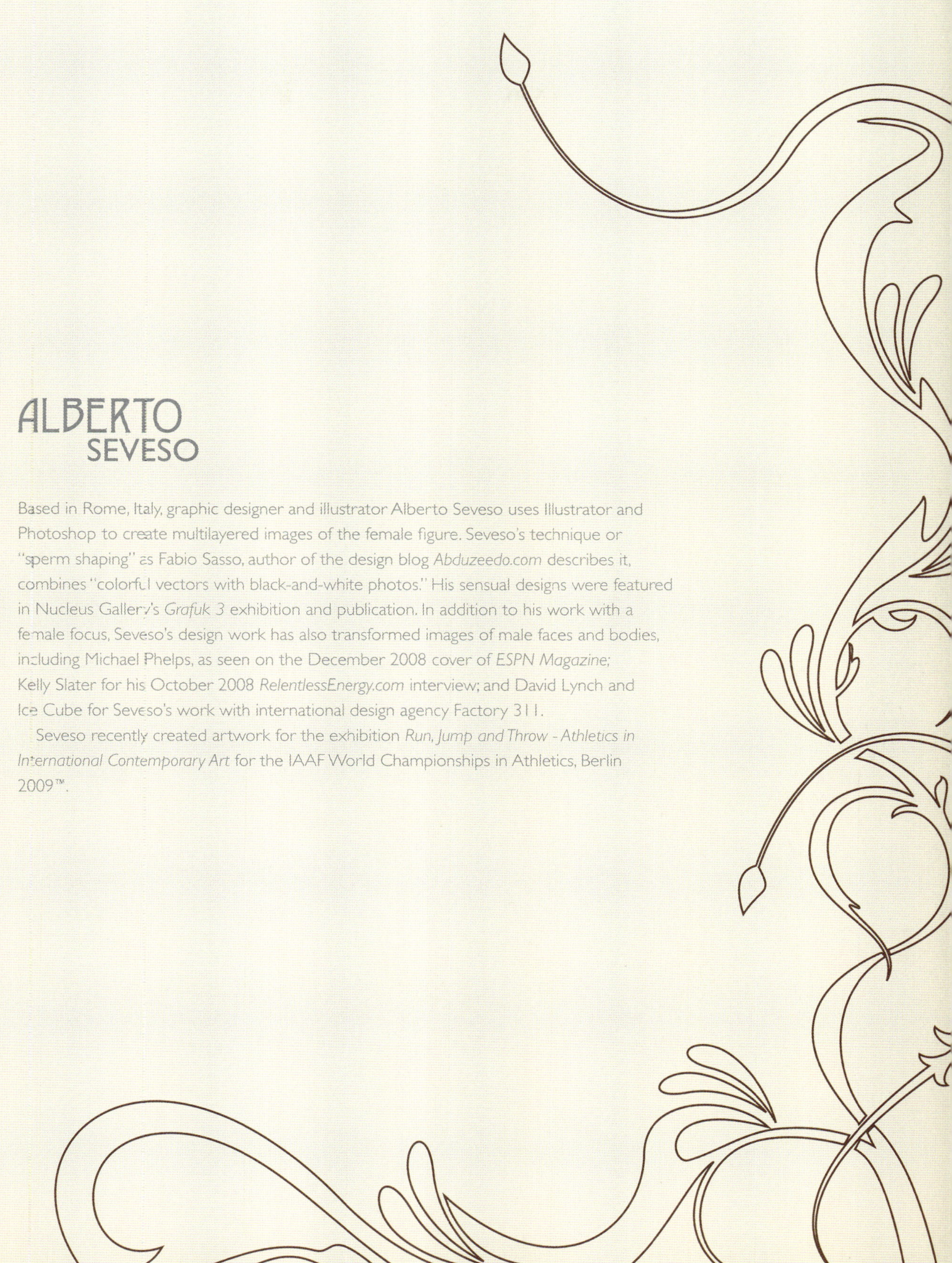

SONYA SUHARIYAN

Rostov-on-Don, Russia

"Suhariyan's work is a layered composite of a global contemporary style on one hand, and a more specific quality of expressive emotion which is distinctly Russian. Her use of overall pattern certainly fits the decorative and Pop traditions of now. Yet there is an obsessive quality to the shapes, and an intensity to specific images which is expressive of an eastern European tradition."

~ Joe Biel, Cal State Fullerton Associate Professor
of Studio Art, 2009

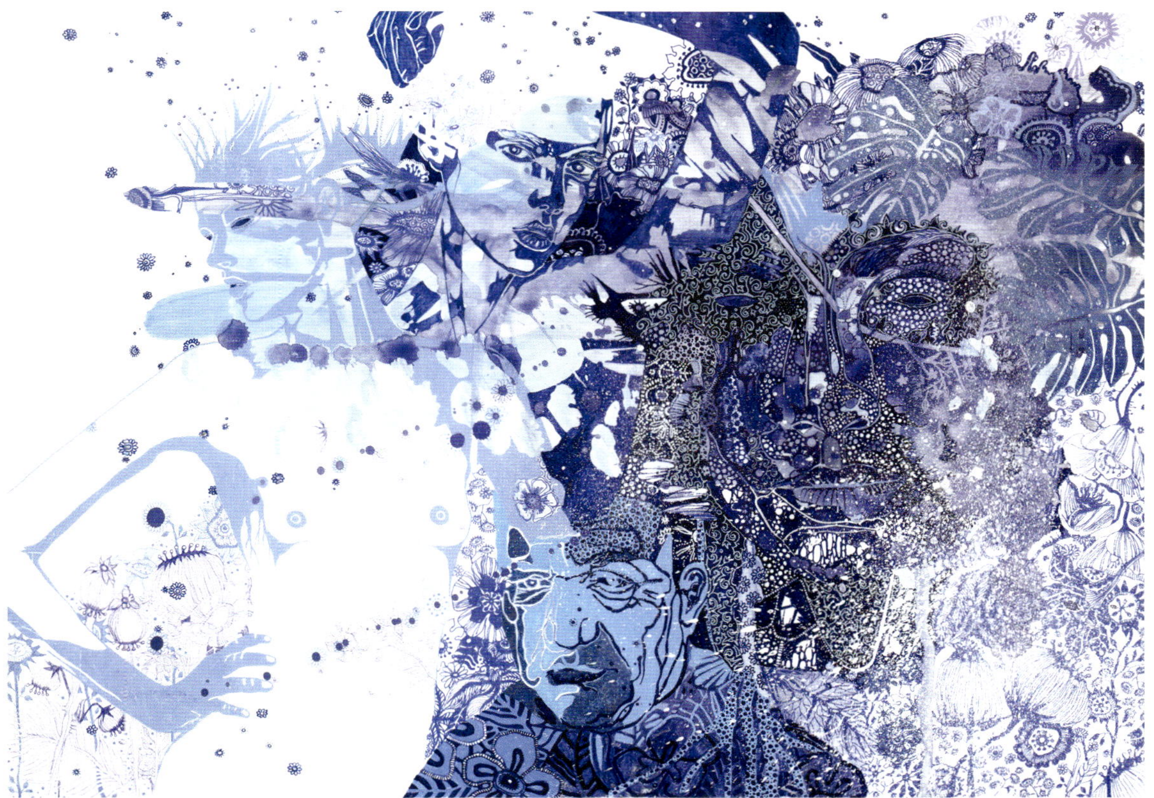

Sonya Suhariyan | *Blue Mask*, 2005 | Gouache, watercolor, and ink on paper
11½ × 16½ inches | Courtesy cf the artist

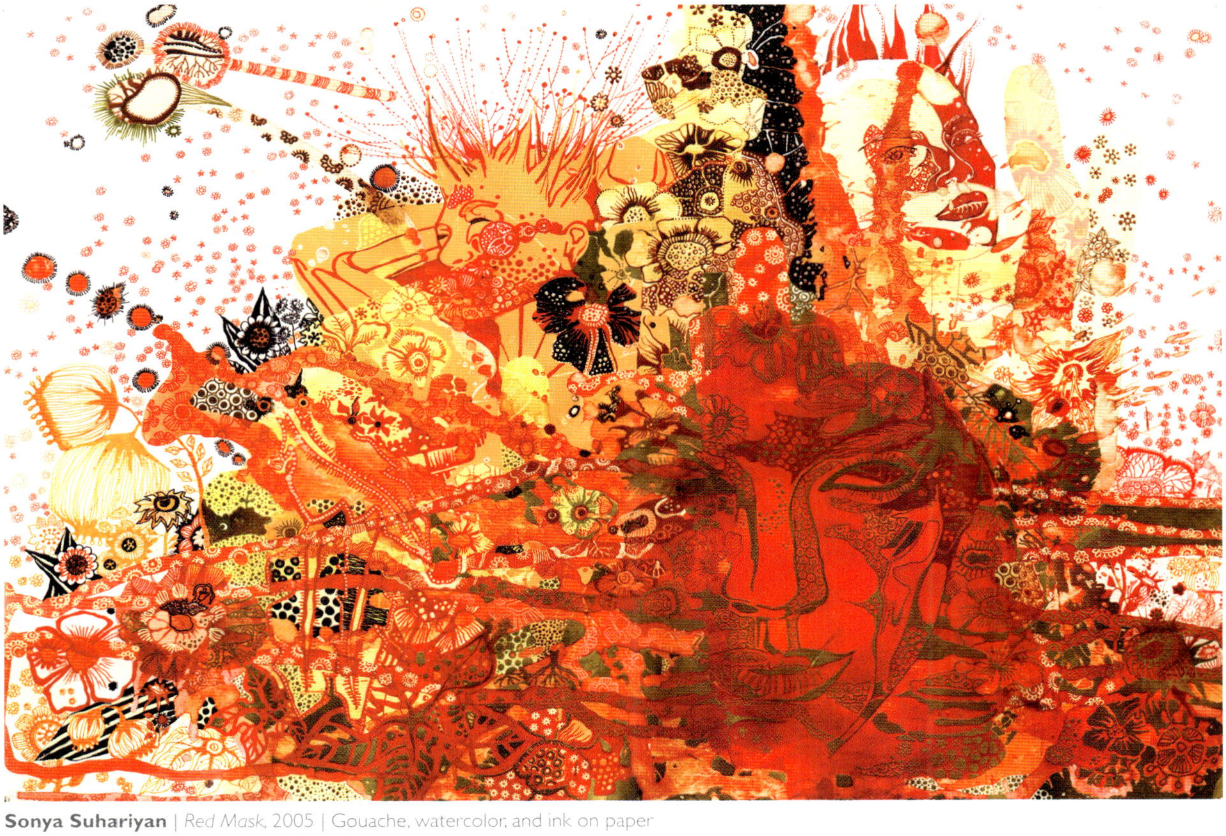

Sonya Suhariyan | *Red Mask*, 2005 | Gouache, watercolor, and ink on paper
11½ × 16½ inches | Courtesy of the artist

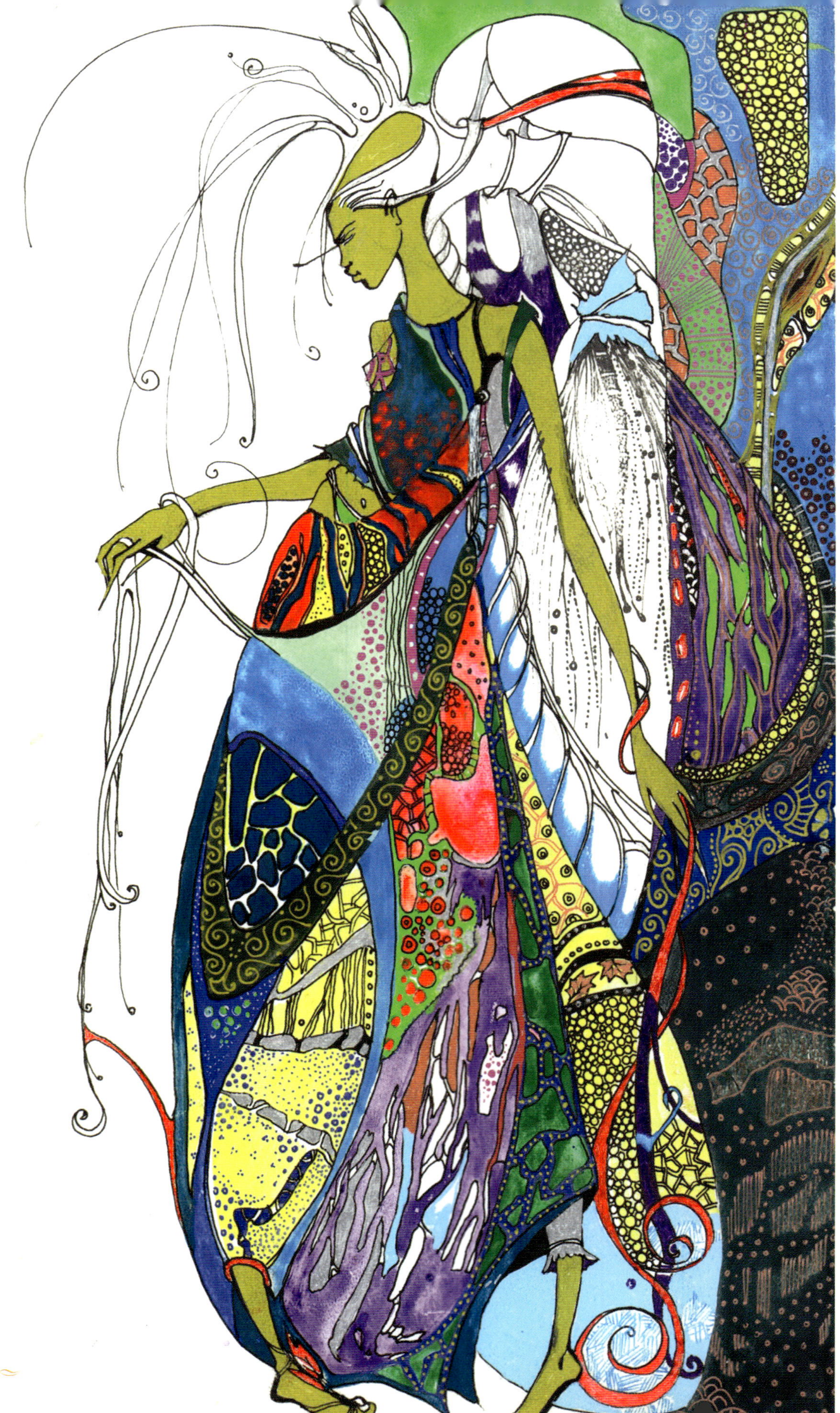

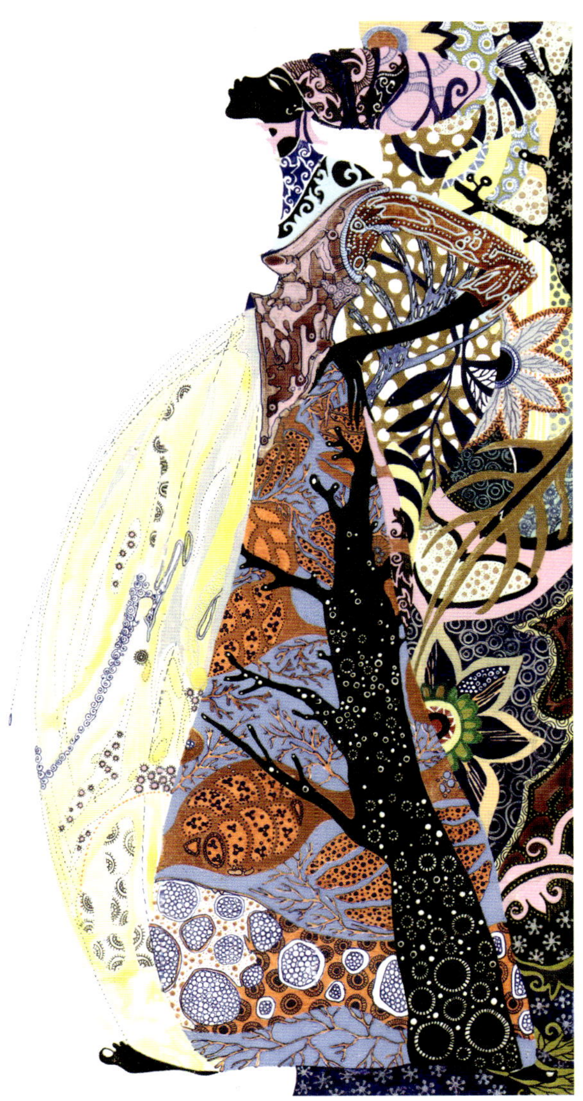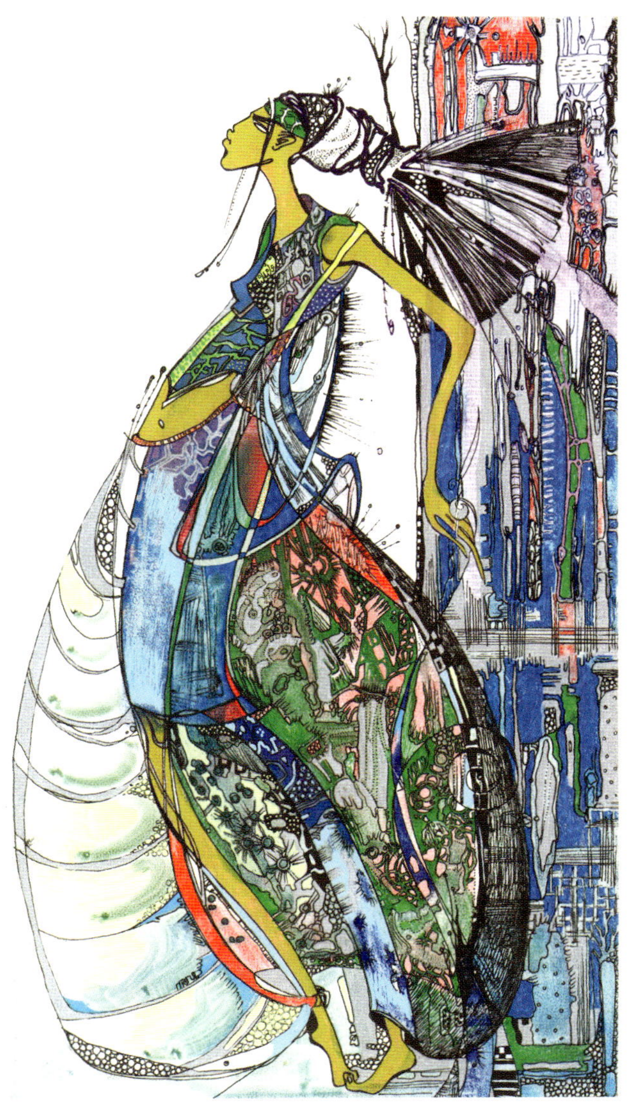

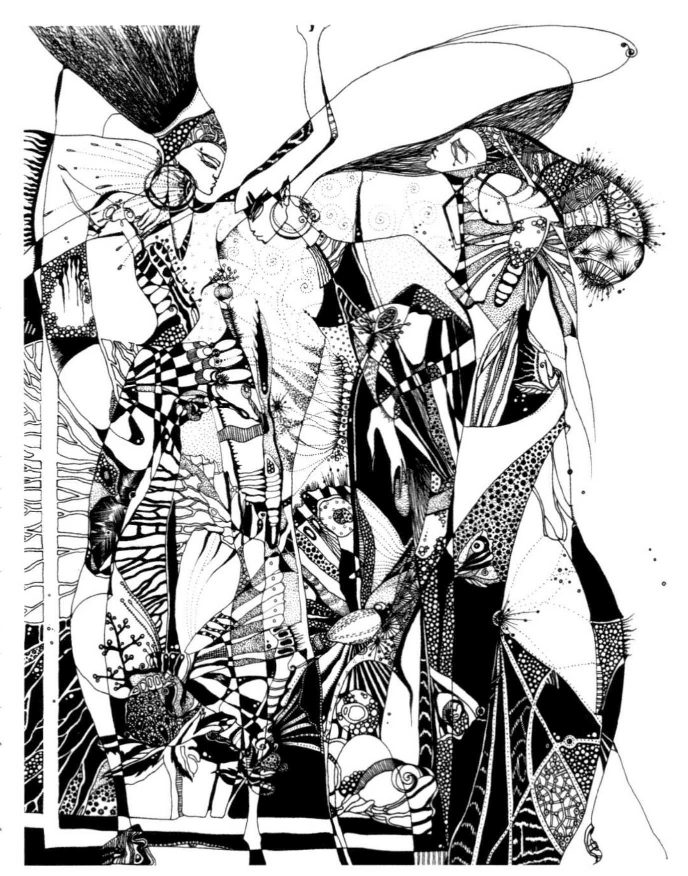

Sonya Suhariyan | *Desire*, 2004 | Ink on paper | 11½ × 16½ inches | Courtesy of the artist

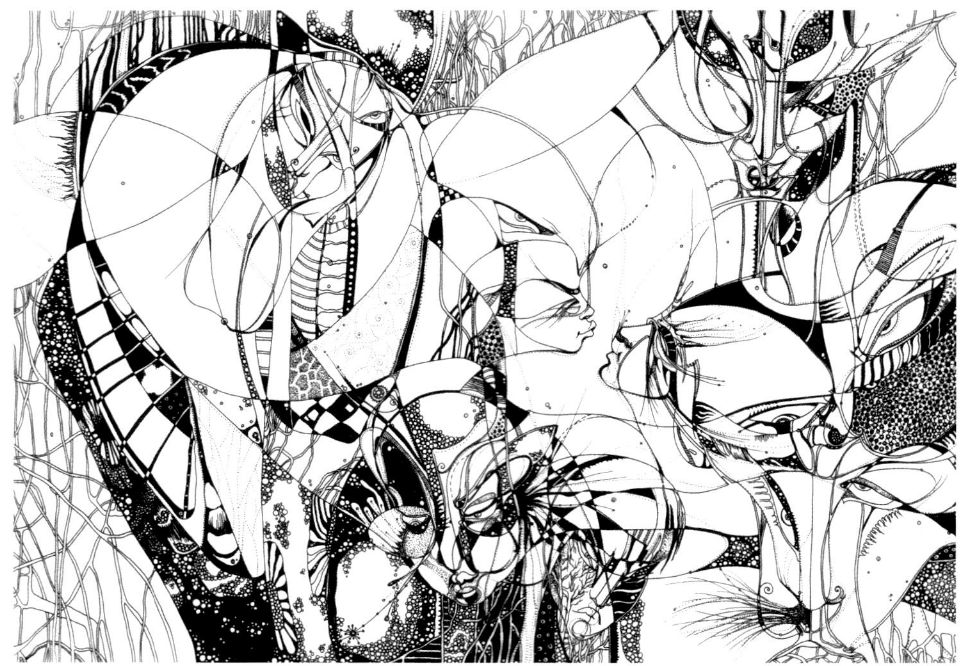

SONYA
SUHARIYAN

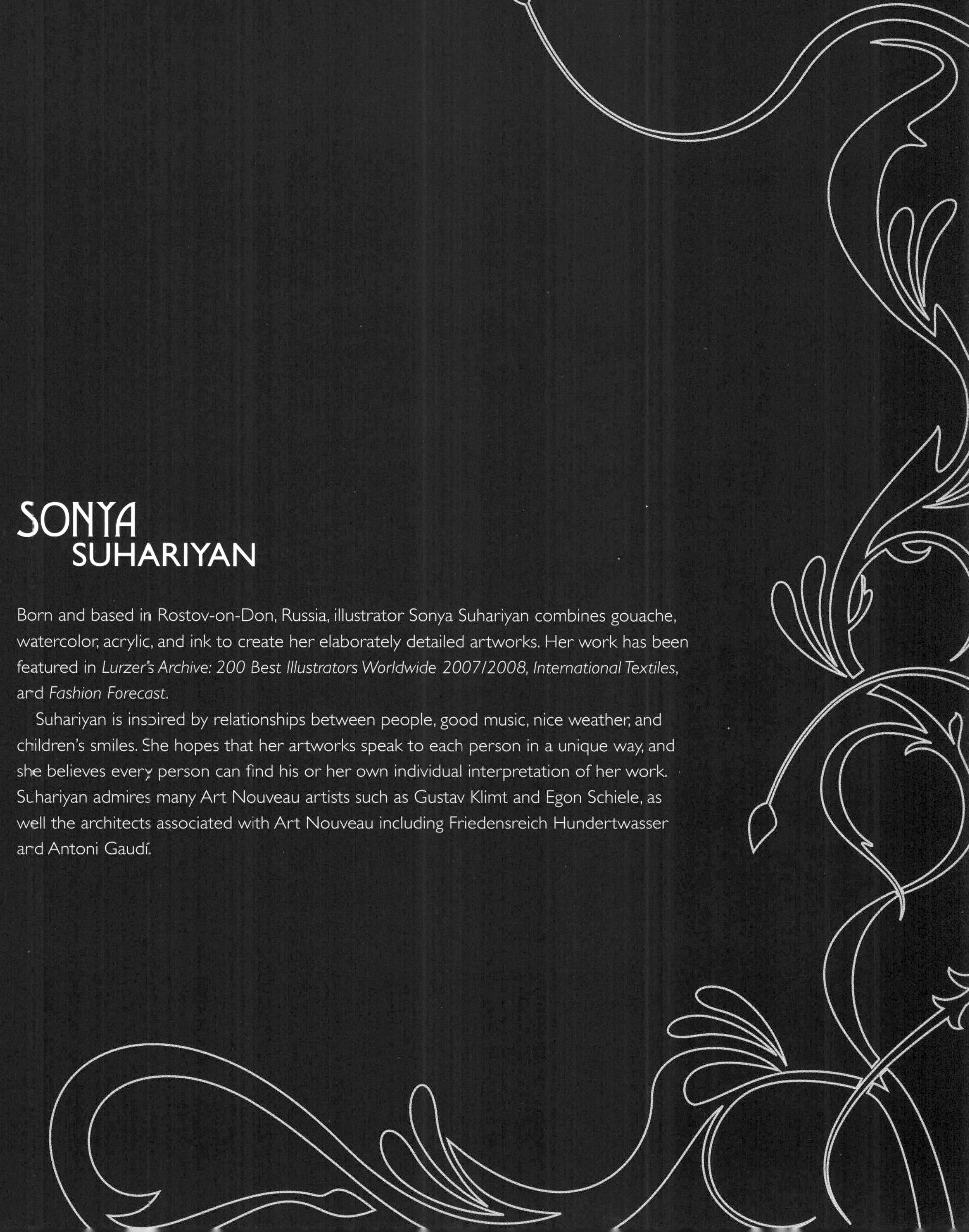

Born and based in Rostov-on-Don, Russia, illustrator Sonya Suhariyan combines gouache, watercolor, acrylic, and ink to create her elaborately detailed artworks. Her work has been featured in *Lurzer's Archive: 200 Best Illustrators Worldwide 2007/2008*, *International Textiles*, and *Fashion Forecast*.

Suhariyan is inspired by relationships between people, good music, nice weather, and children's smiles. She hopes that her artworks speak to each person in a unique way, and she believes every person can find his or her own individual interpretation of her work. Suhariyan admires many Art Nouveau artists such as Gustav Klimt and Egon Schiele, as well the architects associated with Art Nouveau including Friedensreich Hundertwasser and Antoni Gaudí.

YOSHI TAJIMA

Tokyo, Japan

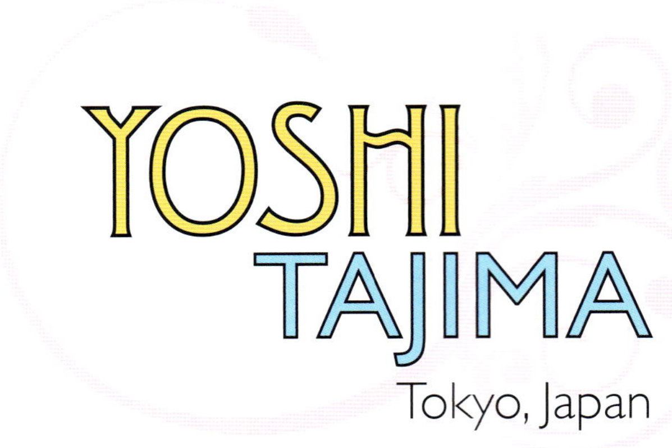

"In his works Yoshi Tajima beautifully merges the poetic delicacy of illustration with the ratio of graphic design."

~ Robert Klanten, Director of Die Gestalten Verlag in
Berlin, Germany, 2009

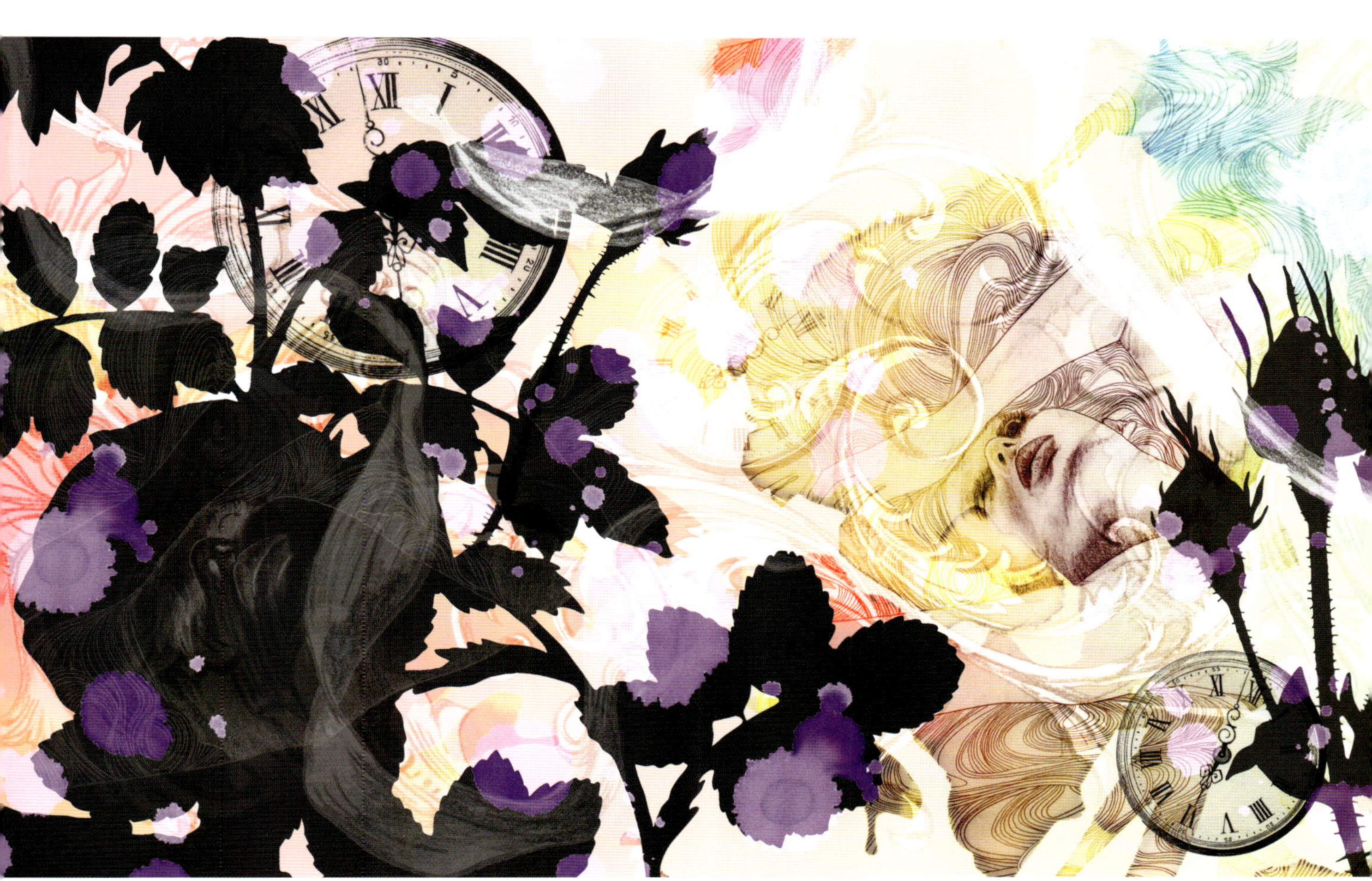

Yoshi Tajima | 6am, 2006 | Pencil, watercolor, Chinese ink, and Adobe Photoshop on paper | 10 × 16½ inches | Courtesy of the artist

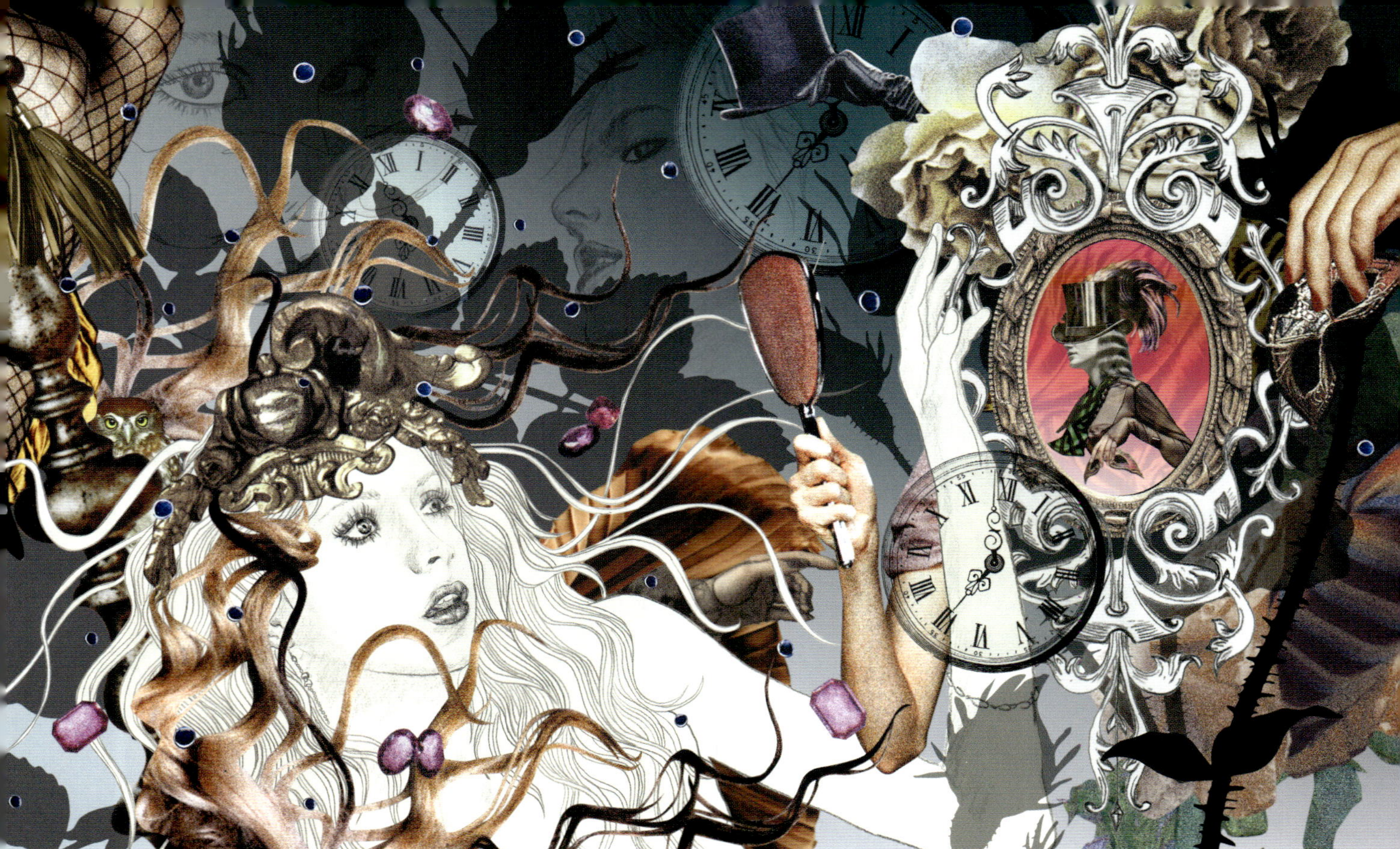

Yoshi Tajima | *Turn*, 2006 | Pencil, watercolor, Chinese ink, and Adobe Photoshop on paper | 10 × 16½ inches | Courtesy of the artist

Yoshi Tajima | *8am*, 2006 | Pencil, watercolor, Chinese ink, and Adobe Photoshop on paper | 10 × 16½ inches | Courtesy of the artist

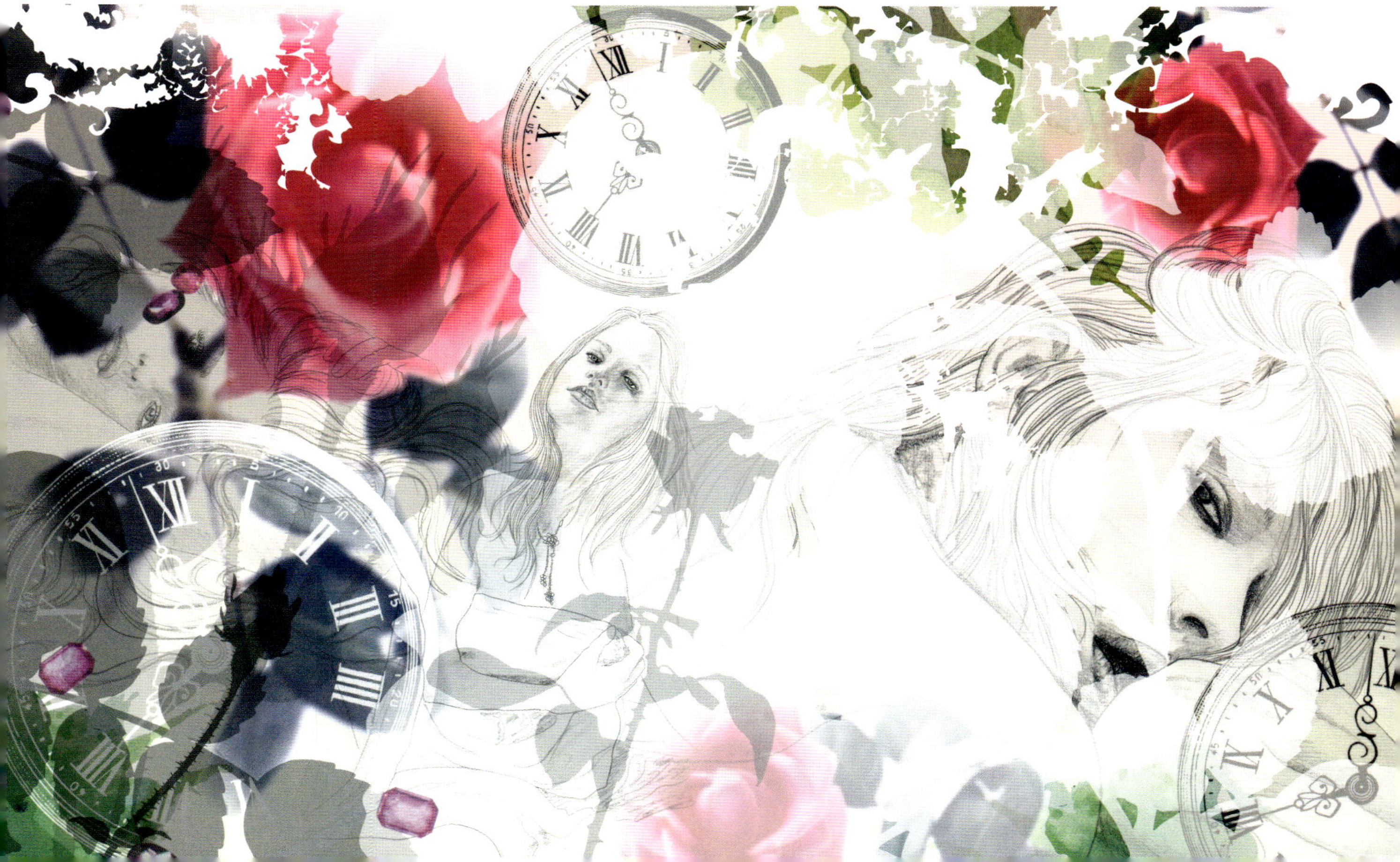

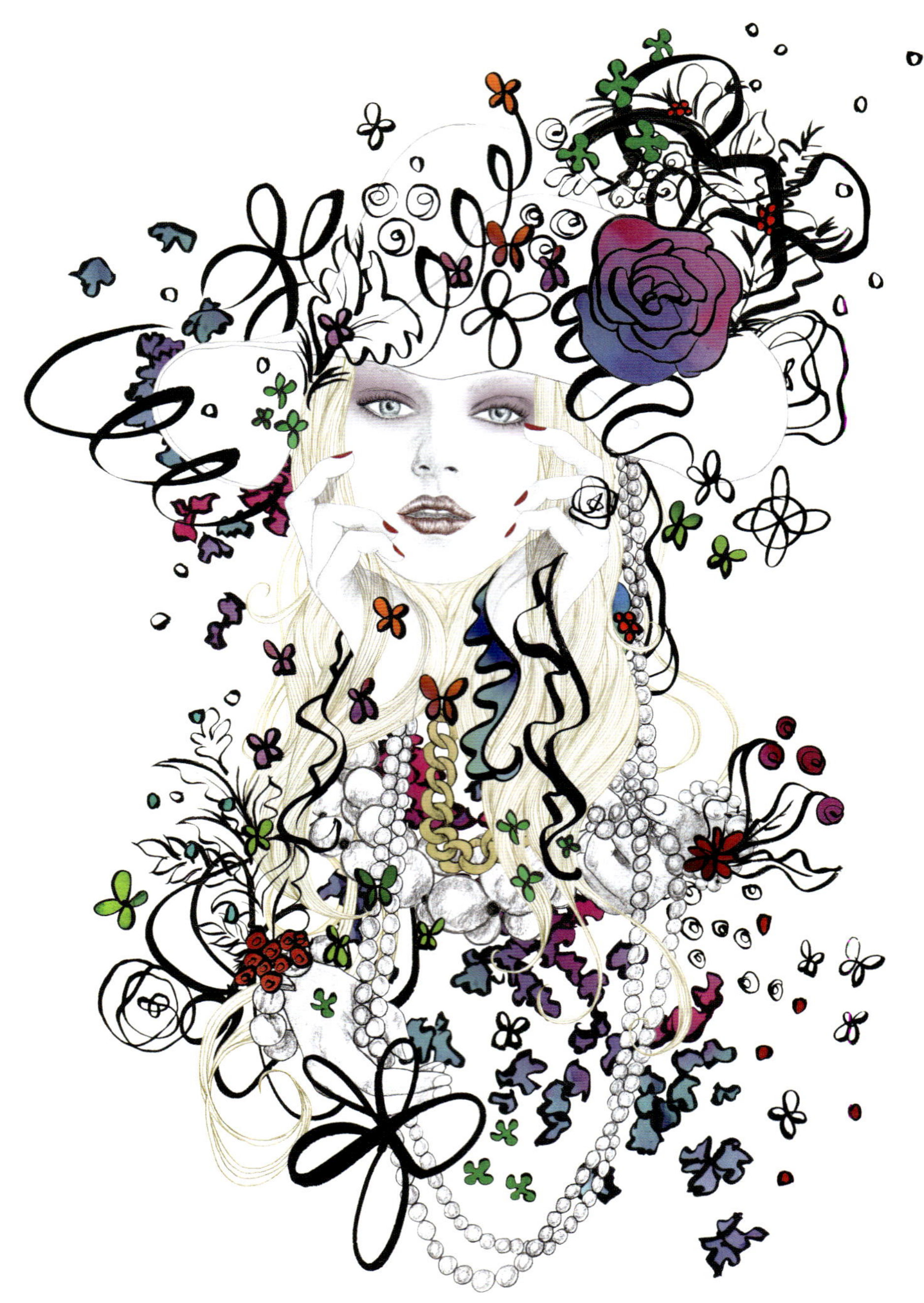

Yoshi Tajima | *Fairy 01*, 2008 | Pencil, watercolor, Chinese ink, and Adobe Photoshop on paper
27½ × 23 inches | Courtesy of the artist

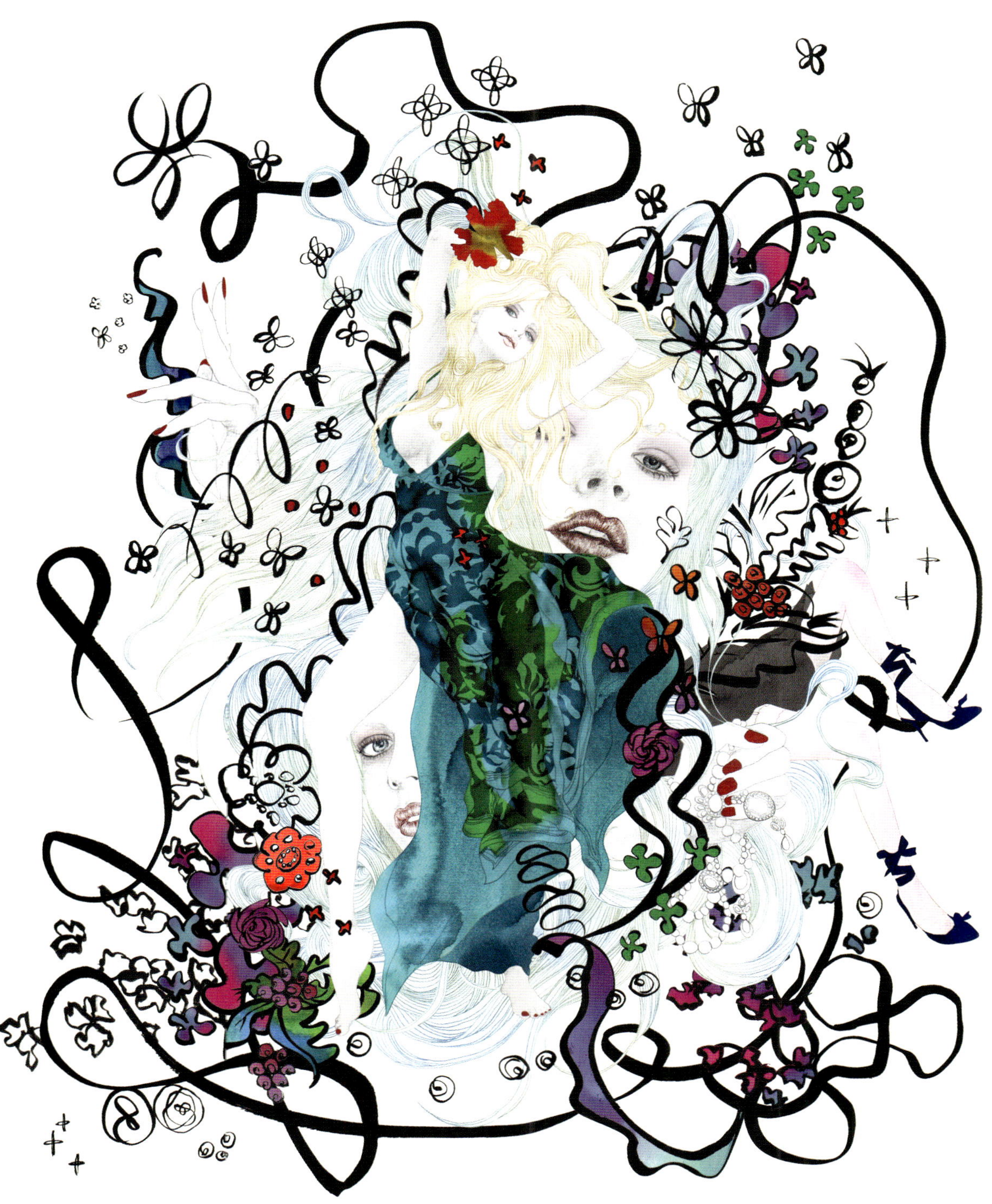

Yoshi Tajima | *Fairy 03*, 2008 | Pencil, watercolor, Chinese ink, and Adobe Photoshop on paper
27⅓ × 23 inches | Courtesy of the artist

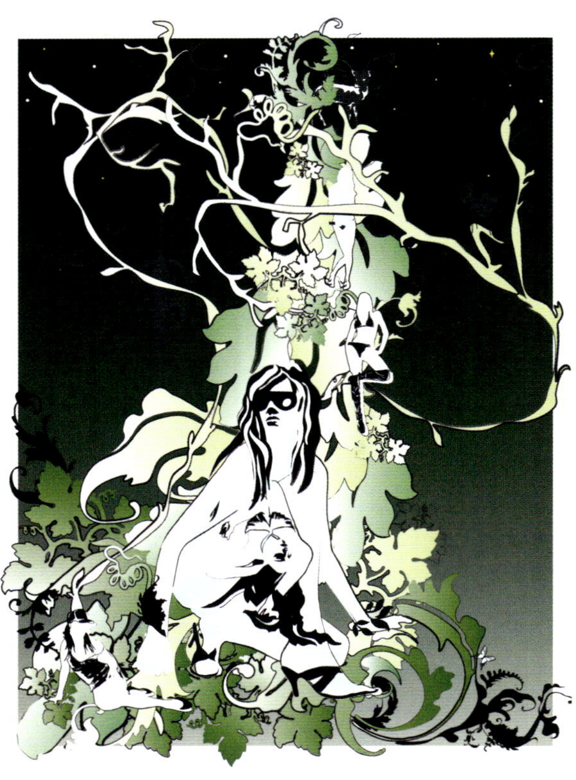

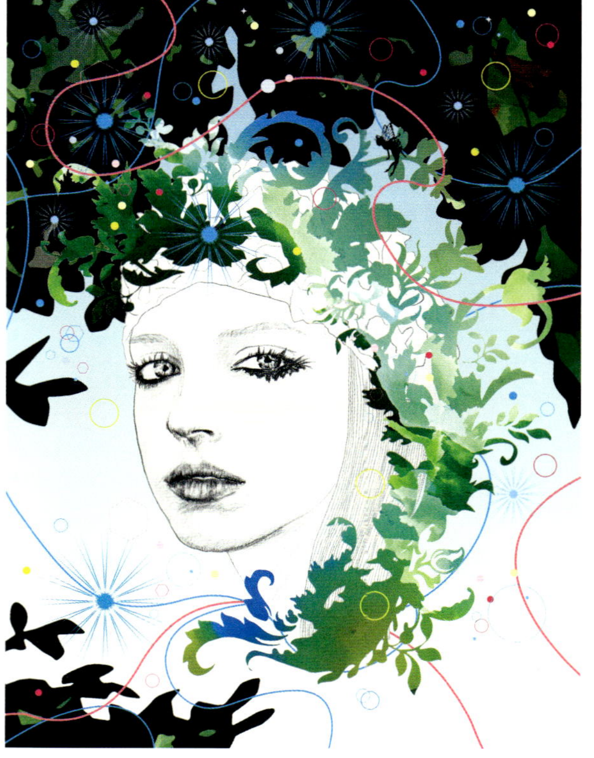

(above) **Yoshi Tajima** | *Dark Forest*, 2006 | Adobe Photoshop on paper
17½ × 13 inches | Courtesy of the artist

(right) **Yoshi Tajima** | *Forest Girl*, 2007 | Pencil, watercolor,
Chinese ink, and Adobe Photoshop on paper
27½ × 23 inches | Courtesy of the artist

YOSHI
TAJIMA

Yoshi Tajima is a designer and illustrator based in Tokyo, Japan. Tajima graduated from The American Intercontinental University in London with a B.A. degree in Communication |Design. His diverse design work encompasses many different styles and media ranging from black-and-white illustration to graphic lettering, logo design, and landscapes.

Tajima's graphic and illustrative works have appeared in many publications, including *Vogue* (Japan), *Numero* (Japan), *Advanced Photoshop* (UK) and *The Age of Feminine Drawing* (Hong Kong) among others.

Freelance journalist and fashion editor Lisa Ibuki asserts that Tajima's female subjects, or "ephemeral muses," are celebrated for their beauty. She describes his creations as "luscious and delicate" in their ability to "capture the elusive moments between fragile beauty and fantasy." Ibuki further notes that in Tajima's work: "elegant flowery lines eloquently express the fashions and sensibility of modern women, which are very common in Art Nouveau-inspired décor."

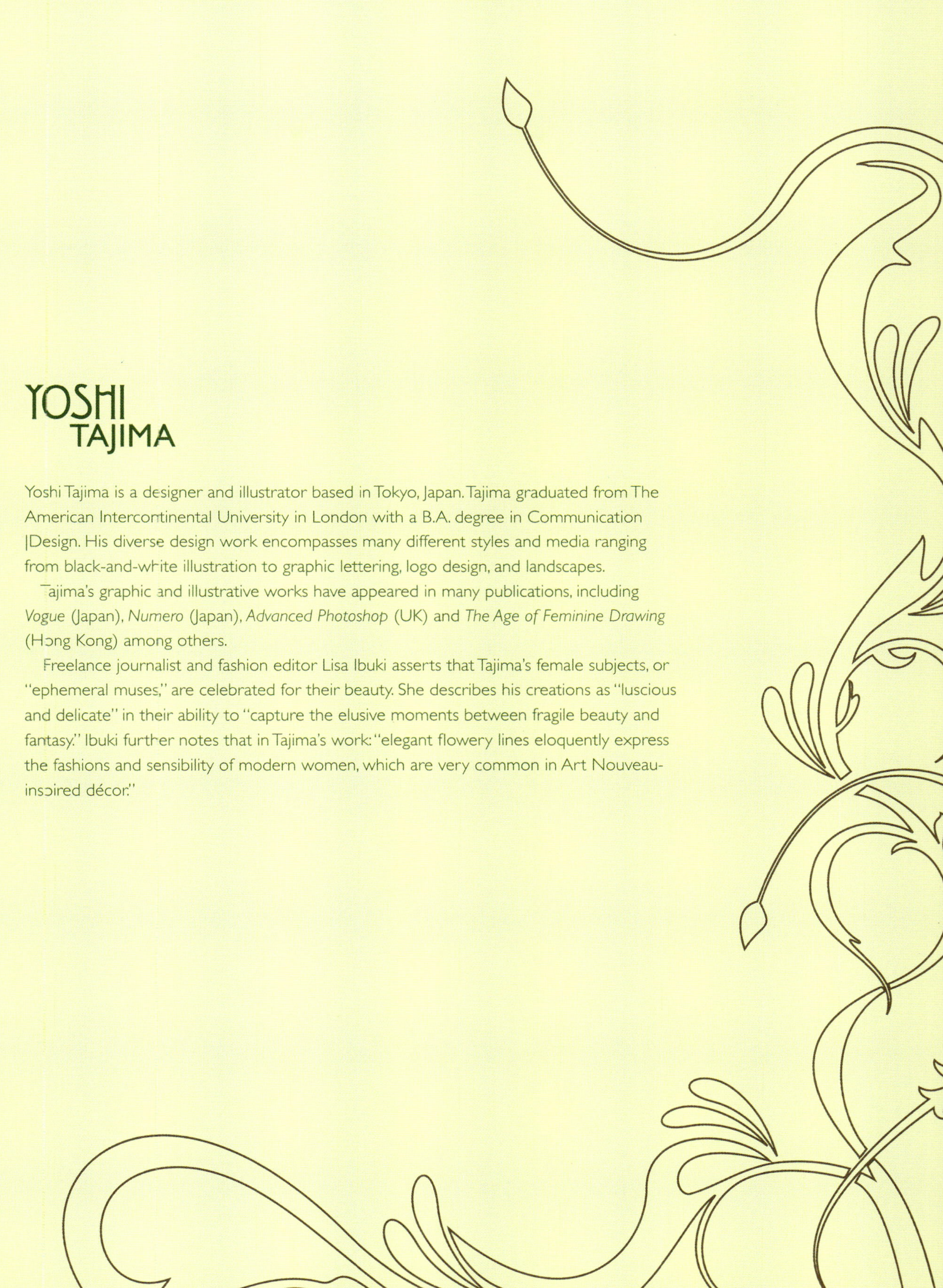

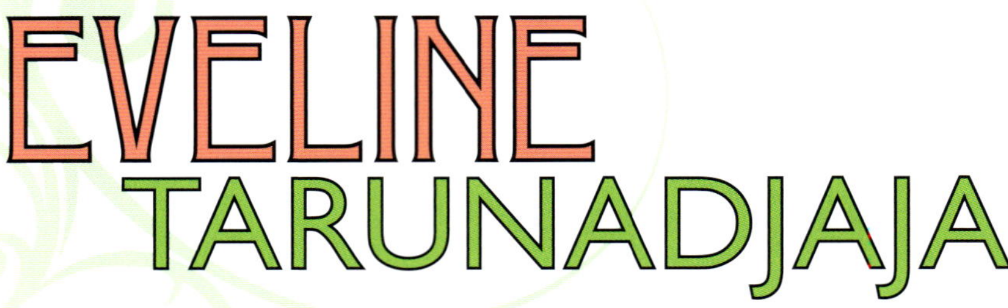

Melbourne, Australia

"I hide secrets in the hair."

~ Eveline Tarunadjaja

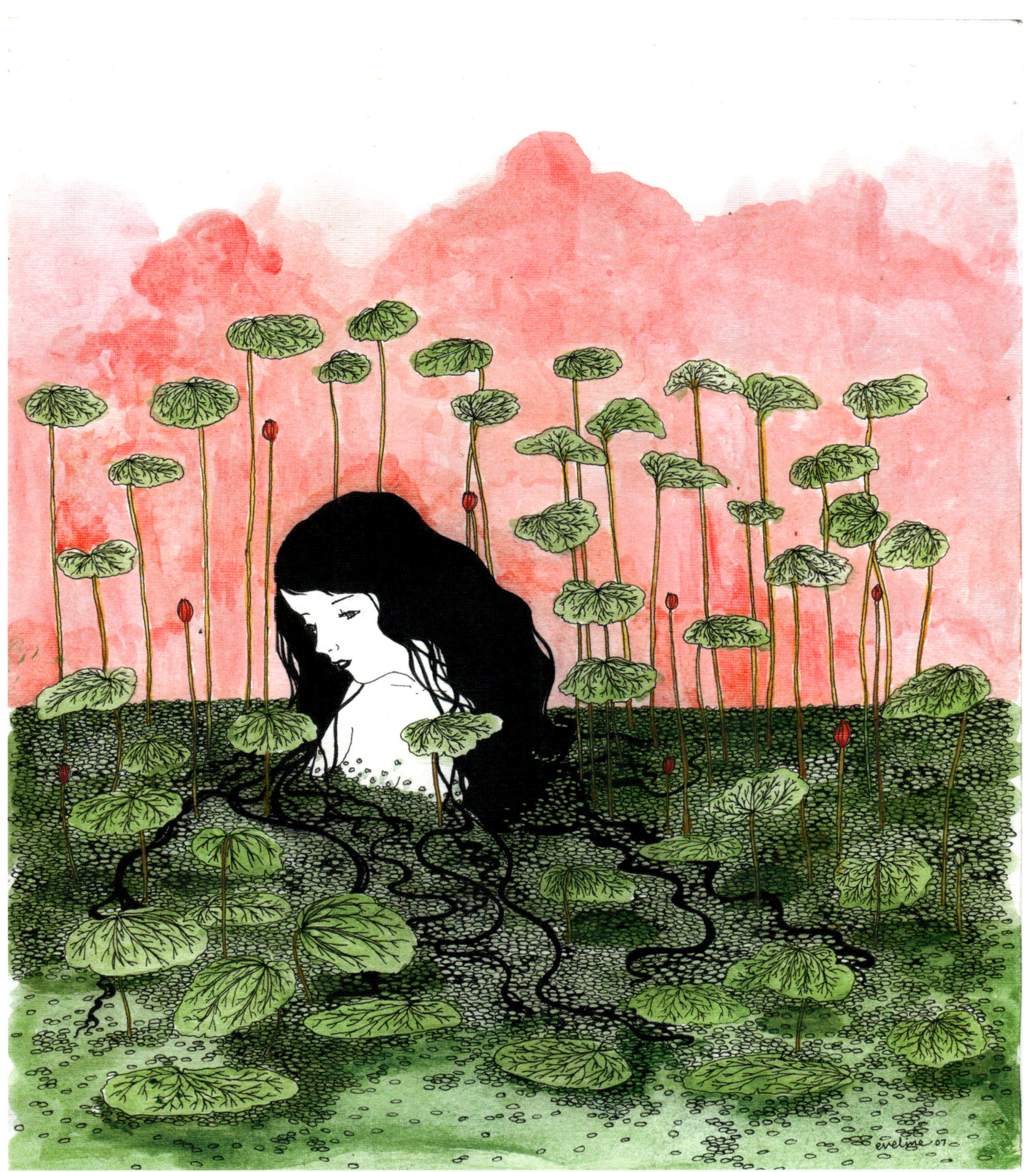

Eveline Tarunadjaja | Lilypad, 2007 | Ink and watercolor on paper | 10 × 10 inches | Courtesy of the artist

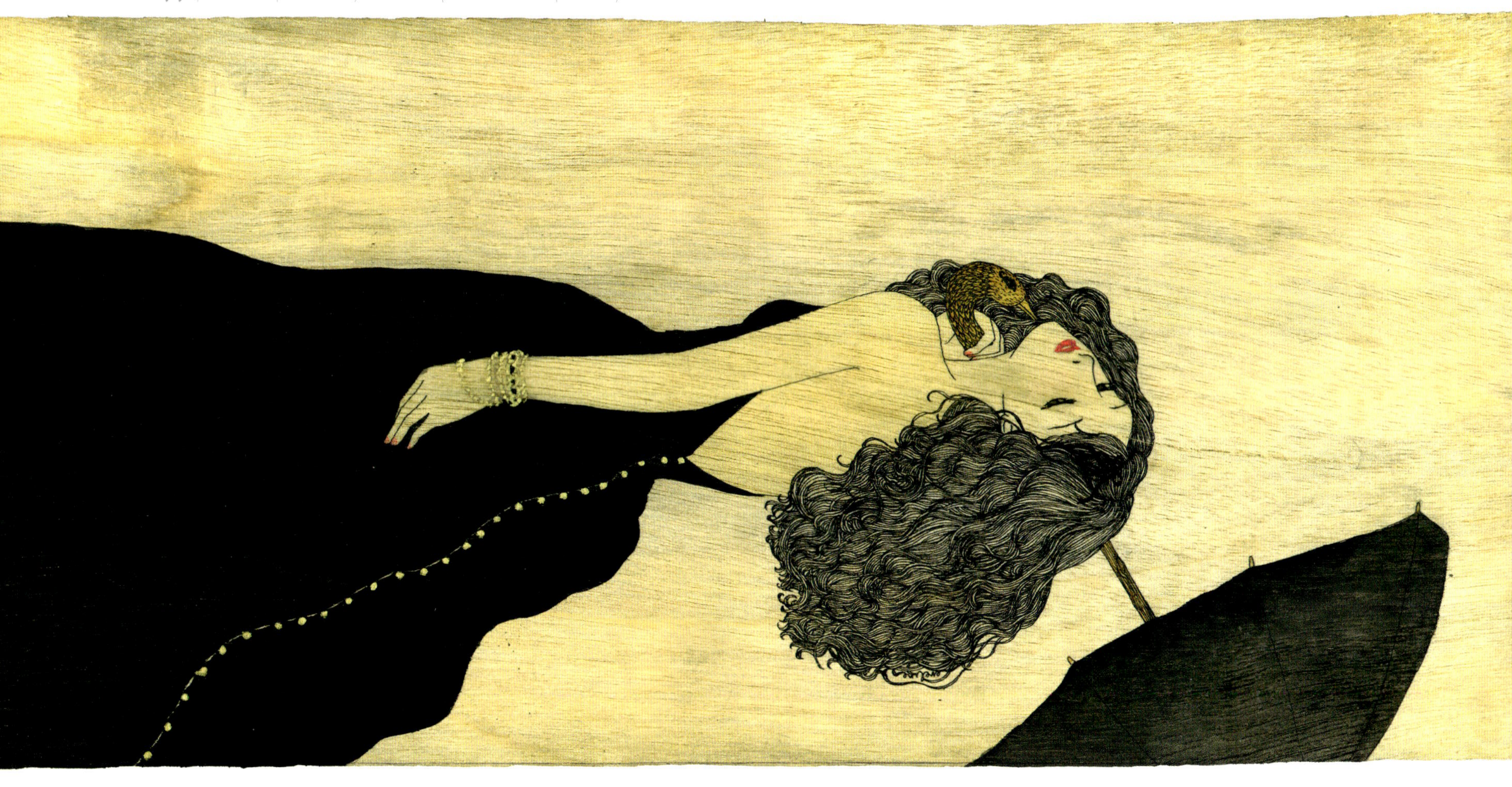

Eveline Tarunadjaja | Gold, 2006 | Ink and acrylic on wood | 19 × 9½ inches | Courtesy of the artist

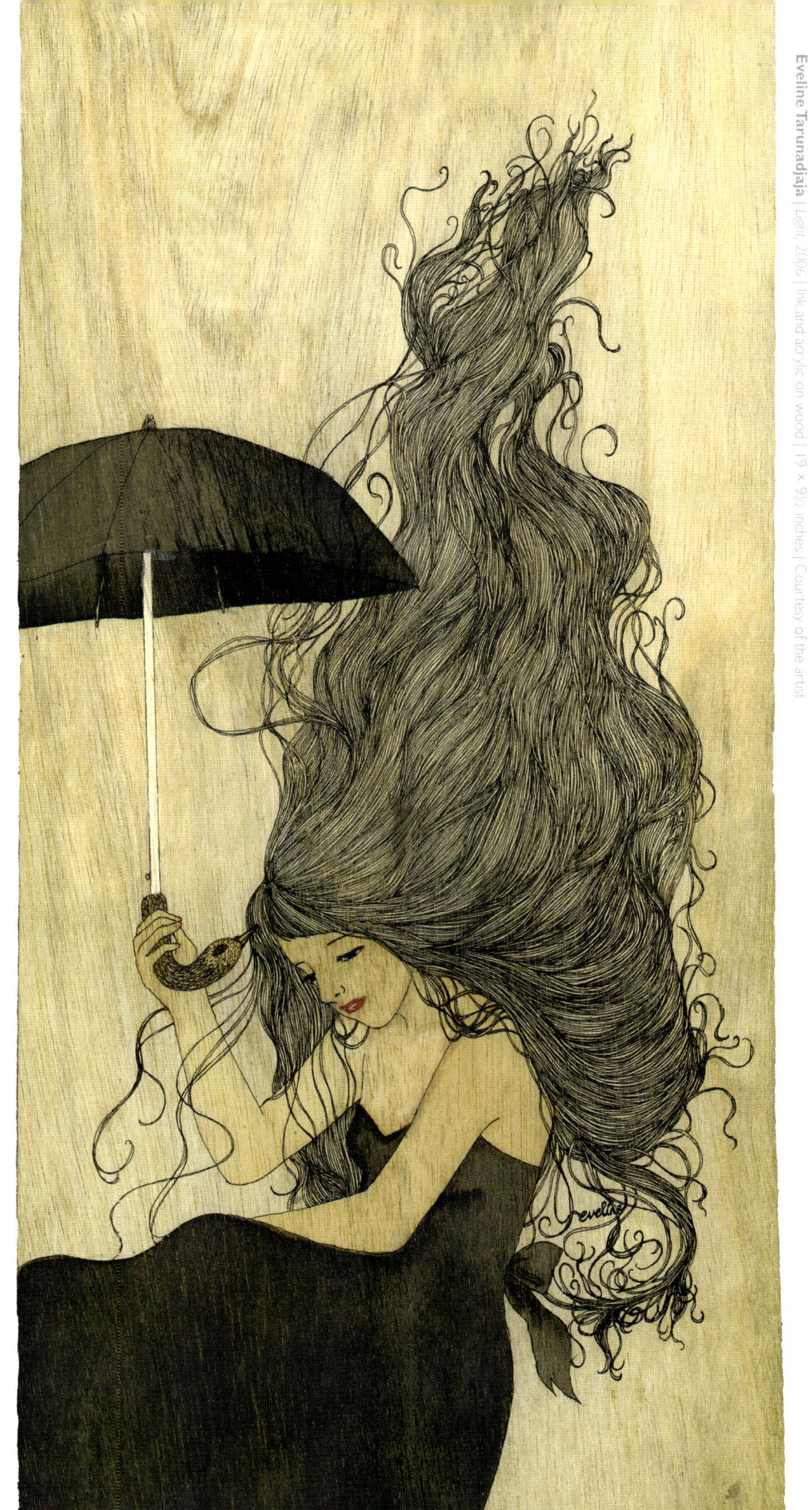

Eveline Tarunadjaja | Light, 2006 | Ink and acrylic on wood | 19 × 9½ inches | Courtesy of the artist

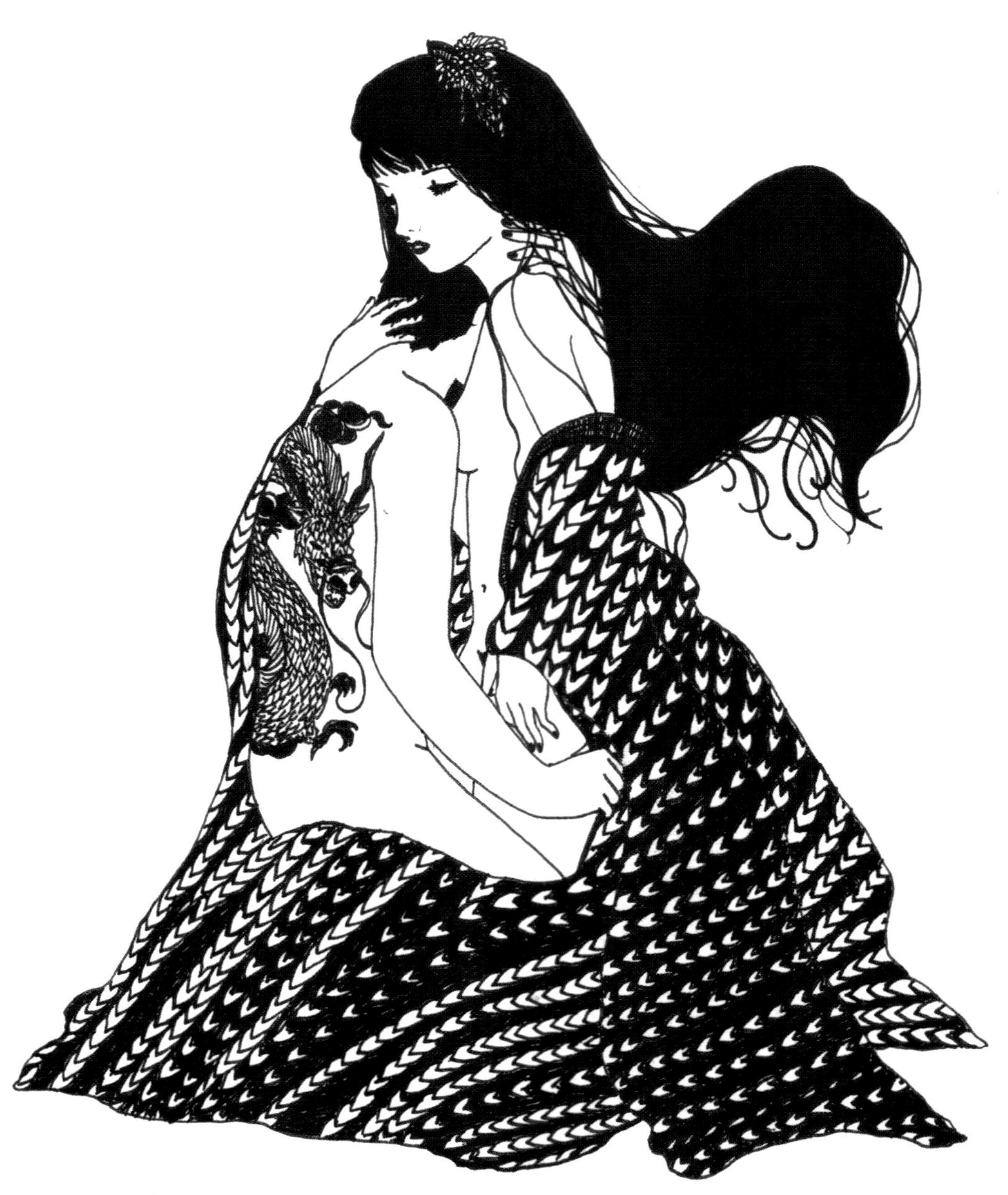

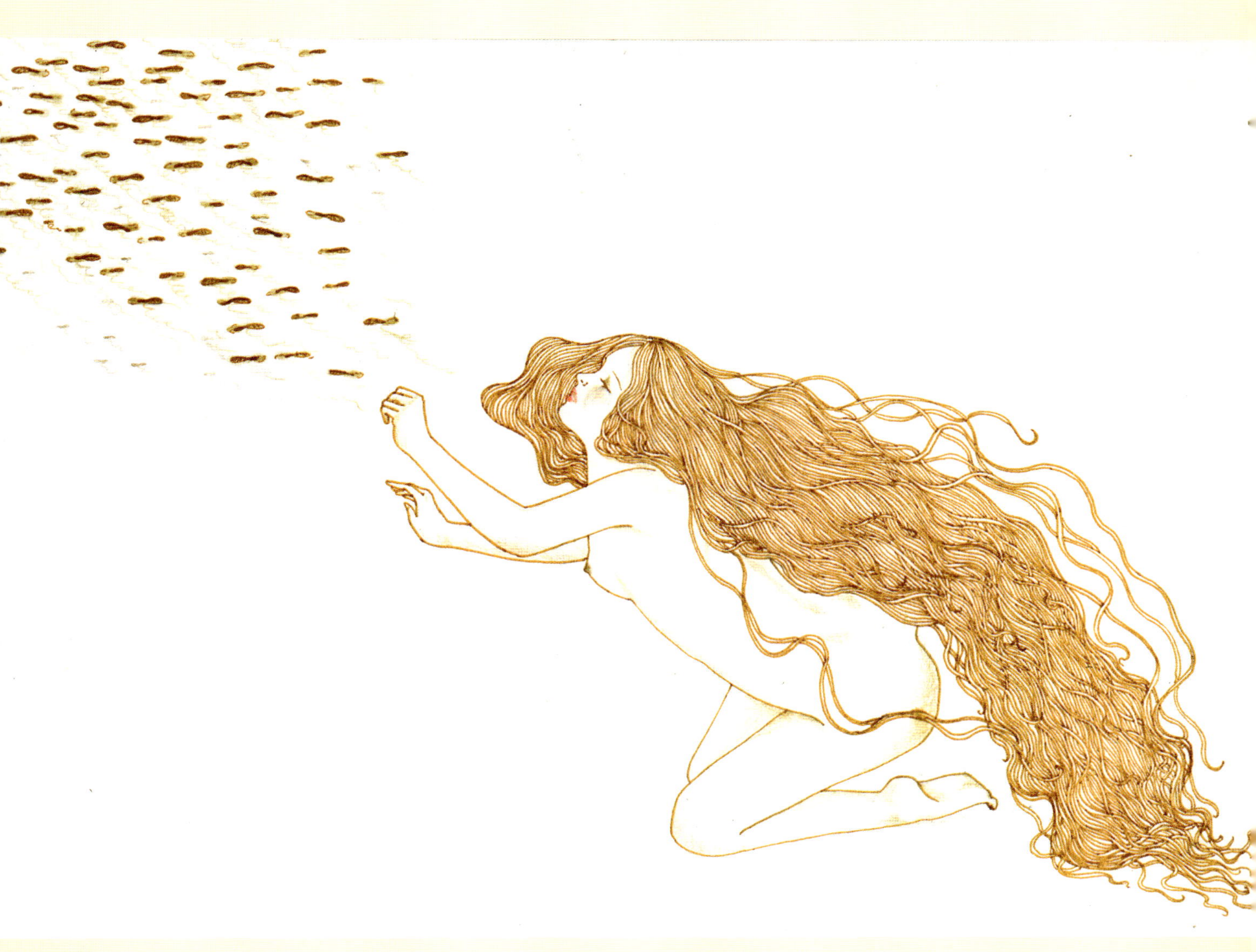

(above) **Eveline Tarunadjaja** | *Sycamore,* 2007 | Ink and color pencil on paper
6 × 8¼ inches | Courtesy of the artist

(opposite) **Eveline Tarunadjaja** | *Dragon,* 2006 | Ink on paper
8 × 6 inches | Courtesy of the artist

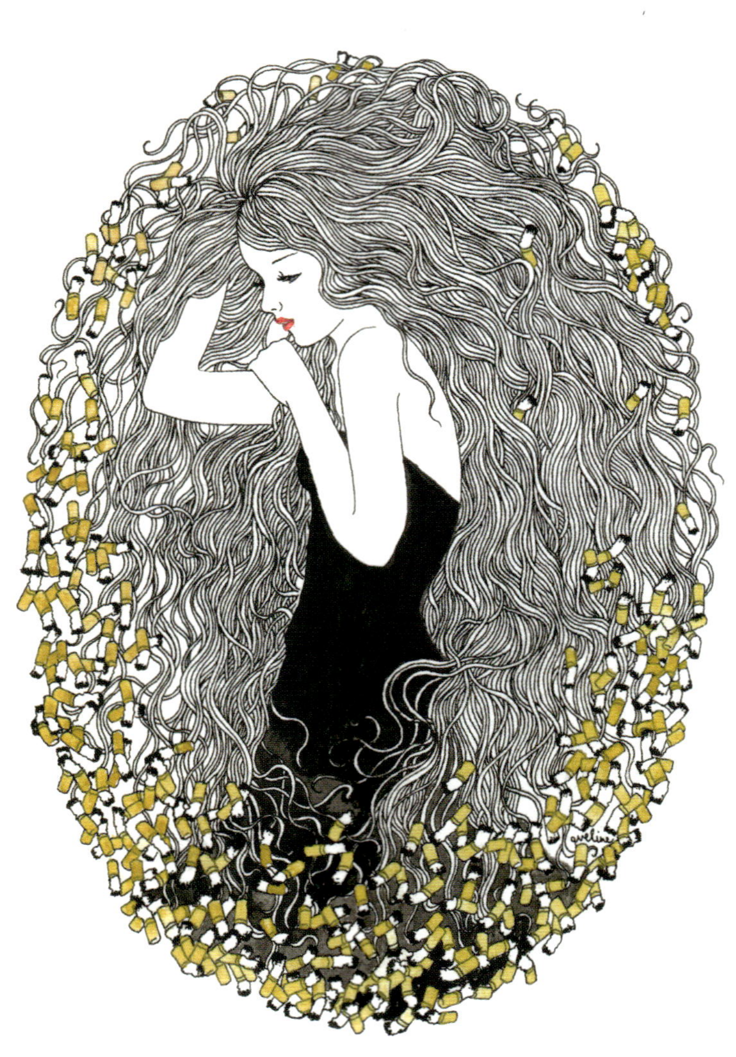

Eveline Tarunadjaja | *V is for Vices,* 2006 | Ink and watercolor on paper
9½ × 7 inches | Courtesy of Bergen O'Brien

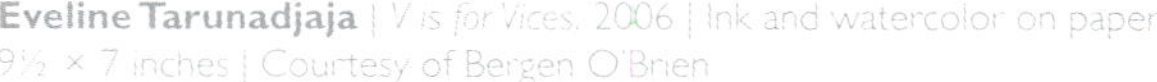

EVELINE
TARUNADJAJA

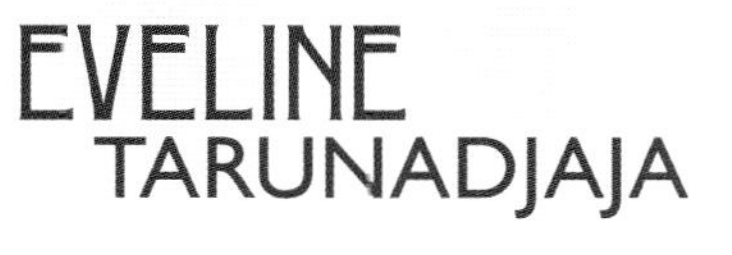

Eveline Tarunadjaja was born and raised in Indonesia and moved to Melbourne, Australia, at the age of fifteen. After she completed her degree in Multimedia Design, she worked for the Australian street-wear label Nique. Her work has been featured in various publications including *Frankie* (Australia), *Singles* (Korea), *Vogue Girl* (Korea), *Elle Girl* (Korea), and *FAR* (Indonesia). Her work was also displayed in Nucleus Gallery's *Grafuk 3 and 4* exhibitions and publications. Tarunadjaja has designed artwork for fashion labels Hurley, Billabong, Gorman, Anna Sui, and French Kitty, in addition to her unique CD and book cover designs for Shock Records and book publisher Penguin.

Intricate detail and cascading hair characterize Tarunadjaja's illustrations. Fiction, unrequited love, and silly notions such as taking a dip in a lily pond inspire her artwork. Eveline injects her love for Art Nouveau into modern day-to-day life to enhance her ever-evolving, delicate yet complex style.

GCAC WORKSHOP
WITH PANDAROSA

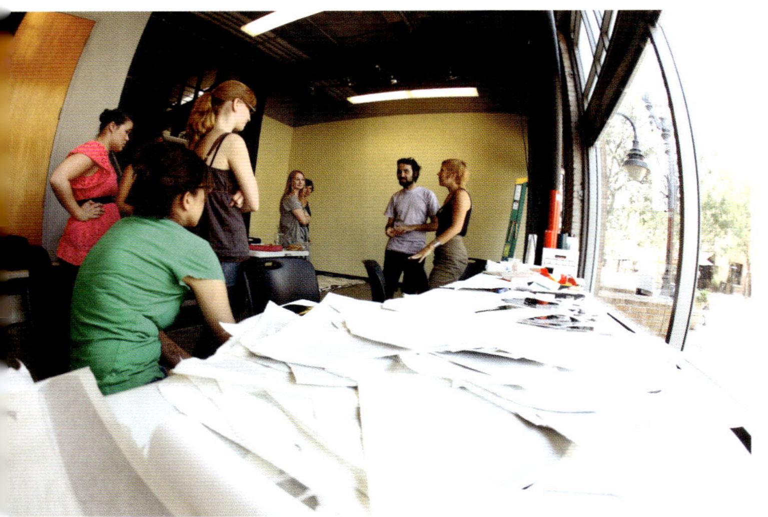

August 31 - September 1, 2009:
Pandarosa introduced audiences to their personal experiences as artists, work methods and ideologies during a lecture at Cal State Fullerton and a workshop at the CSUF Grand Central Art Center in Santa Ana. In response to their vinyl installation from *Redefining the Line*, the artists saved the "leftover" materials from the installation in order "to highlight how waste can often be the staring point for creativity." According to Pandarosa, "the 'negative' or neglected aspect of a visual creation can be re-interpreted to make something new, while also allowing Dada aspects of chance, randomness and fun to take place." Workshop attendees were invited to participate in the creation of a free-form vinyl installation.

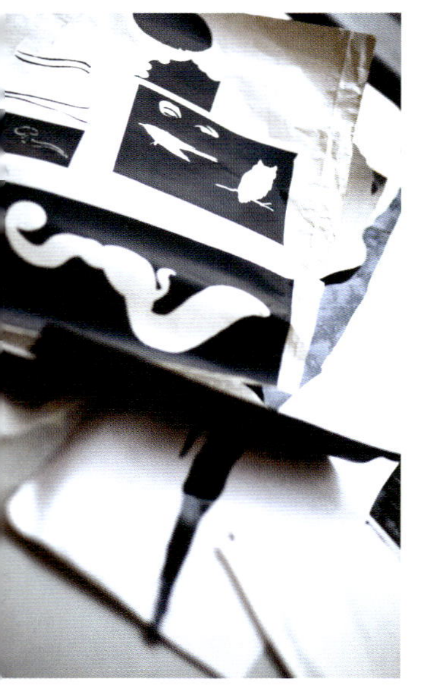

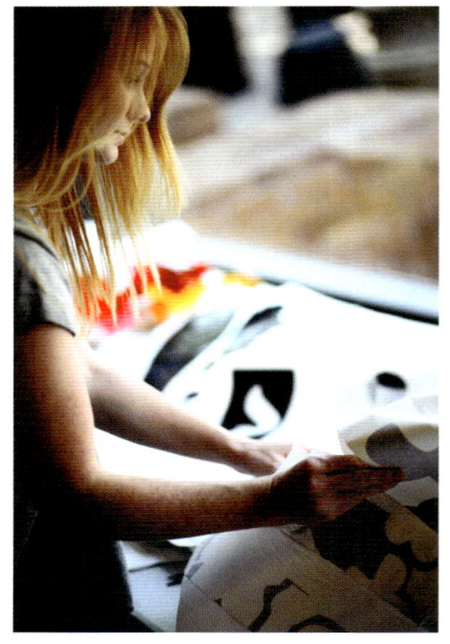

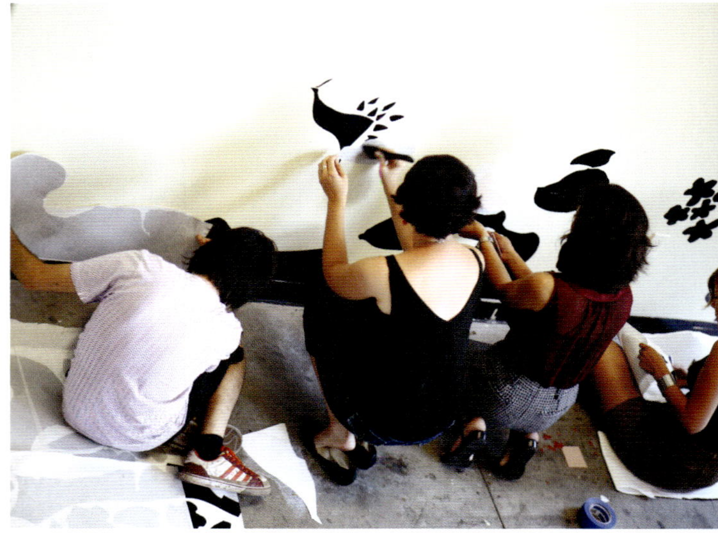

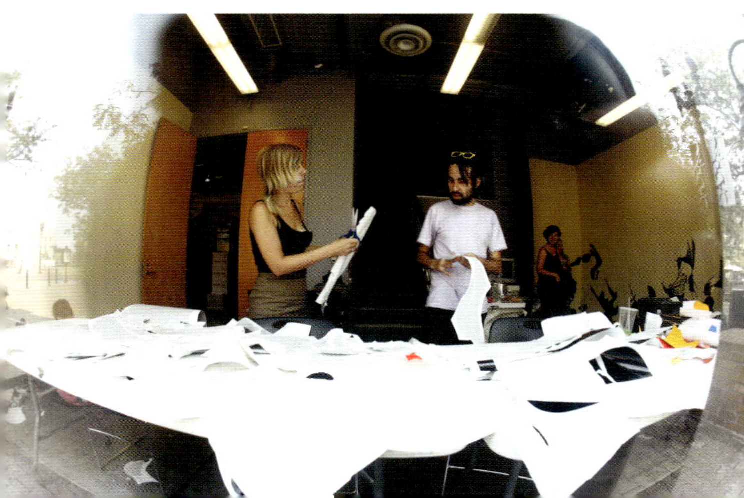

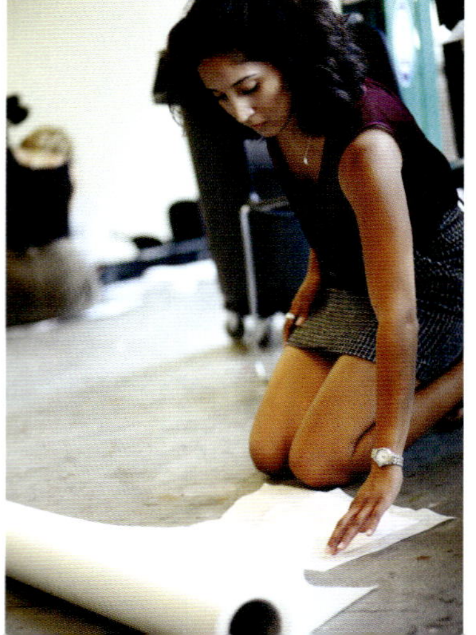

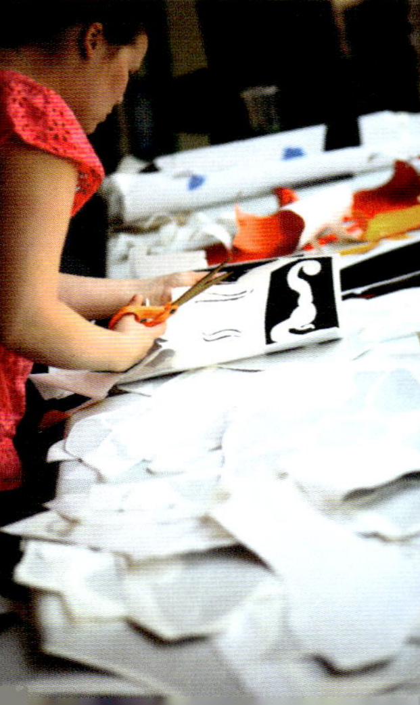

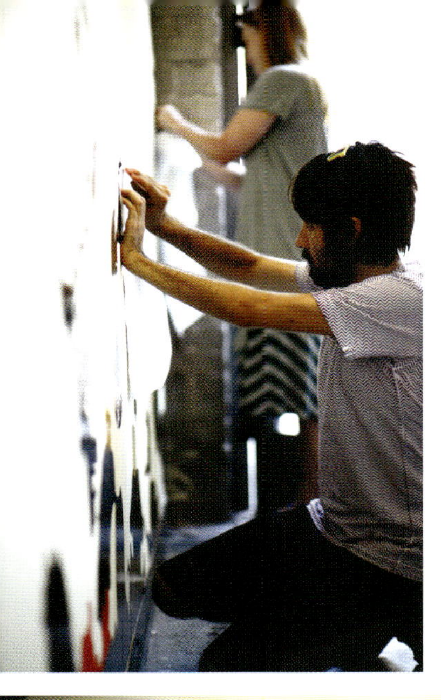
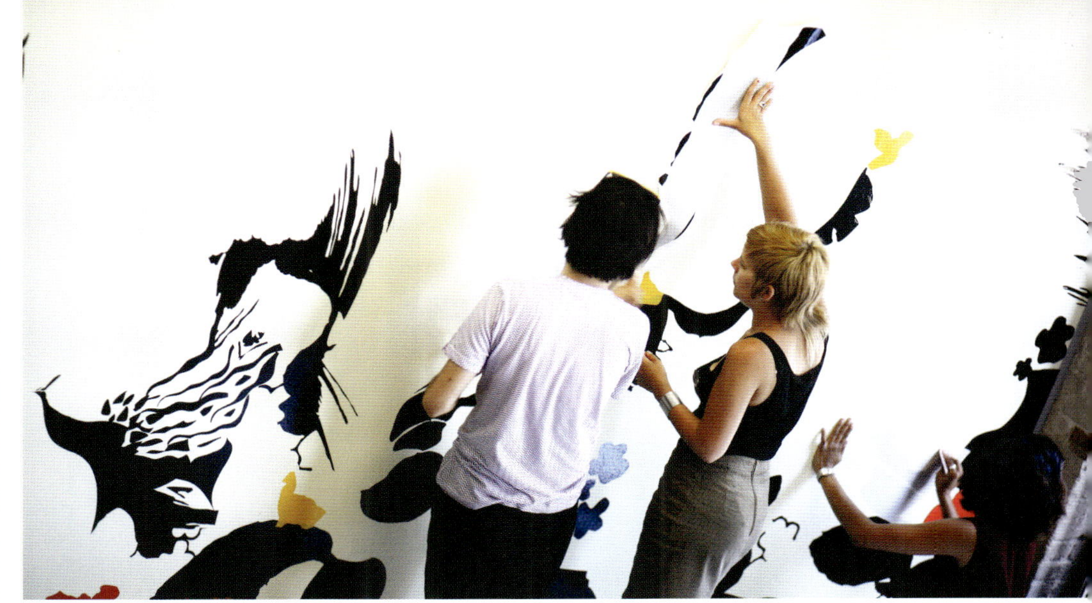
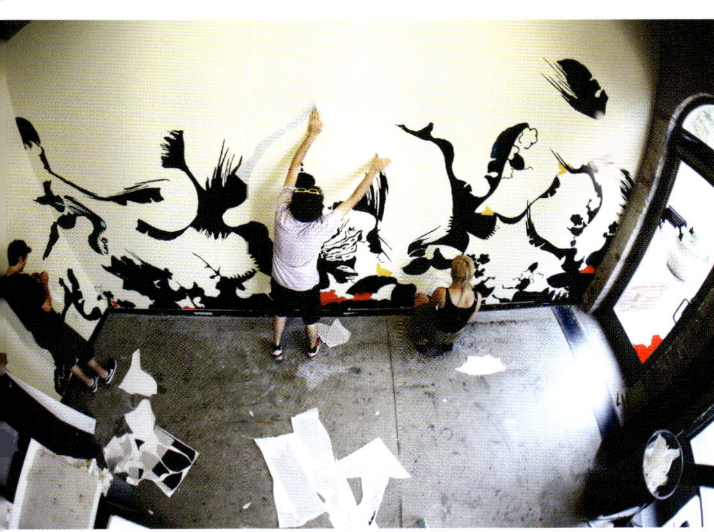
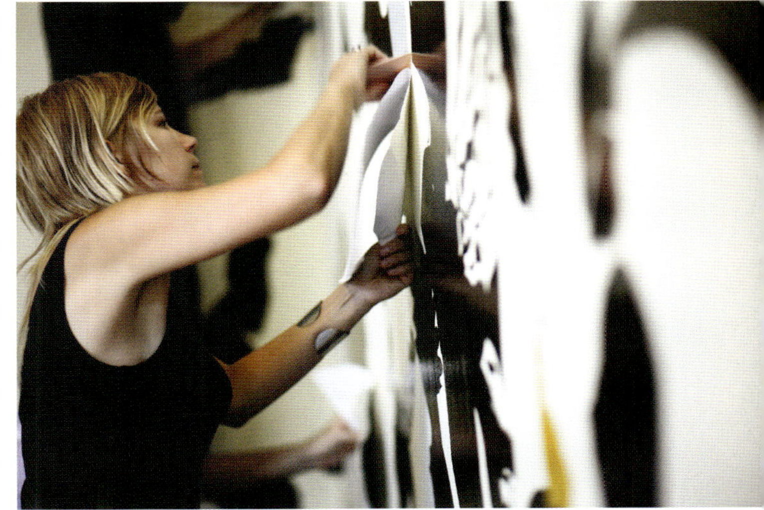
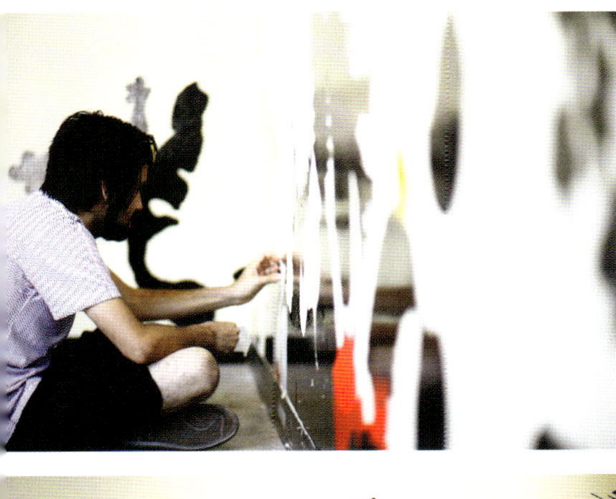
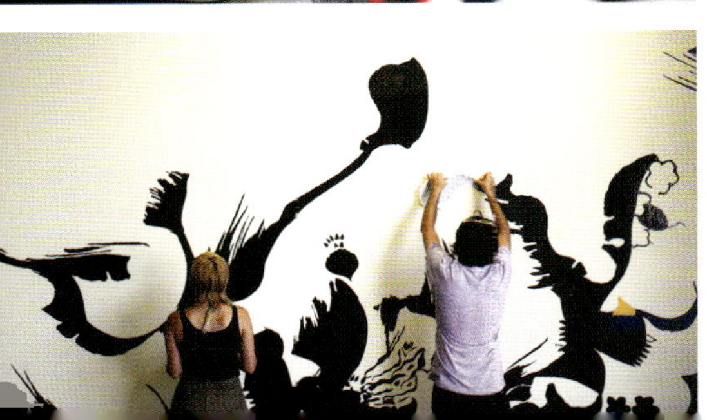
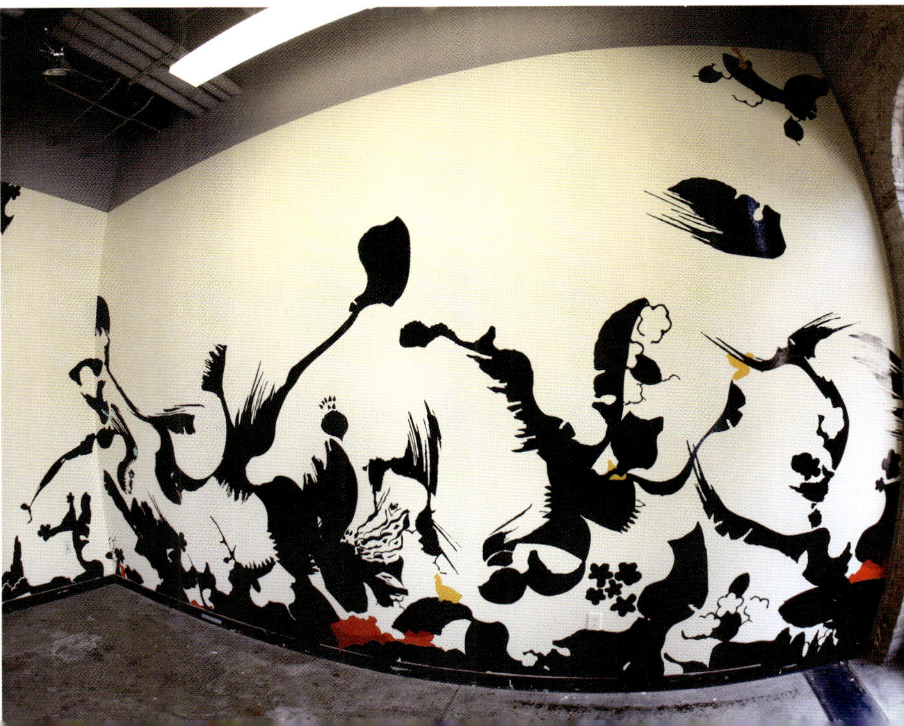

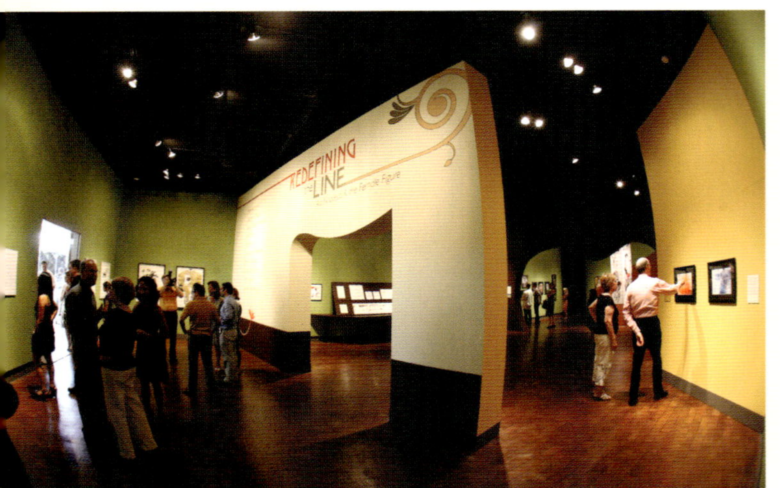

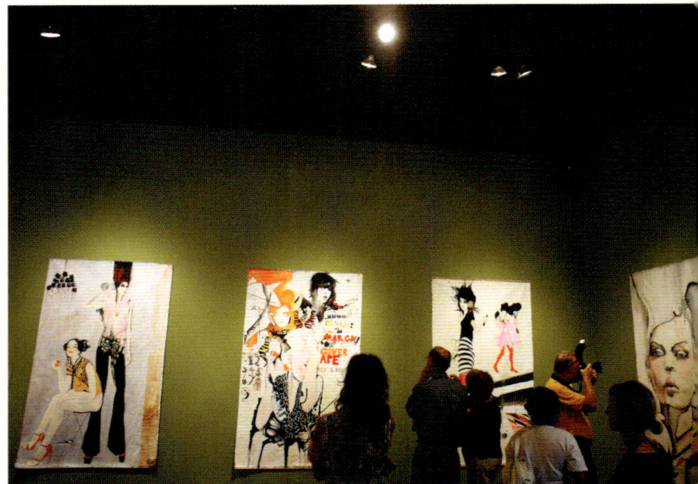

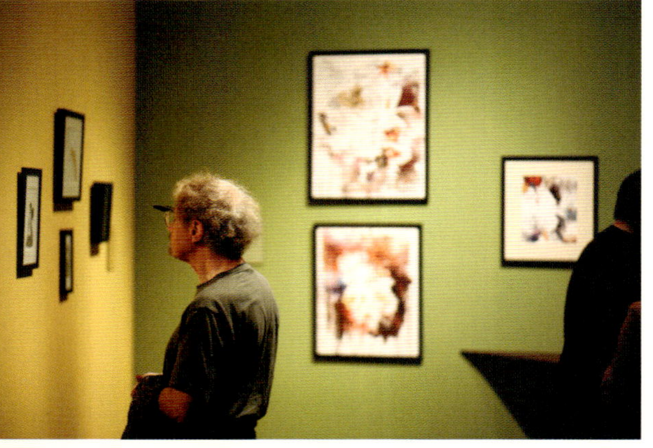

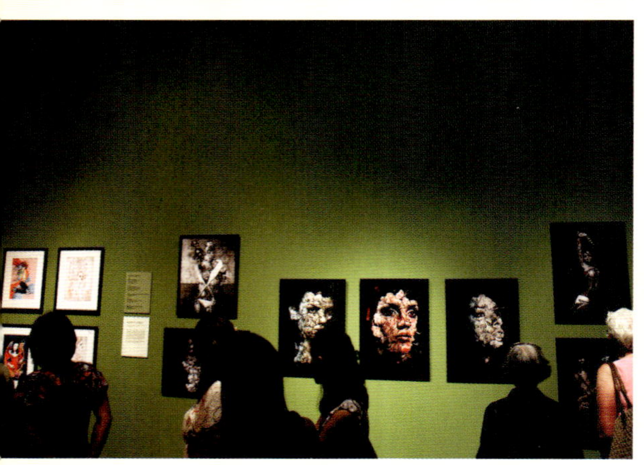

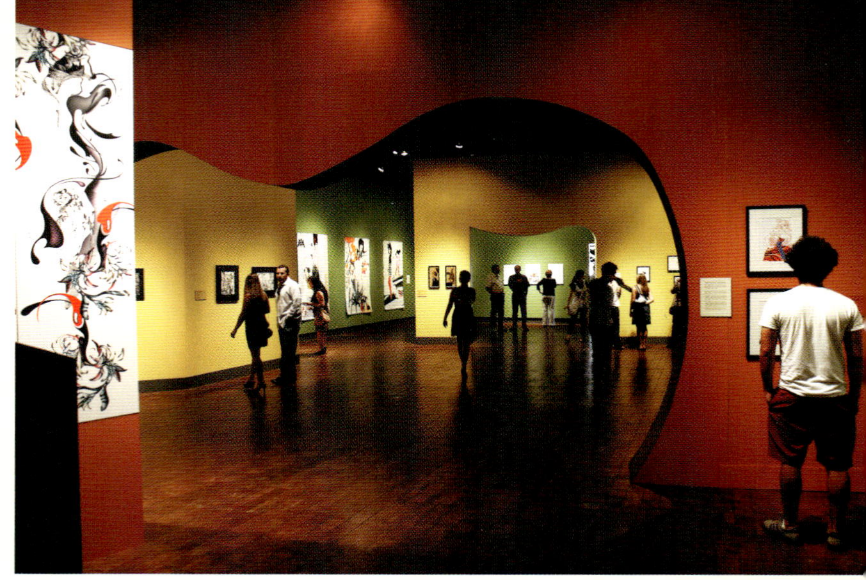

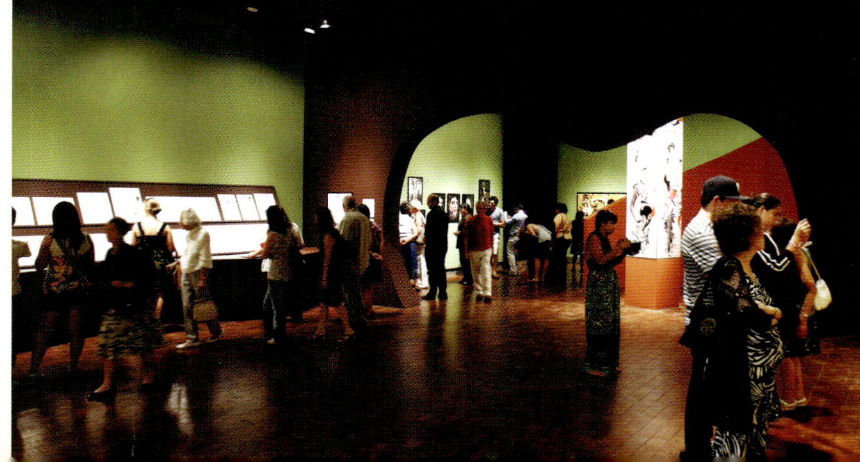

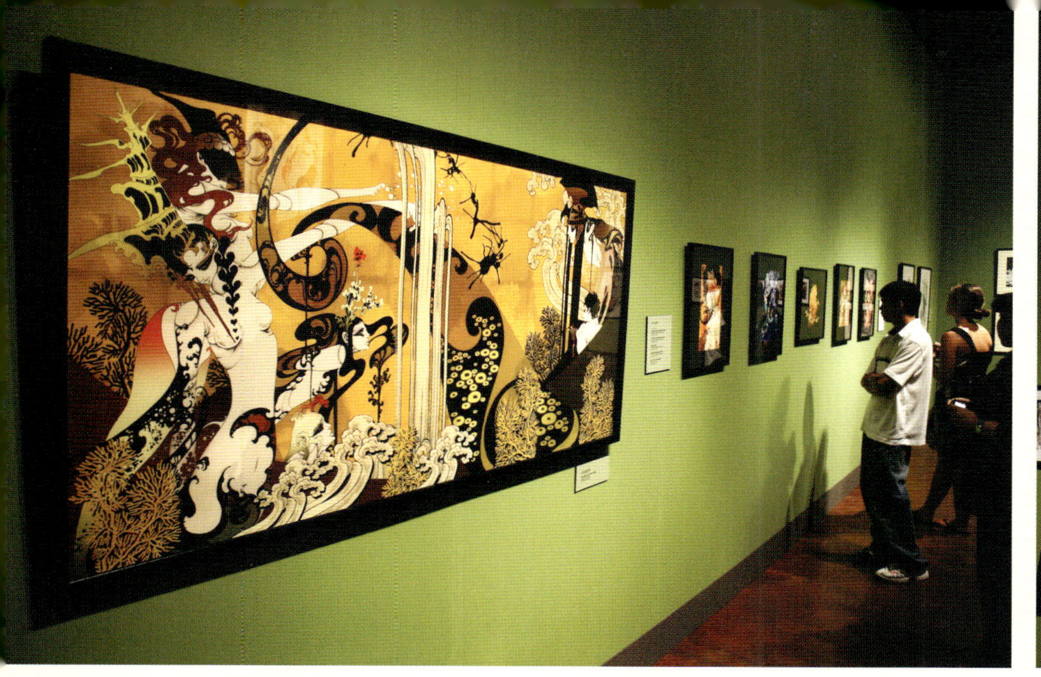
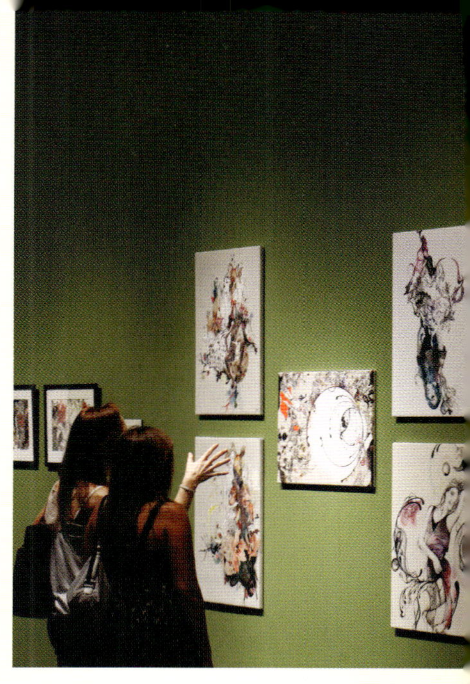
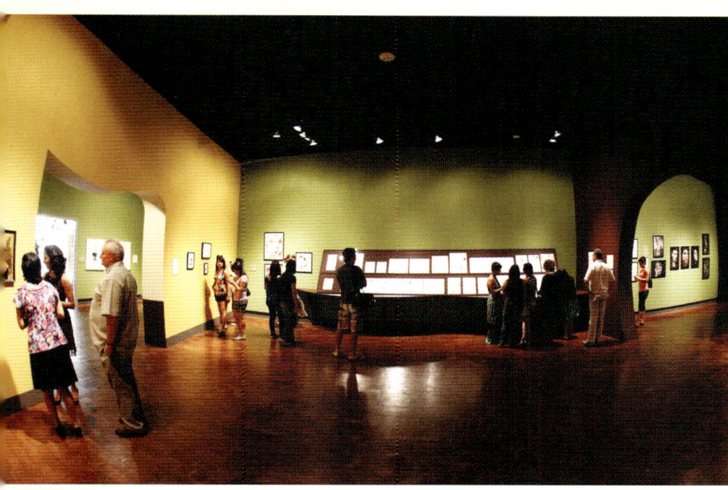
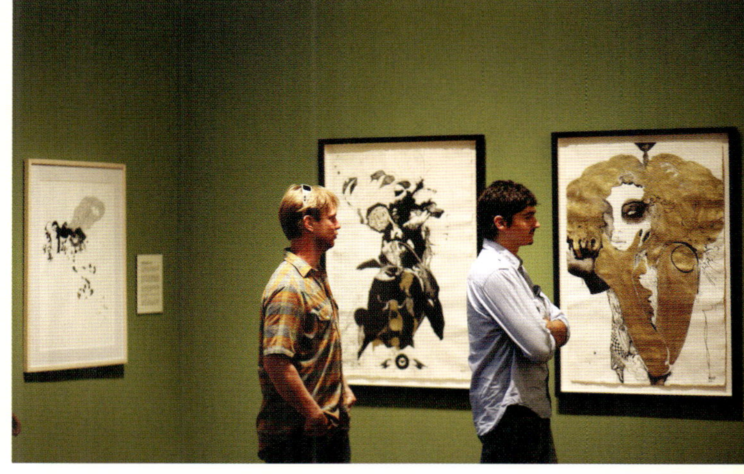
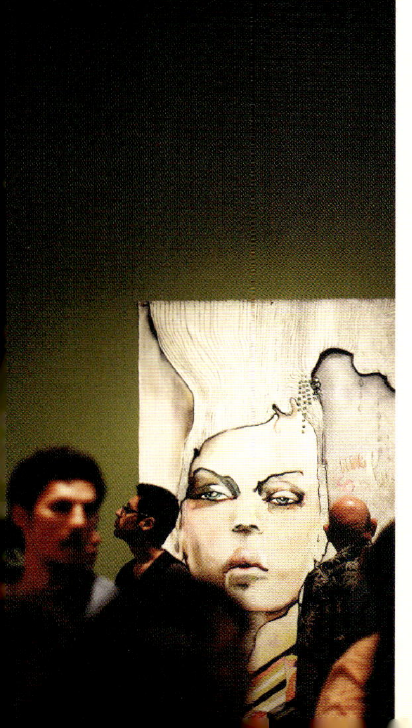
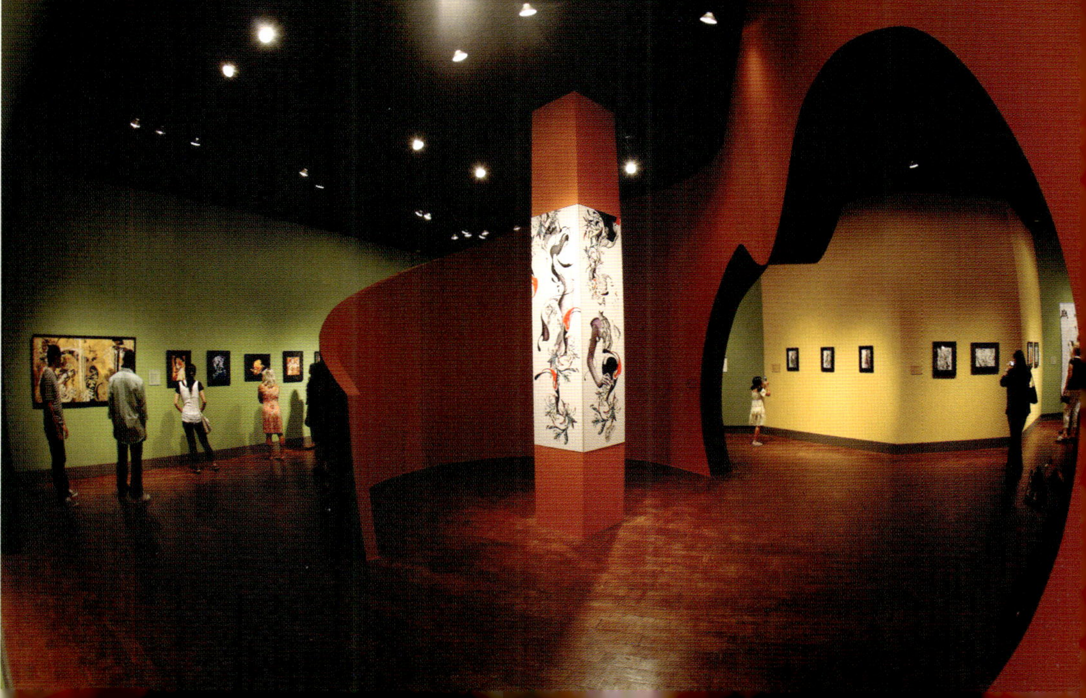

EXHIBITION CHECKLIST

POMME CHAN
www.pommepomme.com

pg. 22 *H.Un.T Project Image #1,* 2007
(Collaboration with Vault49)
Print on canvas (original hand-drawn + photo collage + computer finish)
30 × 25 inches
Courtesy of the artist

pg. 23 *H.Un.T Project Image #2,* 2007
(Collaboration with Vault49)
Print on canvas (original hand-drawn + photo collage + computer finish)
30 × 25 inches
Courtesy of the artist

pg. 21 *Lust,* 2009
Created specifically for *Redefining the Line*
Print on canvas (original hand-drawn + photo collage + computer finish)
30 × 25 inches
Courtesy of the artist

pg. 26 *Secret World,* 2009
Site-specific installation
Prints on paper (original hand-drawn with watercolors + computer finish)
4 parts, 86½ × 23½ inches each
Courtesy of the artist

pg. 25 *She,* 2009
Created specifically for *Redefining the Line*
Prints on canvas (original hand-drawn with watercolors + computer finish)
23½ × 16½ inches
Courtesy of the artist

pg. 24 *Wonder,* 2006
Print on canvas (original hand-drawn + computer finish)
20 × 30 inches
Courtesy of the artist

DEANNE CHEUK
www.deannecheuk.com

pg. 33 *Mushroom Girls Virus,* 2005
Artist book with embroidered cloth cover
64 pages printed offset
Edition 3,000 (out of print)
11 × 9 × ½ inches
Courtesy of the artist

Prepatory prints, drawings and sketches for *Mushroom Girls Virus*
pg. 29 *Elegance Bizarre* (Part 3), 2003
Digital print on archival paper
27 × 21 inches
Courtesy of the artist

pg. 30 *Mushroom Girls Mandolin, On Decayed Wood,* 2003
Digital print on archival paper
24 × 19 inches
Courtesy of the artist

pg. 31 *Psyc Girl,* 2002
Digital print on archival paper
12½ × 10 inches
Courtesy of the artist

pg. 32 *Thank You Girls, In Or Near the Borders of Woods,* 2004
Digital print on archival paper
24 × 19 inches
Courtesy of the artist

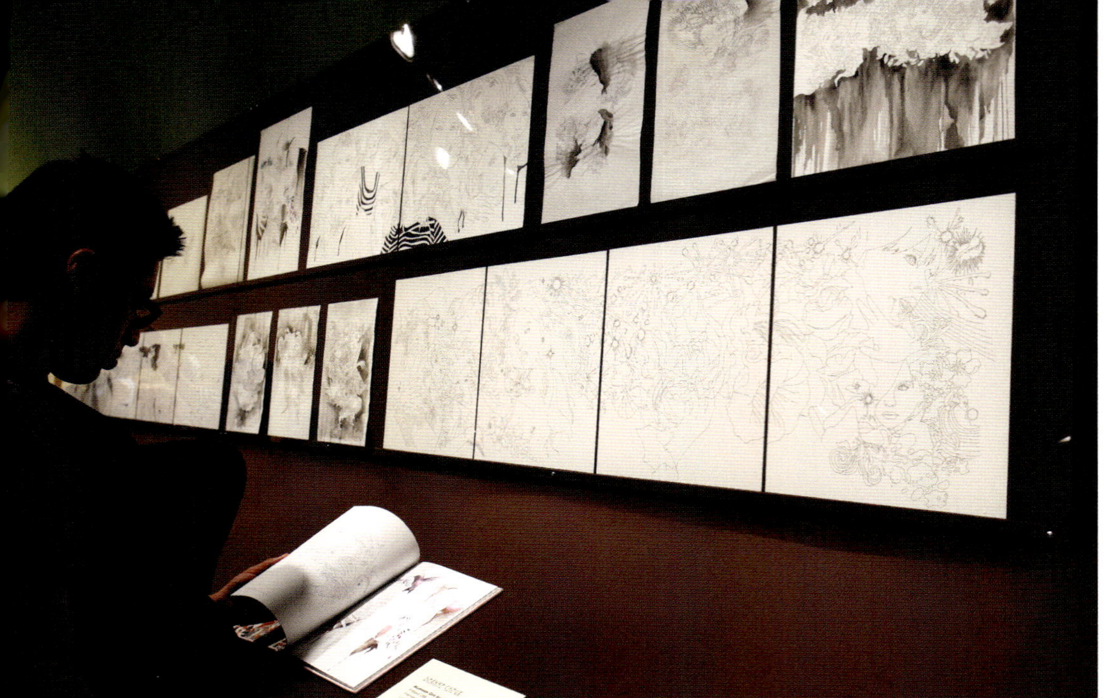

pg. 46, 51 *The Witch's Love (Hero),* 2006
Giclée print on paper
35½ × 71 inches
Courtesy of the artist

pg. 52 *The Witch's Love (Secret Desire),* 2006
Giclée print & silkscreen print on paper
22 × 18 inches
Courtesy of the artist

PANDAROSA
(ARIEL AGUILERA & ANDREA BENYI)
www.pandarosa.net

pg. 56 - 57 *Noir Sunshine,* 2009
Site-specific vinyl installation
6 feet, 4½ inches ×
10 feet, 3½ inches
Courtesy of the artists

pg. 55 *She tangled her hair in the clouds,* 2009
Acrylic and pen on paper
35½ × 27½ inches
Courtesy of the artists

pg. 58 *somewhere between Sunset and Sunrise,* 2009
Acrylic and pen on paper
35½ × 27½ inches
Courtesy of the artists

MARGUERITE SAUVAGE
www.margueritesauvage.com

pg. 64 *Cups of Tea,* 2007
Drawing on paper,
colors on computer
16½ × 11½ inches
Courtesy of the artist

pg. 63 *Dita,* 2008
Drawing on paper,
colors on computer
16½ × 11½ inches
Courtesy of the artist

pg. 60 *Dress and Hair (01),* 2008
Drawing on paper,
colors on computer
16½ × 11½ inches
Courtesy of the artist

pg. 62 *Dress and Hair (02),* 2008
Drawing on paper,
colors on computer
16½ × 11½ inches
Courtesy of the artist

pg. 66 *Jelly Fish,* 2008
Drawing on paper,
colors on computer
16½ × 11½ inches
Courtesy of the artist

pg. 65 *Pudeur,* 2007
Drawing on paper,
colors on computer
16½ × 11½ inches
Courtesy of the artist

ALBERTO SEVESO
www.burdu976.com

pg. 74 *Camera con Vista,* 2007
From the series "A Joint Venture With…"
Photography by Ivonne Carlo
Illustrator and Photoshop on paper
23¼ × 16½ inches
Courtesy of the artist

pg. 73 *Coppia di Bagasce (Incostituzionale),* 2009
(Remake of 2007)
Illustrator and Photoshop on paper
23¼ × 16½ inches
Courtesy of the artist

pg. 72 *Firiyal,* 2007
From the "Bacardi B-Live event in the Netherlands"
Illustrator and Photoshop on paper
23¼ × 16½ inches
Courtesy of the artist

pg. 69 *Non Perderne Uno,* 2007
From the series "A Joint Venture With…"
Photography by Paul Octavious Aka Dunny
Illustrator and Photoshop on paper
23¼ × 16½ inches
Courtesy of the artist

pg. 70 - 71 *The Three Graces (Grazia, Graziella e Grazie al Cazzo!),* 2008
Illustrator and Photoshop on paper
23¼ × 16½ inches each
Courtesy of the artist

SONYA SUHARIYAN
www.sonyasuhariyan.com

pg. 79 *Autumn,* 2006
Gouache, watercolor, and ink on paper
12 × 6½ inches
Courtesy of the artist

pg. 77 *Blue Mask,* 2005
Gouache, watercolor, and ink on paper
11½ × 16½ inches
Courtesy of the artist

pg. 80 *Butterflies,* 2004
Ink on paper
14 × 10¾ inches
Courtesy of the artist

pg. 80 *Desire,* 2004
Ink on paper
11½ × 16½ inches
Courtesy of the artist

pg. 77 *Red Mask,* 2005
Gouache, watercolor, and ink on paper
11½ × 16½ inches
Courtesy of the artist

pg. 79 *Spring,* 1999
Gouache, watercolor,
and ink on paper
12 × 6½ inches
Courtesy of the artist

pg. 78 *Summer,* 1999
Gouache, watercolor,
and ink on paper
12 × 6½ inches
Courtesy of the artist

YOSHI TAJIMA
www.radiographics.jp

pg. 83 *6am,* 2006
Originally designed for
The Creator Studio, Vol. 9 (Spain)
Pencil, watercolor,
Chinese ink, and Adobe
Photoshop on paper
10 × 16½ inches
Courtesy of the artist

pg. 84 *7am,* 2006
Originally designed for
The Creator Studio, Vol. 9 (Spain)
Pencil, watercolor,
Chinese ink, and Adobe
Photoshop on paper
10 × 16½ inches
Courtesy of the artist

pg. 85 *8am,* 2006
Originally designed for
The Creator Studio, Vol. 9 (Spain)
Pencil, watercolor,
Chinese ink, and Adobe
Photoshop on paper
10 × 16½ inches
Courtesy of the artist

pg. 88 *Dark Forest,* 2006
Adobe Photoshop on paper
17½ × 13 inches
Courtesy of the artist

pg. 86 *Fairy 01,* 2008
Pencil, watercolor,
Chinese ink, and Adobe
Photoshop on paper
27½ × 23 inches
Courtesy of the artist

pg. 87 *Fairy 03,* 2008
Pencil, watercolor,
Chinese ink, and Adobe
Photoshop on paper
27½ × 23 inches
Courtesy of the artist

pg. 88 *Forest Girl,* 2007
Pencil, watercolor,
Chinese ink, and Adobe
Photoshop on paper
27½ × 23 inches
Courtesy of the artist

EVELINE TARUNADJAJA
www.lovexevol.com

pg. 94 *Dragon,* 2006
Ink on paper
8 × 6 inches
Courtesy of the artist

pg. 92 *Gold,* 2006
Ink & acrylic on wood
19 × 9½ inches
Courtesy of the artist

pg. 93 *Light,* 2006
Ink & acrylic on wood
19 × 9½ inches
Courtesy of the artist

pg. 91 *Lillypad,* 2007
Ink and watercolor on paper
10 × 10 inches
Courtesy of the artist

pg. 95 *Sycamore,* 2007
Ink and color pencil on paper
6 × 8¼ inches
Courtesy of the artist

pg. 96 *V is for Vices,* 2006
Ink and watercolor on paper
9½ × 7 inches
Courtesy of Bergen O'Brien

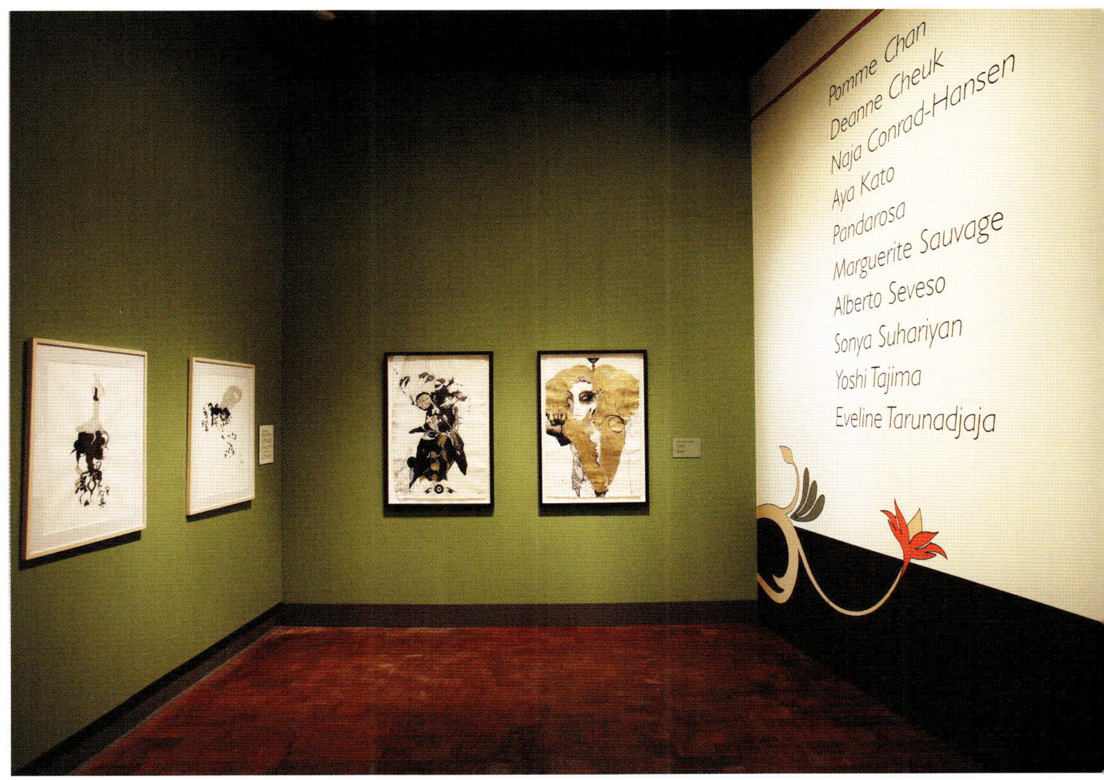

ACKNOWLEDGMENTS & SPECIAL THANKS

ACKNOWLEDGMENTS

Dean, College of the Arts: Dr. Joesph H. Arnold, Jr.
Chair, Department of Art: Larry Johnson
Director, Main Art Gallery: Mike McGee
Assistant to the Director: Marilyn Moore
Gallery Technician: Martin Lorigan
Exhibition Curators: Alexandra Duron and Sarah Strozza
Installation Assistants: David Brokaw, Kimberly McKinnis,
and Martha Rocha
Graduate Committee: Joe Biel and Joanna Roche
Cal State Fullerton Grand Central Art Center, Santa Ana, California

EXHIBITION SPONSORS

California State University Fullerton Art Alliance
Life Members: Nicholas and Lee Begovich, Robert Cugno,
Patricia Dolson, and Robert Logan
Benefactors: Gene and Shirley Laroff
Donor: Joyce McCleery
Patrons: Floyd and Maxine Allen, Dr. Joseph and Voiza Arnold,
Lois Austin, Renaud and Martha Bartholomew, Gary and Lynn
Chalupsky, John and Jeanice DeLoof, Jean Fischer, Nancy Fix,
Leonard and Sylvia Garber, Tallya Geiger, Bill and Milly Heaton,
Bill and Joyce Leong, Drs. Russell and Glory Ludwick, Peggy Martin,
Mike McGee and Andrea Harris-McGee, Charlotte Oliva, Dr. Martin
and Suzanne Serbin, Margaret Starks, David and Cathrynn Thorsen,
Carole Wakeman, Lorraine Walkington, and Chiki Yamamoto

CSUF Department of Art and Associated Students

Albert and Virginia Duron, Alex and Gloria Duron,
Eleanor Everett, Ted and Anne Kucklick, Mauricio Martinez,
Robert and Gloria Martinez, Jeff and Michelle Ponce, Liz,
Veronica and Danielle Martinez-Romero, Rich and Donna Varesi

EXHIBITION DESIGN STUDENTS

Jennifer Frias, Krystal Glasman, Loriann Hernandez,
Lilia Lamas, Elizabeth Little, Jillian Nakornthap, Heather Rose,
Lynn Stromick, and Elizabeth Tallman

CATALOG PRODUCTION

Essayists: Annie Buckley and Joanna Roche
Art Director: Theron Moore

Catalog Designers: Paul Lam, Shana Lengyel, and Sawako Naganuma
Catalog Cover Design: Paul Lam, Shana Lengyel,
and Sawako Naganuma
Announcement and Poster Design: Paul Lam
Editor: Sue Henger
Photographer: Eric Stoner
Printer: Permanent Printing Limited, Hong Kong, China
Typefaces: Crown Jewels, Desdemona, Gill Sans,
LimeGloryCaps, and Nickelodeon
Prototype Designers: Jenny Goodwin, Jimmy Hsieh, Leon Ingram,
Paul Lam, Shana Lengyel, Sawako Naganuma, and Jeanette Sawyer

SPECIAL THANKS

Thank you to all the artists of *Redefining the Line*.
It was a pleasure and honor to work with you.

Website Design: Chris Varesi
Lender: Bergen O'Brien
Assistant to Aya Kato: Akinori Kojima
Assistant to Marguerite Sauvage: Iris Tal
Italian Translator: Martino Strozza
Exhibition Development: Janet Blake, Jacqueline Bunge,
Christian Hill, and Johnny Sampson

MATERIAL SUPPORT

Jenson Printing & Litho, Irvine, CA
Martinez Framers, Santa Ana, CA
One-Day Signs, Anaheim, CA
The Enlarger, Santa Ana, CA

Book © 2010 California State University Fullerton, Main Art Gallery
Artwork © Featured Artists
All rights reserved. No part of this publication may be reproduced
or transmitted in any form without the written permission of the
publisher and artists.

California State University Fullerton, Main Art Gallery
800 N. State College Blvd.
Fullerton, CA 92834-6850
www.fullerton.edu/arts/art

ISBN: 978-0-935314-76-2

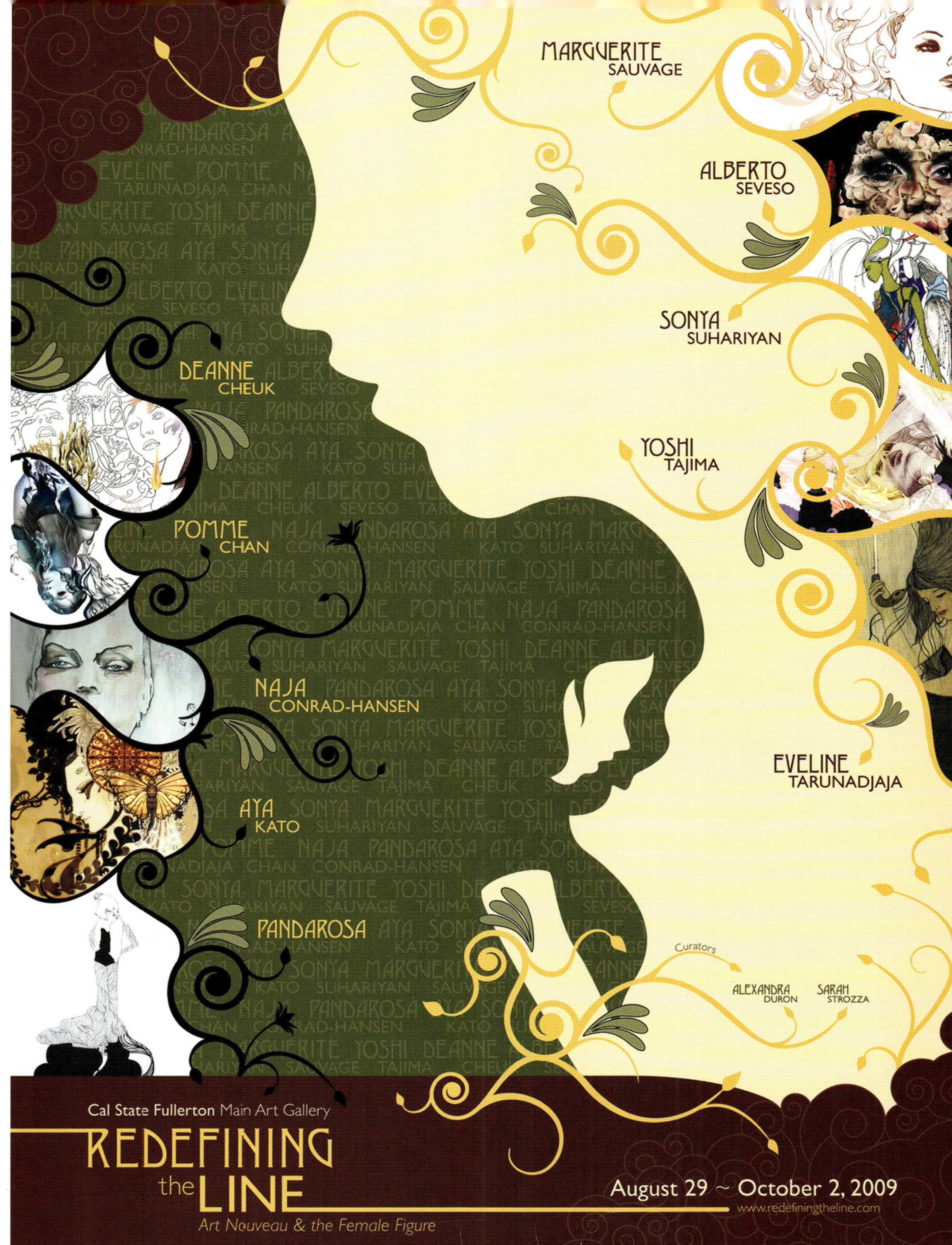

MARGUERITE SAUVAGE
ALBERTO SEVESO
SONYA SUHARIYAN
YOSHI TAJIMA
EVELINE TARUNADJAJA
DEANNE CHEUK
POMME CHAN
NAJA CONRAD-HANSEN
AYA KATO
PANDAROSA
Curators
ALEXANDRA DURON
SARAH STROZZA
Cal State Fullerton Main Art Gallery
REDEFINING the LINE
Art Nouveau & the Female Figure
August 29 ~ October 2, 2009
www.redefiningtheline.com

REDEFINING

the LINE

Art Nouveau & the Female Figure

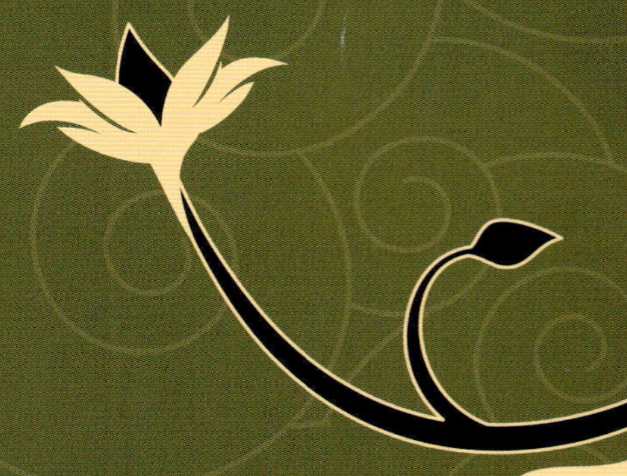